Stranger and Brother

STRANGER AND BROTHER

A Portrait of C. P. Snow

by

Philip Snow

M

MACMILLAN LONDON

ISBN 0 333 32680 6

First published in the United Kingdom 1982 by
MACMILLAN LONDON LIMITED
4 Little Essex Street London WC2R 3LF
and Basingstoke.
*Associated companies in Auckland, Dallas, Delhi,
Dublin, Hong Kong, Johannesburg, Lagos, Manzini,
Melbourne, Nairobi, New York, Singapore,
Tokyo, Washington and Zaria*

Text set in 10/12pt Linotron 202 Bembo, printed and bound
in Great Britain at The Pitman Press, Bath

For
Philippa
and her generation
whom Charles would like to have known

Note. The first eleven chapter titles are taken from chapter titles used by C. P. Snow in the *Strangers and Brothers* sequence of novels.

Contents

List of Illustrations

Acknowledgements

So many friends and relatives have been generous with their time, corroborating evidence and generally giving me encouragement, that I hope the following list does not omit anybody.

First of all the family and in particular Charles's wife, the late Pamela Hansford Johnson; his son, the Hon. Philip C. H. Snow; our brother, E. Eric Snow; my daughter, Mrs Stefanie D. V. V. Waine and her husband, Peter E. Waine; Charles's stepdaughter, Lindsay Stewart, and our cousin Mrs Peggy Rhodes.

Friends and colleagues include Mrs Lucy Wilde (née Parker); Harry S. Hoff (William Cooper); Anne Seagrim; Mrs Janet Nalder; Mrs Doris Cadney; Freda M. Haddy; Donald O. Gould; Herbert W. Wells; Frank Oldham; Reginald Symington; Edwin B. Chapman; Clifford A. E. English; Arthur H. T. Richmond; Vincent O. McQuillin; Donald H. Herbert; Leslie Stewart; Sir George Deacon; T. John Whall; Frederick T. Watson; Professor Sir Jack H. Plumb, Master of Christ's College, Cambridge; Professor Louis Hunter; Professor George R. Potter; Professor A. Roger Manvell; Mollie Rippin; Dr Mary Waddington; Norah Waddington; Eric Swift; Leicester University Library; Derek Deadman; The Marquess of Exeter; Leicestershire Record Office; The Master of Emmanuel College, Cambridge (Derek Brewer); Cynthia Levene; Dorothy Sterling; Janet Plomer; Count and Countess Giacomo Antonini; Professor Ian S. MacNiven; Wilfred Wooller; Joseph F. Maloney; Professor Thomas Burrow; Dr Anthony Storr; M. A. Sholokhov; Lorimer Fison; Sir Ronald Millar; Mrs. Nancy Poland; Mrs Ronnie Schwartz; E. M. Horsley; Professor Derek A. Long; Mrs Mollie Menzies; Darby Perry; Susanne Kirk; Kenneth C. Harlow; Seymour Krim.

For generous permission to quote material of which they hold the copyright I thank: Rt. Hon. Harold Macmillan, PC, OM, FRS; Rt. Hon. Sir Harold Wilson, KG, PC, OBE, MP; J. B. Priestley, OM; Anthony Powell, CBE; Sir Ronald Millar; Sir Anthony Wagner, KCB, KCVO; Rt. Hon. Earl of Longford, KG, PC; Nancy Poland and *The Harvard Magazine*; Mrs Dorothy Laurie; Mrs A. B. Wyatt.

Every effort has been made to trace all holders of copyright in material quoted and in illustrations: I apologise to those whom I have been unable to find.

Three remaining debts are acknowledged – to the editing skill of James Wright for separating the light from the dark so imaginatively and amiably, and to my publishers, in particular Alan Maclean (a friend of the subject of this portrait), for the warm encouragement, for the final editing from his rich experience and for kindness well beyond the normal. My inexpressible gratitude to my wife, Anne, for typing a series of drafts of this her sixth book and for her tolerance, encouragement and valued comments on it at all stages.

Angmering, Sussex.   P.S.

Note

From a letter by C. P. Snow to Mrs M. Lanius dated December 1961.

'The phrase Strangers and Brothers is supposed to represent the fact that in part of our lives each person is alone (each of us lives in isolation and in such parts of the individual life we are all strangers) and in part of our lives, including social activities, we can and should feel for each other like brothers. . . . Socially I am optimistic and I believe that men are able to grapple with their social history. That is, the brothers side of the overall theme contains a completely definite hope. But some aspects of the individual life do not carry the same feeling. Have you ever seen anyone you love die of disseminated sclerosis? This is the strangers part of the thing. I don't believe we subtract from our social optimism if we see the individual tragedies with clear eyes. On the contrary, I believe we strengthen ourselves for those tasks which are within our power. . . .'

Foreword

This book is a portrait of my brother. I was ten years younger than Charles Snow, and I cannot be said to have known him until I was about seven and he was seventeen; but from then on until his death in 1980 the only prolonged period of separation was the war and its immediate aftermath. For this period I have had to rely on our correspondence and what he told me later.

He knew that I would write this book, and welcomed it; his only stipulation was that it should not be published in his lifetime. The definitive biography has yet to be written; it will be a monumental task for somebody, and must be some way off. In the meantime, without attempting any sort of analysis of his work – though I have identified many of the characters in the *Strangers and Brothers* series – I have set out to paint an informal picture of a man who has been the main influence in my life.

1. A Sense of the Past

Introducing himself in the House of Lords to the Marquess of Exeter (the former Olympic hurdler, Lord Burghley), the newly-created Baron Snow could not resist telling him that his not too distant ancestor had been gamekeeper to the Marquess's not too distant ancestor. It was a belief persistently held in our family, although 'gamekeeper' on the Burghley House grounds would sometimes be changed to 'poacher'. A less dramatic account of this grandfather, our mother's father, indicated that he used to gild and paint Burghley House's imposing main entrance. Perhaps he was both poacher and painter, the one occupation relieving the tedium of the other. What is certain is that Frederic (*sic*) William Robinson was a minor portrait painter who, like others of his kind, turned to photography when the camera came along. Consequently his branch of the family is more photographed than is generally the case. The birthplace of his eleven children (he married twice) in the minute Georgian house of 21 St Martin, High Street, Stamford, Lincolnshire, belonged – and still does – to the Burghley House Estate: he had to leave it late in life through inability to pay the rent. His self-portrait gives the impression of a not entirely reliable man. Nothing is known of his antecedents. He fitted in well with Charles's concept of what an ancestor of his would be like – variously enterprising, far from grand, and unsuccessful materially.

F. W. Robinson had, however, married into the Wigmore family who were impecunious with tenuous pretensions to grandeur. To start with, Charles's life was steeply uphill and he wanted this recognised. He didn't want to believe in Wigmore accomplishments, maintaining that his social and economic base was almost at the very bottom. But one cannot accept his thesis that the Wigmores were then rather a run-down lot without mentioning the family belief,

1

based on the evidence of an early eighteenth century family tree, that they are descended from Edward IV. Lord of Stamford and Lord of Wigmore were among the king's titles. He had made what was termed a precontract marriage with Lady Eleanor Talbot, daughter of the Earl of Shrewsbury, about 1463. They had a son, Edward de Wigmore. Did his line continue via our mother to Charles? He was always amused by this speculation, but as one who had risen by his own effort from the edge of the working class to a position of eminence, he would have been less than pleased to have it verified. Nevertheless when he had to select for Garter King of Arms a territorial title on the conferment of his peerage in 1964 he seriously thought about being made Lord Snow of Stamford.

Charles was more comfortable with the Snow side of the family. He was proud of the fact that great-grandfather John Snow, born in 1801 in Devon, was illiterate. John moved to the Midlands as part of the Industrial Revolution. Charles was intrigued by the idea of John Snow as peasant-turned-engine fitter, unable to sign his name. He was also immensely interested in our grandfather, William Henry, born at Engine Street, Smethwick and often talked to me about this radical, nonconformist figure who had largely educated himself. William Henry became Foreman Engineer of the Leicester Tramways, supervising the transformation from horse-drawn to electric trams. He died in 1916 when Charles was eleven. A photograph shows a neatly-bearded, rather haughty looking man who wore a wing-collar, cravat and tiepin to show that he was a cut above the ordinary artisans. Charles was proud of our grandfather's wide reading, and grateful for the encouragement he gave him.

Of W. H. Snow's children our father, William Edward and, less so, his sister, Kate (Aunt Cissie), are depicted in the *Strangers and Brothers* sequence of novels, the latter as Aunt Milly, an unattractive, acid character. Born at Monks Coppenhall, near Nantwich, Cheshire, William Edward was the first Snow known to have artistic gifts. A tiny man, only five feet two, with rather protruding light blue eyes, pale reddish hair, moustachioed but beardless, he became an Associate, then Fellow, of the Royal College of Organists. Unhappily he couldn't make a living as an organist and he had to go where the money was. It took him to Leicester, where he became a clerk in a boot and shoe factory. There he bought a semi-detached house, number 40 Richmond Road, half of a tall building which had once been a Liberal Club.

He married in 1897, at the age of twenty-eight, Ada Sophia

2

Robinson, the eighth child of F. W. Robinson and Sophia Palmer Wigmore. The wedding was at St James's Church, Aylestone Park, Leicester; this red brick building which still stands facing the end of Richmond Road, was where father was organist and choirmaster from 1910 to 1930. Six inches taller and two years younger, Ada Snow was a handsome woman; she might even have been beautiful if her nose had had less of a downward curve: it was Charles's nose too. She had a dignity of bearing which Charles, amongst the four sons, perhaps most strongly inherited. He could bear down on someone he was meeting in the same way, slowly and impressively. Mother's combination of black hair and kindly but discerning light-blue, almost pale violet, eyes was equally striking. Charles's descriptions of her as Mrs Lena Eliot in *Time of Hope* catch her almost exactly. Both Charles and I suspected that the marriage for mother, thinking more of her Wigmore than her Robinson descent, was strictly downhill; father, absorbed in his music, was quite unaware that she thought she'd demeaned herself. But in fact she had left Stamford with a brother to find work; when father met her she was a seamstress in Leicester.

Mother's brother George, with grandfather Snow, had an enduring influence on Charles. He is described by Charles as 'Uncle Will' in *Time of Hope*, confusingly since there was a real Uncle Will, a younger brother of George Robinson. Rubicund, not in the least swarthy like other male Robinsons, George was imperious. As an unqualified solicitor he gathered in enough clients among the farming, fox-hunting community of Melton Mowbray to live in reasonable style. His house at Thorpe End was late Georgian: its contents, at least in the parts that were on show, were suitable for receiving middle-class landowners. In the hall and on the staircase were Victorian sporting prints. In the upstairs front room, which served both as drawing and dining room, Uncle George, invariably dressed in a long white tie and white waistcoat, would serve breakfast from a sideboard covered with large joints of beef, ham and game and an entire stilton, to follow the bacon and eggs. He had three daughters: pathetically 'County' Edith, as straight-backed as Queen Mary; the intelligent, quick-witted Florence who, also unqualified, later carried on her father's practice; the dreamy, rather simple but most cosy Mabel. None of them, as eligible in point of style as Jane Austen's girls, ever married. They lisped, their complexions were florid, their natures excitable. When the Prince of Wales (later

Edward VIII) and Prince Henry (later Duke of Gloucester) were known to be out hunting the sisters would sit in the full-length windows hoping to catch royal eyes as they passed the house.

There was always one absentee. George's extremely handsome wife Thirza or Za (pronounced Zay), it was explained to me on my visits before the age of twelve, was never well enough to join us. I did once see her flitting across an upstairs passage, frail and rather demented-looking, like a senior Alice in Wonderland figure. Charles told me that she was a hopeless alcoholic. He himself was greatly admired in this household, except by the one son, eldest in the family. He showed his independence by marrying and, after his father's death, struck Charles off the list in their family Bible because he was not a Conservative. Monty had a lisp too: he was also florid and excitable. Charles got on splendidly with Uncle George, despite the latter's pseudo-aristocratic poses which included the stand that none but the landed gentry were good enough for his daughters.

Our parents' marriage produced four sons. All, except me, were known by their second names. William Harold, born on 10 October 1898, was black-haired, blue-eyed and took after mother, though he had the heavy paternal jaw. Father was too old for the First War but Harold enlisted underage in 1916 in the Leicestershire Regiment where, passed unfit for active service because of weak eyesight, he was principally on local guard duties. Afterwards he became a clerk in the Inland Revenue. He was the first of the brothers to show an interest in cricket but, though he had a profound knowledge of the game, he was no performer. Sartorially he left the others far behind. A tall spare figure in trilby hat with walking cane, shiny shoes, spats, a nearly perpetual cigarette silhouetted in an ivory holder, he was the height of 1920s elegance. His was a benevolent, dignified influence. At the age of twenty-eight he died of pneumonia complicated by diabetes, both killing diseases at that time.

Charles Percy Snow was born on 15 October 1905. To the immediate family for the first forty-five years he was Percy, and he remained so to distant relatives. Percy became Charles on his marriage in 1950 to Pamela Hansford Johnson who had initiated the change; it took me all of the next two years to get used to it. Up till then most of his friends knew him as Snow, a few as CP. This wasn't the end of Charles's mildly tiresome confusion over what he was to be called. When he was made a life peer he decided that for all

4

purposes connected with the writing side of his life he should continue to be styled C. P. Snow. Nevertheless, at lectures and interviews he was often referred to as 'Lord Snow' and after a time he ceased to worry about it.

Unlike Harold, Charles was golden-haired; at a very early age he had to wear glasses. Two more sons arrived at five-year intervals. Edward Eric Snow, born 13 March 1910, was like Charles and our father in shape of head and their early need for glasses. Eric was closest to father in colouring, his hair being darker and more truly auburn. I was born five years later on 7 August 1915, had brown hair and was said to look more like my mother. I was named after the family doctor, Philip Snoad, and the country's 1914 hero, King Albert of the Belgians. William and Edward were family names, as was Charles, after a Romany-looking uncle who was close to his sister, our mother. The reasons for Harold, Eric and Percy are obscure.

It was a full house for mother to cope with since it also included her father-in-law until I was a year old. She did not know of the Edward IV ancestral theory but would have totally approved of it; ultra-conservative, she was opposed to everything her father-in-law, William Henry Snow, stood for. They shared for many years the same house but little else. Charles, aged ten or eleven, observed this with relish and later told me of their endless arguments. Mother was deeply religious while grandfather Snow was an unbeliever, careful to keep in the single bookcase in the house the occasional theological volume which he would read diligently so as to pull the faithful to pieces with quotations from their own dogma. He was pro-Boer, more out of mischief than conviction, and after 1914 asserted that Kitchener, our mother's hero, was monumentally stupid. She in retaliation would attack her father-in-law's absolute confidence in the capacity of Belgian fortresses like Liège to keep back the Germans. He was not easily contradicted before the event since he was the only member of the family to have ventured outside England; he had been a technical adviser to several Belgian towns, including Brussels and Liège, on the installation of electric tramways. This gave him special authority when the crucial, if short-lived, extent of resistance in Belgium was in everyone's minds. He lost his fortresses and mother lost Kitchener; then the spirited adversaries were parted by grandfather's death – a great loss to Charles. When he was dying mother expected him to abandon his agnosticism but he retained it, and mother graciously conceded: 'I

5

grant him this, he didn't go back on his word. You couldn't say he didn't make a good end.'

Father kept well clear of it all, helped by the fact that for fifteen years, 1895–1910, he was organist and choirmaster at All Saints', Wigston Magna, and he had to walk the five miles each way (twice on Sundays). He walked speedily with tiny steps, as in an animated cartoon, wearing the bowler hat from which he could not bear to be separated. During the week he would daily take the tram the four miles to the boot and shoe factory beyond the centre of Leicester, and in the evening, after a meal, teach the piano in the back room (always known as the study); it was surprisingly unobtrusive, or perhaps our ears were accustomed to it.

Our relationships with William and Ada Snow were wholly amiable and uncomplicated. We took pride in being seen with a mother of such dignity and were patient with her when she fussed. From early on father could be relied on to provide us with amusement – not always intentional. Our relationship with him was less one of respect and more one of 'we are all boys together'. 'Merry gentlemen' was how he would address us. Charles's fictional portrait of father as Bertie Eliot, principally in *Time of Hope* and the *Sleep of Reason*, was not far removed from the truth. William Snow was certainly meek but, as the son of a Radical, he didn't toe the line without showing flashes of independence. We suspected that he voted Labour, not daring to tell our mother. Her High Toryism, I believe, was initially responsible for Charles's support of the Labour Party, which lasted all his life; nevertheless, like all his brothers, he was very fond of her. William Snow neither swore nor drank, except for a minute glass on special occasions. He was easy-going except with male music pupils, for whom he had little patience. He had naturally tried Charles and Eric on the piano but quickly abandoned them, Charles being tone-deaf and Eric nearly so. I had a little more sense of tune but not enough; the lessons were the only occasions when father got cross with me, and I too was eventually released. The only tune Charles ever acquired was the opening bar of Offenbach's *Barcarolle*; on one occasion, sitting in the front row of the stalls, he saw no one rise to their feet and therefore did not recognise the National Anthem.

Life at 40 Richmond Road under mother's leadership was not precisely puritanical, but certainly genteel. Only the rarest sips of brandy and Wincarnis would be indulged in by her and then only for medicinal purposes. I never saw my brothers drink in the house. As a Rechabite, mother made liquor invisible. Harold was the only smoker. Luxury took the form of occasional sweets; chocolate and ice-cream were a special treat. At the paper shop we bought *Magnet* and *Gem* – and our favourite, *Nelson Lee*, which added to a school background the eponymous hero, an amateur detective.

2. Inside a Family

The Two Cultures, a phrase coined by Charles and likely to be used for a good many years yet, was a product of his upbringing; it was partly the result of the range of his early reading, partly of the lack of educational opportunity at a crucial stage which forced him towards science. Both these factors are part and parcel of his origins.

When I suggested to him that he should write his autobiography he would always firmly reject the idea, saying that he had written quite enough about himself either by way of direct or indirect experience. In particular, he felt that *The Search*, *Time of Hope*, *The Sleep of Reason* and *Last Things* conveyed a lot about himself first-hand that was not submerged or concealed by the fictional Lewis Eliot, who also exposed certain facets of the true Charles in some of his other works. Not only was he determined never to write an autobiography but he discouraged the appearance of any biography while he was alive. But how accurately did he depict his origins in his writings? Because his early struggles were hard, Charles wanted no one to overlook them and, perhaps because of this, he placed the family background just a shade lower in the social scale than it actually was.

There is no doubt that we were lower middle class. We were also poor; not so badly off as some of our neighbours but poor enough to impede our progress. In the evenings we all congregated in the front room of our overcrowded semi-detached house, except our father who escaped into his study. Our mother spent much of her time reclining on a sofa; she had a heart condition brought on by rheumatic fever when young. We also had a lodger; the wonderfully kind and adaptable Lucy Parker turned up one day at the wrong address, seeking accommodation – with the happiest results for the family. Tragically, she became engaged to Harold not long before he died.

She has recently recalled to me how high-spirited and good-natured we brothers were; but she of course contributed hugely by fitting in so well. Graduating from Nottingham University College, she taught geography and physical education in Leicester schools. She would join us at the single table where we did our homework, under the two hanging pale-lemon, incandescent gas mantles (the house never had electricity) with a pile of books to mark. The effect of that gas-lamp holder on the family sight is incalculable; I was the only one in the family not to wear glasses.

The first-floor bedroom up steep stairs was our parents', the back room Lucy's. On the attic floor, up almost perpendicular stairs, were three bedrooms, involving some doubling up of brothers when mother's health required living-in help. There was a coal cellar, dimly lit by an open gas flare; our diminutive father, with his shiny delicate hands, was the uncomplaining, permanent coal hewer, I am now ashamed to relate.

There were at least four unpleasant features about the house. One was a narrow corridor (the parental air-raid shelter during the war) with a naked gas flare sometimes lit, connecting, after three danger-ous steps, the living part of the house with the single-storey arm comprising the kitchen and minute scullery. Other drawbacks were no hot water taps or wash-basins, no bathroom (only a partitioned-off section of an out-house near the scullery where buckets of water heated on a stove had to be lifted across to the bath) and in the backyard a single lavatory which was scarcely less than arctic in any season.

Around us were terraced houses, sometimes split by a common rear entrance, occupied by bricklayers, foremen stokers, shoe click-ers, framework knitters, compositors, hosiery trimmers, ware-housemen, tram conductors, travelling drapers, punctuated by those in marginally superior professions like petty shopkeepers, minor joiners and builders, heel manufacturers, cobblers, dressmakers, vergers, self-employed painters and decorators, prison warders. The street directory for Richmond Road in 1904, the year before Charles's birth, reads like a roll-call of the strata of artisanship, checked uniquely with the entry 'Wm. E. Snow, FRCO, music teacher'. This, the brass plate outside the house pro-claiming the same entry, and the exterior style of the house marked the social frontier for our origins between that of lower middle class and working class. There were other extra touches. The family doctor, Philip Ephraim Snoad, had us as his only patients in the street. It was only outside our house that Dr Snoad's carriage would draw up; from it would descend a bowler-hatted, bespatted, pin-striped trousered figure. Powdered and superbly mannered, he was a great favourite of mother's, whose children he'd brought into the world; whether he removed his seemingly incorporated white kid gloves for the purpose is not recorded. He dressed for dinner with his brother every night. Once, on some emergency, he reflected con-siderable credit on us by arriving in evening dress, top hat and cape. He was the vicar's churchwarden – in mother's eyes there could scarcely be a more august office – at St James's, Aylestone Park, that spireless, undistinguished edifice just out of sight of 40 Richmond Road. His appointment contrasted with that of people's churchwar-den, which cut no ice in mother's estimation.

Following father's twenty years at St James's as organist and choir-master, another inscribed clock joined the modest household orna-ments and he went to St Mary de Castro, a church with a fine organ in the most historic part of Leicester. No doubt at his wife's prompting, he had much earlier attempted to set up his own boot-making busi-ness; but he had little drive as a businessman and soon went bankrupt. This was a disaster with four sons to bring up. From his music lessons he could add at best nothing but a few pence an hour to his wage as a factory clerk and a stipend of twenty pounds a year as a organist; we were always in danger of crashing through the slim frontier into the lowest economic level of the working class. Father never bore the world a grudge, dispensing respect broadly and expecting the same in return – even his one or two remote male friends he addressed as 'Mr' – but his financial failure had a profound effect on Charles, Eric and myself; caution with money was something that never left us. Father and mother took no holidays together, except very early on and invariably to Llandudno. Indeed, they never accompanied each other anywhere after that, even going to, and returning from, St James's at different times. We occasionally went with mother to relatives or to a resort, but father could never absent himself from the organ. He seldom travelled outside the county, and if he went to London it was to hear the organists at St Paul's and the Abbey: he was proud of shar-ing the Fellowship of the Royal College of Organists with them. At home he would chant 'W. E. Snow, FRCO', enjoying the rhyme, and then laugh at his own joke, uttering his special euphoric adjective, 'Capital!'

★

10

On the same elitist principle which he was afterwards to support, Charles was kept away from the primitive and, it has to be said, predominantly philistine Board schools which were the government's non-fee paying form of education. He went to a school with a side access exactly opposite the grim Board School in Lansdowne Road.

Miss Martin's establishment fronted on the more appealing view of the Aylestone Road tram route, meadows and the River Soar. It was for girls and boys from five to eleven, calling itself grandiloquently Beaumanor School after the terrace in which it was one of five houses, and consisted of three small rooms. Beaumanor School underlined its status with blazers and a monogram entwining B and S. Fees were modest but no doubt a real financial burden on father. Miss Martin, who took the older children, was rather fierce in contrast to Miss Maud Sadler, embodiment of gentleness for children just starting school. Charles was quickly recognised as years ahead of his age; at Miss Martin's he absorbed all that there was to be learnt, with bespectacled eyes close to the page, and looked for more.

Our own library at home was contained in a glass-fronted rosewood bookcase (which I still have). It was nonchalantly miscellaneous. *The History of Music* by Neumann, *Arthur Mee's Children's Encyclopaedia* in eight volumes (we devoured them all word by word; Charles never ceased to laud it as close to perfection), *Discoveries and Inventions of the Nineteenth Century*, *Ports of Britain*, two or three Wodehouses, *Gentlemen Prefer Blondes* by Anita Loos, *Heroes of the Great War*, bound volumes of *The Penny Magazine*, a huge Bible with a family tree inside, some boys' books with decorative covers (like Ballantyne's *Ungava* which left an impression on Charles and me), *Prince Ranjitsinghji's Jubilee Book of Cricket*, P. F. Warner's *My Cricketing Life* and a few paper-covered cricket volumes. The library did not amount to more than fifty books in all, though it was larger than most in our neighbourhood. Fortunately there was a public library in Richmond Road itself; its part in our lives cannot be overestimated.

Built in the 1890s, it was an unassuming single-storey building. Open only in the evenings and Saturday afternoons, it housed, for anyone beginning to develop an interest in literature, enough to satisfy him. It still does, but gone is the wealth of weekly and monthly magazines bound in leather with gold lettering: *The Tatler*, *The Graphic*, *The Illustrated London News*, *John o' London's*,

Wide World, Bystander, Strand, Punch. These were for sitting down to. Standing up, one could read the daily papers, *The Times, Morning Post and Daily Telegraph, Daily Herald, News Chronicle, Leicester Mercury, Leicester Evening Mail, Leicester Chronicle,* held in position by a brass rod on what can only be described as a continuous lectern. In my time it was a good place for picking up girls; but this had no appeal for Charles who was seemingly unaware of these diversions until relatively late – his university days.

To satisfy his sporting interests Harold bought *The Athletic News,* shared avidly by Charles; this publication's annuals were inherited by the next two brothers. All of us would have excelled in a sporting *Mastermind* in our youth. Charles was also an expert on Sir Walter Scott before he was eleven. When he discovered Scott in the library, a volume at a time was brought back to the house, and it is perhaps not surprising that his mastery of that writer's prolific works caused eyebrows to be raised when he went to his secondary school.

There were other advantages in living where we did. Number 40 was at the top of a gentle hill; it was higher than the other houses. From the attics, front and back, we had excellent views. Over the rooftops in front were the meadows of the combined River Soar and the canal. At the back the panorama took in the chimneys and slates stretching, with large areas of greenery, to and away from the town. It was high enough to be visible from the Leicester–London LMS railway line, together with St James's Church and the Primitive Methodist Church at opposite ends of Richmond Road. To one of those green spaces less than two streets' distance father would take the young Harold and Charles; later, mother took Eric and me for picnics there. This was the Recreation Ground, an important breathing space for us across a then-countrified Saffron Lane where countrified cricketers gathered; Eric and I played the game on rough pitches with friends and pick-ups. The ground extended almost up to the railway viaduct. As a very small child I believe I once saw on the viaduct an ambulance train with a large red cross on the carriages, full of heavily bandaged soldiers. The river and canal meadows, in the opposite direction, were not so easily reached; just as well perhaps as none of us, except Eric, could swim. Although in a straight line only a street away, access was barred by hostile gypsies. A treat was to board a tram at Cavendish Road, passing large houses in handsome grounds, for the Aylestone Terminus where we disembarked for the short walk to the hump-backed canal-cum-river bridge in open country. The Aylestone Boathouse with its café, regarded by the working class as rather raffish, was a meeting place for Charles and his circle, as it was for me in my role of post-adolescent philanderer. It held, in my pre-Cambridge days, a magnetism for me.

Number 40 was the only house to have room for a laburnum and lilac tree on each side of the front bay-window. This was my favourite view of the passing world: the now forgotten sound of workhorses and their carts on the cobbles; the doctor's carriage; floats with huge containers of milk; the street gas lamp opposite ignited at dusk by the brisk lighter with his hooked pole; whistling errand boys who made shopping largely unnecessary. I tended, as the youngest, to be the family errand boy, notably for Charles whose milk chocolate flakes I would fetch, with no reward or acknowledgement of any kind other than an imperious nod. The trees would stand out in season, golden and purple in an otherwise drab set of house fronts.

But it was at the rear of Number 40 that the cricket-loving Snows had an inestimable benefit. A small slabbed yard with an apple and two plum trees was virtually enclosed by the low kitchen, scullery, 'bathroom' and lavatory on one side, a six-foot boundary wall on the opposite side, the study at one end and a lower garden at the other. Here we played with a stump for a bat and a sorbo (hard rubber) ball, delivered underhand. In the lower garden, twice as long, a version closer to the true game was devisable between two apple trees and higher boundary walls, one framed by a small boot and shoe factory. Next to it were gardens whose owners flatly refused to send back the ball or let us look for it. The first part of Leicester to be bombed in the Second War were these Cavendish Road houses when a string of bombs was dropped all along the road not far from the gasometers. Amongst the dead were the owners of houses at the bottom of our cricket pitch; pieces of these houses and the surface of Cavendish Road flew up to shatter some of our rear windows. We certainly had not expected Number 40 to be a casualty of the first attack on Leicester (and one of the first attacks on England).

Harold and Charles picked up the game from the odd manual in the library and by watching the county play; Charles and Eric in turn instructed me. The full-size bat was too large for me and Charles added to the complication – with the best intensions because it made me an unusually able defender – by arranging both my wrists behind the handle, so that it was painful to do anything but

13

play back. Charles's method which, it is only fair to say, he adopted himself, set me back as a batsman some years. It was one of the very few instances of brotherly misguidance. An imperturbable batsman himself, Charles would disdain to score runs; elegance and pure survival were his aims. As a bowler he was altogether different. He was histrionic; gestures of hope and despair, grunts, cries of 'My God!' and 'Good shot!' intermingled with vicious spin, beaming and scowling. He played the game hard; and I learned to do the same. Lucy would sometimes be coerced into accepting bruises from the really hard composition ball in the lower garden on a pitch of soil that was never grassed nor was anything but unpredictable. And there would be a rest from cricket when father was induced to join us in catching the sorbo; this he would do by bringing, not ineffectively, one hand down on top of the other as it grasped the ball, to the accompaniment of his own guffaws of laughter. He seldom seemed to be in anything but a state of mild euphoria. Mother would be using these outdoor diversions of the family to rest inside. She was not as lighthearted as he was; she often looked quite solemn, perhaps because she had the greater sense of responsibility.

Charles left Miss Martin's when he was eleven. Seldom can there have been an example of such eagerness to extend mental horizons than his at that age. Financial restraints apart, ours was a good background for an enquiring mind. Pure excitement lay ahead – and lasted in a sense for almost the whole of his life.

3. Towards Ambition

The buildings of Alderman Newton's two schools, for boys and girls, still stand in Peacock Lane. Recently the boys have joined the girls in a building far from the city centre; the girls had moved there in 1959 and it was opened by Sir Charles Snow, as he was then. In the Leicester secondary schools hierarchy, Newton's was the second most expensive: the fee was £5 a term and remained so throughout most of our schooldays. It was in fact a grammar school of eighteenth century foundation in a mid-Victorian building, but was known as a secondary school until after the Second War; in Charles's time nobody had managed to get to university level directly from the school. The science side was stronger than the arts where Latin, a prerequisite for the older universities, had barely started.

Charles excelled in every available academic subject, astonishing the staff for years afterwards. A master, H. E. Howard, recorded in *The Newtonian* that, on arrival at the school, he 'speedily attracted attention by his fantastically high marks in the term examinations; indeed, during his career he averaged 508 marks out of a maximum of 560'; the loss of marks where in Woodwork and Gymnastics. Perhaps his principal gifts were an astonishing memory, which he never lost, and his ability to eliminate everything from his mind except the subject in hand. Such introversion in abnormally gifted children tends to earn them the contemptuous label of 'swot' and a degree of ostracism, but that was not so in Charles's case. His contemporaries agree that the boy with unruly hair, his tie as lopsided as his smile, was too friendly and gentle, despite a core of toughness, to attract criticism. He acquired no conceit to offend his fellows or antagonise the staff.

Before he went to Newton's he had had no need for friends outside the family. Now he started bringing them back to 40 Richmond

Road where mother always made them welcome. Don Gould, a year younger than Charles and living nearby off Aylestone Road, was friend, protégé and eventually a County chess player. He recalled the awe mother inspired in him and his astonishment at the way Charles treated father. A request by father for information from Charles was rewarded with a gruff, concise reply. Father would smile and ask for further enlightenment. Charles's response, even more succinct, rose now from a growl to something close to a roar. Don Gould was amazed; fathers were not spoken to like that. But later he realised that he was watching something of an act, father enjoying the pretence of juvenility and Charles playing up to him in the omniscient manner expected of the worldly prodigy.

Charles's worldliness was evident even at that age. In 1918 a school cadet corps was belatedly established and Gould in his first year was surprised to see that Charles had enlisted, parading in khaki uniform, greatcoat, puttees and a wooden imitation rifle. Charles explained away this unexpected jingoism by maintaining that there were a few extra marks to be obtained by this route – an assertion never to be corroborated from any other source as the corps was disbanded after the November Armistice. Don Gould was also impressed, when the England cricket team was touring Australia in 1920, by Charles buying three successive editions of the evening paper (news was slower coming through then) to obtain the latest score; it was the beginning of a life-long habit.

By his second year at school, Charles had made his mark not only in the academic but the organisational field; he was given offices, such as secretary of the football and cricket XIs, previously held by boys two or three years senior. It entitled him to share with the captain and vice-captain the distinction of a tassel on his cap and attracted some leg-pulling, but his matter-of-fact acceptance of the honour soon quelled that.

Although thought to be worth cultivating by his seniors, Charles was singularly unprepossessing in appearance, making him not one for the girls. In their walks home together, saving tram fares, Don Gould remembers Charles chiding him for 'running after small females'. Gould commented that the smallness of the quarry seemed to increase his contempt and that Charles declined to discuss the sexual consciousness which Arthur Miles, a part portrait of himself in *The Search* (it preceded the *Strangers and Brothers* series), registered when about fourteen.

He remembered Charles's lively sense of fun (a word much used by him), which frequently took the form of seeing the absurd (another word for which he had a predilection) in what he read or heard. He seized delightedly on ludicrous expressions; in those days they often came from schoolmasters.

In the school's Oxford Senior Local Examination (replaced in turn by Matriculation and GCE O Level) Charles was placed in the first class honours list and passed with credit in English, History, Geography, Religious Knowledge, French, Maths and Chemistry, and with distinction in Physics. But his success never made him sentimental about Newton's; he would often talk to me about its failings, among them the sadistic and homosexual tendencies of a handful of the staff of our time. To some he gave credit for helping him, others he labelled buffoons.

One of the chief influences in his life was Herbert Edmund Howard, who joined the staff in 1922 towards the end of Charles's school days. By this time Charles was in full swing, being head prefect, captain of cricket, founder of the debating society, captain of chess and winner of the Chairman of the Governors' Prize. Howard, Bert to his intimates, Bill to the rest of the school, was jovial, fresh-faced and goodlooking, only five years older than Charles. Son of a postmaster in Fakenham, Norfolk, he retained some typical Norfolkese, particularly in his rages; he came straight to teaching from King's College, London. It was to be his life's work, and he entered into it with zest, starting the school debating society (with Charles), running the chess club, founding and editing the first issue of *The Newtonian* and creating the weekly *News Supplement*; besides school news this contained satire and cartoons, which attracted much attention among the boys and even some of the staff who regarded Howard with suspicion. He provided the original of George Passant, after whom the first book of the *Strangers and Brothers* series was named. He found in Charles just the inquiring, active first-class mind necessary to help establish his own ideas. Although Howard was an historian and did not come into academic contact with Charles they spent many out-of-school hours together, often at cafés late at night, when they missed the last trams and had to walk a couple of miles home in different directions. Their partnership extended over the weekends when they and one or two other senior boys took junior boys for walks in the country. Theirs was a friendship for life, although Charles's career led him away from Bert's supreme insularity at Newton's where he stayed

17

until he retired. Unlike Charles, I knew Bert as a teacher since he was responsible for getting me direct from Newton's to Cambridge on a History Exhibition. His methods were unconventional and he inspired original thought. He ignored textbooks, encouraging classes to enact incidents of history and appointing a different person to be 'in charge', entirely without rehearsal, for the forty-minute lesson. His use came in directing us what to read and to avoid dull works. He seldom set essays and when he did rarely looked at them.

Towards the end of his life, soon after retirement from Newton's, we were sad to mark the decline in looks, vigour and responsibility of a man who should have gone far. His influence on boys was remarkable, but any advances in his career were inhibited by awkwardness at interviews. He achieved distinction as one of the two resident Midlands' representatives in the Round Britain Quiz, wrote under the name of R. Philmore six detective novels featuring C. J. Swan (a disguise for Charles) as a writer-cum-detective, and established a succession of loyal coteries of disciples. But for a man of such character he made remarkably little impact on the outside world; this may have been partly because he was bisexual, if that carries schizoid personality problems; perhaps also his intolerance played a part. He considered most people 'sunkets', a splendid East Anglian expression meaning 'despicable creatures'. He would bellow out this word when moved, as he often was, by the stupidity of the world – as time went on the overlay of Leicester intonation came inexorably to hang around his fundamental Norfolk dialect. Nevertheless, he was marvellous for Newton's and the catalyst Charles needed to widen his already strikingly broad interests.

Charles regretted that we could not have gone to a public school. I would stress the benefits of daily contact with home and of escape from what were then the rigours of public school life; but he argued for the undoubted advantages that, say, Rugby, where I was later Bursar, could offer, the most important being the pupil-teacher ratio – in Rugby's case about 10 to 1 as against 35 to 1 at Newton's until reaching the sixth form. Then there was the wide range of subjects offered at a good public school, drawing out whatever latent talent one had, and the wealth of out-of-school activities. Charles would have extracted every ounce from these but he would have missed the experience of pioneering the few that he had enjoyed at Newton's. What clinched the debate in favour of public schools was that they all have superb cricket facilities – a coach, pitches that you could trust, proper pavilions, all the refinements that had been lacking at Newton's. Perhaps we would have opted to be day-boys at a public school, having the best of both worlds.

Charles was approaching the end of his time at Newton's. He was there longer than anybody else for reasons to be explained shortly, and consequently overlapped with Eric. Eric proved to be the best footballer in the family and managed, on the atrocious wickets, to be outstanding at cricket. Unfortunately he was deprived of academic opportunity at a higher level by father's financial predicament and was obliged to go immediately into a profession. The only Snow to be good with his hands – he made our first crystal set, a feat quite beyond Charles and myself – he went into the heating and ventilating industry, eventually becoming chairman of his own firm in Leicester. He also made himself the leading authority on Leicestershire cricket. Nothing, Charles once said to me, can perhaps be as satisfying as to know that one is the acknowledged expert on a particular subject; with his two histories Eric has achieved this. Charles included me in this observation as the acknowledged authority on cricket in Fiji and on South Pacific bibliography. In how many subjects might he himself have achieved world mastery? Perhaps there are some in which he might claim preeminence; but his was such a broad canvas that it is difficult to isolate a specific field. Certainly he was one of the most knowledgeable persons of his time on both American and Russian cultures.

Don Gould remembered the important part that conversation played in Charles's life from these early days. It was almost an obsession with him and he had theories on almost anything. He also had theories, culled from obscure sources, on games which he played strictly according to these rules hoping to catch his opponent unawares. He played chess, table tennis and billiards at the Leicester YMCA with Howard, Gould, Edwin Chapman and others. He would try esoteric, outrageously complicated gambits at chess, sometimes achieving dramatic victory, which he accepted with sangfroid. Ingenious variations of spin were applied to both table tennis and billiards with sometimes cataclysmic results, though as regards the former the new pimply rubber sponge of the racquets helped him considerably.

But, while always amused by theories of older men, he was never bemused by them. He believed that one should run through the gamut of them while young. Charles had a general distrust of those in authority who were dominated by theories that must adversely affect their activities; we shall see this coming to its most famous paradigm with Professor Lindemann in 1960. Intuition – that was acceptable; but not overwhelming and preponderant theory. His knowledge of so many theories had been acquired – if only for most of them to be discarded – in the central reference library in Leicester. This Valhalla represented an apex of excitement that he had sensed would be his on leaving the Richmond Road milieu. At school, where there were no books worth speaking of, he might be bound to his science, but by his middle teens he had become sure that he would be a writer, with C. P. Snow's books joining those in the huge shelves that he was now systematically going through – or with perhaps a journal or two edited by him adding to the Central Reading Room galaxy in their gold-embossed leather folders.

Of all Charles's millions of words in print, *The Newtonian* of 1923 contained the first. Hardly epoch-making but it was not the time and place for that:

The ill-success of our 1st XI at cricket is difficult to explain. The actual playing record, however, is gloomy enough: played 13, won 4, lost 8, drawn 1. The bad luck the team experienced far exceeded that any Newton's team has had for years . . . And yet, despite all this misfortune, many good things were accomplished . . .

The rest of this article is in much the same strain. What strikes me about it is that his style is already recognisable. There are phrases and words which recur throughout his work: 'a capital win' (the word 'capital', now little used, was father's favourite), 'with but a little luck' (he was ever a great believer in luck), 'the 1st XI wickets are abominations unto the Lord' (again one of father's expressions), and 'as near infallibility as mortal man can be' (a phrase I often heard).

Then follows surprisingly an article by him on soccer; it was the only period of his life when he was interested in the game. There was a lack of lustre in the ambiance of the higher grades, with professionals monopolising what he recognised as plainly a scientific game. Because it is football with its relative literary paucity, his style is not typically premonitory although he is able to say 'unless disaster is awaited with equanimity steps should be taken now . . .'

He was eighteen and laboratory assistant at this time. In the next issue of March 1924, over the initials H. E. H. (Bert Howard), Mr

20

C. P. Snow is thanked as a member of the staff helping to raise the tone of the debating society and described as a model for the aspiring public speaker. He is described under 'Shining Lights of the Junior Old Newtonian Society' as 'C. P. Snow – the great Percy. Need we say more?'

For the next issue, July 1924, he was editor and I cannot resist quoting his brief editorial:

TRADITION

'There were giants in those days'. So might say a Newtonian of the times that were, and so might say any schoolboy in England, for the arbiters of fashion have decreed that in the past no wrong was done. Yet this is unreasonable – evolution is a law of nature, and it is foolish to consider that it is suspended in man-made institutions. Indeed, all who are honest with themselves know that tradition-worship is but a pleasing survival of the dim ages when man, finding evil in the conditions of his day, turned to a flawless past for solace and forgot often to look to the future. Thus a heritage has come to us and, rampant in our schools, it may conduce to a proper reverence and the persistence of good institutions but, blind and indiscreet, it may most assuredly hamper the progress of needed reform. Therefore let us keep a sense of proportion; let us revere and strive to emulate the good our predecessors have done, but at the same time let us profit by their errors and improve the present, so that we may be worthy of the future.

CPS

Nothing apocalyptic about this, but it was a credo of the value of balance from which he never moved very far.

His articles on the cricket teams and individuals are models of their kind, depicting a maturity of expression that one might expect but is still surprised to see. But then he always was old for his years (I was often taken for his son). This, and the issue of June 1925, were the only ones he edited: he eschewed any articles by himself on literature. In the last issue of December 1925, while still with Newton's, he limited himself again to cricket and football contributions. In that issue there was this valediction to him:

He was the greatest Newtonian of his generation and he so overshadowed his contemporaries that they appeared small and petty men by his side. He gained that complete ascendancy by his tremendous courage, which led him to attack abuses without regard

21

to the cost; by his complete forgetfulness of self in seeking good of the school; by his knowledge of the world and statesmanship that enabled him to do all things well; above all, by his culture, his command of English which no Newtonian has approached, and his gifts that have already won him a name among accomplished people of the town. There is no doubt that very many Leicester men and women have certainly revised their opinion of Alderman Newton's since Snow came to the fore; they recognise in him a cultured gentleman of no mean oratorical powers – dogmatic, perhaps; so are all people worth knowing. He enriched the School by his long association and set an example that all can follow if few can equal; our regret at his loss must be tinged with rejoicing that he has gone forth to give us repute abroad.

HEH

Although Charles obtained his Intermediate Examination in Science as an External student of London University in 1923 he had to remain at Newton's until the end of 1925, when Leicester University College Chemistry and Physics Department was established. The headmaster gave him the job of laboratory assistant to bridge the gap of two years.

In many ways, the enforced wait was serious. Charles was always conscious of those years slipping by with nothing concrete in his career to show for them. Trying to catch up later was, as will be seen, to set him close to a disaster course.

Laboratory assistant was a humble, breadline post, and Charles's enforced continuation at Newton's was made tolerable only by the stimulus of Bert Howard. Impatient for the next horizon, he fatalistically accepted that his life could not extend for the immediate future beyond Leicester, which he had now also outgrown. To help pass the time, he immersed himself in literature of every description, notably in reading and rereading Dostoevski, Tolstoi, Proust, Balzac and Wells, and everything Wodehouse had ever written.

Another younger friend at Newton's was Edwin Chapman who shared with Charles many YMCA games-playing evenings containing vivid, unfading memories. He confirmed that Charles 'could hold forth brilliantly on any subject' and disclosed that one of his early ambitions was to be a journalist. Chapman told me, too, that his 'most poignant memory' was of a 'late-night confession when we were walking home together from the YMCA. There had been some mutual baring of souls. Suddenly Charles

22

said: "I'd like to be known as Snow of Leicester . . . then Snow of England . . . finally, just Snow." And he made it, didn't he?'

4. Last Tram from a Provincial Town

Charles was the first to go directly from Newton's to a university college. This he did in 1925 with a senior scholarship and an Education Committee grant in recognition of his merit. It would not have been possible to do this from the school's Arts side to which, he told me, he would otherwise have transferred as early as he could. If he had not taken Science as far as he did because he had to, one can only conjecture what effect this would have had on his priority of interests, his career, and on The Two Cultures in particular.

A chemistry master at Newton's warned the professor of chemistry and physics at Leicester University College that, when asked as laboratory assistant at the school to dismantle the equipment after a lesson, Charles's idea of doing so was to open a top drawer just below the demonstration bench and, stretching his arms round the apparatus, sweep it towards him straight into the drawer. It was soon apparent to Professor Louis Hunter that while in Charles he did not have the best handler of equipment he did have a first-class student, at least in theoretical chemistry and physics. On the practical side, Louis Hunter told me, Charles was simply hopeless; those slender fingers and flipper-like hands could not assemble equipment. An external examiner for London University told me that he had marked an experiment by students who had to prepare a dye stuff, malachite green, from supplied chemicals. It was normal, at the end of the experiment, for hands and fingers of all students to be covered with the dye: Charles managed to emerge distinctively with the addition of a green face and green hair. Achieving virtually maximum marks in theory meant, however, that his practical awkwardness could be counter-balanced more than comfortably. Louis Hunter always thought that this practical ineptitude would hamper his scientific progress; one should bear this in mind when considering Charles's later work at Cambridge. It was the real reason for his abandoning scientific research, especially as some of his technical predictions turned out to be false. Nevertheless in 1927 Charles obtained a first in Chemistry at Leicester University College, in those days an external degree of London University.

At the age of twenty-one he became the eldest brother on Harold's sudden death in 1926. By then I was of an age to join in most family activities at Richmond Road. We brothers had a good deal in common. Apart from table tennis on a minute table, we talked about what we had read. As a family we never went for walks; on Lucy's bicycle I acquired the not too testing trick of balance, quite beyond Charles and Eric; Charles never did learn to ride a bicycle or attempt to drive a car. His lack of physical coordination was not evident of course in his quite athletic playing of certain ball games. He became distinctly good at billiards; I am not sure that potentially it was not his best game. But with mechanical devices, even a cigarette lighter, he was anything but deft. He never referred to this disadvantage; it was as if he regarded his inability to cope with gadgets as the price to be paid for being an intellectual. At eleven I went through a phase of tending and reorganising our infinitesimal garden; he derided me for wasting my time when I could have been playing cricket.

After Harold's death Lucy stayed on for a while but Charles left Richmond Road for the greater privacy of lodgings near the college. It was on one of his infrequent visits home that he extracted from me the fact that I was miserable as an acolyte (candle-stick bearer) and deputy thurifer (incense-swinger) at St James's. I told him that I no longer believed; I'm not sure that I ever did. He immediately told mother, and I ceased to attend church, obviously causing her great pain. It was with immense relief that the red cassock and surplice were discarded. I could not have done it if Charles had not interceded for me. He had abandoned church-going at about the same age, later becoming, as he described himself, a 'pious agnostic'.

The college's official title was the Leicester, Leicestershire and Rutland University College. Built as the County Lunatic Asylum in 1837, it became a military base hospital from 1914 to 1918; but that gives a wrong impression of what was, at least on the ground floor, a presentable Georgian-style residence. Much of Charles's energies went into extending the activities of this very small college (founded only in 1921, it became a university in 1957). There was debating to be started, some tennis (the only time he played, although he was completely captured by it when later he was to see Wimbledon on television), chess – and acting; Charles played a wise counsellor in Lady Isabella Gregory's *The Dragon* and Chigi, a merchant, in Louis N. Parker's *The Cardinal*, produced by Roger Manvell who went on to make an international reputation in drama and film history. He recalls Charles performing with tremendous bravado, if no great flair, obviously loving every minute of it.

Many years later when *The Affair* ran as a play in America it was suggested that he should tour as one of the cast; the presence of the author in American theatres would be good publicity. The same temptation presented itself again quite seriously in 1975 when *In Their Wisdom* was dramatised by Sir Ronald Millar as *The Case in Question*. The judge's lines in it were very good; the actor manqué saw himself uttering them with relish for nights on end. It took concerted family efforts to prevail on Charles not to exhibit himself; he complained ruefully that he was being deprived of a lot of fun.

In 1927–8 he edited *The Luciad*, the college magazine, and was the first editor of *Wave*, a typewritten broadsheet. On his visits home he would show me these publications, though they were beyond me at the age of thirteen. He was pleased to wear – as much on the streets as on the grounds – the college cricket blazer, white, with thin green and brown stripes. He had become captain of the team and quickly built up its strength. Sometimes I would go with him to the ground (I was too young to play but Eric occasionally made up the XI) and to the college itself.

One might have thought that there was quite enough here to absorb Charles's energies. Not so. There was still Bert to argue with. The regular meeting place was the saloon bar of The Victoria, a pub which still exists on London Road. And there was the YMCA nearby. In this rather dingy Victorian building Charles played table tennis with vigour, delight and skill. He was later to play contemporaneously with me for Cambridgeshire – and for Cambridge University before I did so. But he played for Leicestershire too, a noteworthy treble.

Four men from Newton's represented the county. Bert Howard, very agile, either totally on the offensive or defensive; Charles, extremely nimble and mixing retrieval with attack judiciously; Ken

Bradley and Bert Wells, both younger and aggressive players. One evening, the four of them, walking down Granby Street from the YMCA, passed a leading men's outfitters, Knight's, under the Grand Hotel. In the window was a model in frock-coat and very old-fashioned top hat. Bert Wells reports that Bradley, to whose mischievous personality Charles responded, remarked quite casually, knowing that Charles had no dress sense: 'That's the sort of hat you should wear, Percy.' Charles agreed that it might suit him, whereupon the others bet him 2/6 each that he would not wear one like it for a week, stipulating that he should carry on just as usual and not go out on the streets without it. Charles promptly appeared on the following Monday in a large grey overcoat and grey flannels surmounted by a motheaten top hat. He kept his side of the bargain to the letter, although the others were too embarrassed to walk with him, following him through the town about four yards behind. When asked how he felt when people stared at him he replied: 'I just stared back at them as though *their* headgear was out of place.' It was discovered subsequently that, although he had won 7/6 on the bet, it had cost him 10/– to hire the hat. I remember seeing him in this attire walking along Aylestone Road on a visit home. From the top of a tram I was astounded by the sight and relieved not to be recognised as his brother. All the other passengers moved to one side of the tram to share the spectacle and I am sure the driver slowed down, prolonging my agony.

There seemed to be no limits to Charles's capabilities. At the YMCA one evening an official of a mixed hockey team was complaining that they had no umpire for their game the following afternoon. Charles at once volunteered. When Bert Wells pointed out that he knew nothing of the game Charles assured him that if he could borrow a book of rules he would be quite capable of umpiring the match. A book of rules being produced, Charles took it home to read. The next day he took charge of the match and, according to players, did not put a foot wrong. That evening friends congratulated him on his performance. He thought it strange that they should be surprised; he had read the rules and, once read, they were embedded in his memory.

While at the University College he joined the Leicester Parliamentary Debating Society which met weekly at the YMCA. There were about sixty with Charles in its Labour Party and equal numbers of Conservatives and Liberals. Run on parliamentary lines with printed Bills, speeches were limited to ten minutes by a Speaker. Governments were arranged and Cabinets appointed. When there was a Labour Government the Prime Minister, Frederick Watson, tells me that Charles was always a minister, often President of the Board of Trade, frequently intervening in a markedly forthright manner on scientific subjects. Bert Howard was also a minister (Foreign Affairs) in the Labour Government. Both were considered to be close to Fabianism or the centre of the party. Their experience in this sizeable society appreciably added to the oratorical power which had been demonstrated earlier at Newton's. Charles was never known to refer to any notes.

He always believed in public speaking for anyone for whom it was not too formidable a test of nerve and as long as it did not take up too much time. When I was president of the Milton Society (Christ's College debating society) I was approached by the secretary of the Cambridge Union with the offer of a place on the committee, although I had not spoken there. Charles's advice was to think hard as to whether I really wanted to go into politics, for which the Union was a start of inestimable value, weighing the time that would be swallowed up. Having no ambitions in that direction I took no further action. For similar reasons, active as he had been in debating at school and at Leicester University College, it is not surprising that Charles himself never spoke either at the Milton Society or the Union. However, in 1970 he could not resist an invitation to be a principal speaker at the Cambridge Union on a special occasion. He was asked to be the fourth speaker on the motion 'That this House believes that technological advance threatens the individuality of man and is becoming his master'. Two undergraduates proposed and opposed and the seconder was the eloquent Professor George Steiner. The Prince of Wales, then an undergraduate and making his only speech at the Union, followed Charles; he stayed neutral and was followed by Earl Mountbatten on Charles's side. The motion was carried by 218 to 184. Charles mentioned to me that it was not easy for anyone to follow Steiner or his (Charles's) special brand of 'anti-rhetoric' but that the Prince of Wales coped remarkably well. There was afterwards a dinner for the principal speakers and officers during which Mountbatten, frequently consulting his watch, was most concerned that Prince Charles should not be shut out of Trinity when its gate closed at midnight.

The YMCA in Leicester was the scene of somewhat idiosyncratic action by Charles on more than one occasion. But only once did he decide to appear at a Saturday night dance there. Charles was not regarded as a ladies' man in his late teens. He was to have his conquests rather late in life and then embarrassingly simultaneously. His teeth were less than good, his tie haphazard, his shoe laces invariably undone. Slow to lose a lopsidedness in the jaw and mouth, his face had not developed its later well known shape. On this occasion he turned up with temporarily tamed hair in a dinner-jacket and bow-tie. He was quick to defend his appearance, explaining that his doctor had advised him in a period of stress to take up dancing as well as tennis and conversation with the opposite sex. With his then oblique smile he left for the dance room and as he went Edwin Chapman noticed that he was still wearing street shoes thick with dust. Edwin Chapman remarked, 'In anyone else it would have been reprehensible. In him it was endearing.' For a six-foot and (later) fourteen stone man Charles was extremely light on his feet, but he had no sense of rhythm whatever.

It was also at the YMCA that he showed evidence of that tunelessness which he never lamented, when taking part in a debate on schoolday myths. Edward Chapman recalls that Charles was scornful of sickly sentiment and, coming to his peroration, suddenly began conducting himself with both hands and burst into a hoarse rendering of the Harrow School song. This was only recognised as such by the words 'Forty years on . . .', and received as a brilliant parody, bringing the house down. He had no ear for music but a fine one for verbal nuances, the *mot-juste* and the nice character-revealing phrase.

I was too young to be present at these performances at the YMCA, but I did witness a monumental table-tennis tussle with Bert Howard. I had not seen the game in any setting except our cramped front-room table. In the spacious room of the YMCA the snappy clatter of celluloid ball on the emery-paper-covered bats gave way to the mellow sound of the ball on sponge-rubber rackets; they added a new dimension of hitting power and subtlety of spin. Bert would serve fast and attempt full-arm smashes while Charles's vicious underspin and overspin frustrated the hapless Bert whose aggression increased with diminishing success. It was a battle of Titans. A few years later I was to take on Bert's role with Charles in, I believe, even more Titanic struggles.

Nevertheless Charles was overtaxing his resources. In 1928 he gained his MSc (still as a London University external student) and obtained the Keddey-Fletcher-Warr Studentship of £200 a year (no meagre figure then) for three years at any university. Open to graduates from the whole country, it was among the highest scientific prizes. For these and his sights on Cambridge he had worked intensely hard. Too hard. He had exchanged Richmond Road and mother's watchful eye for lodgings and seclusion in which to work. The college had no facilities for subsistence and he was quite unable to look after himself – throughout his life he never prepared a meal or part of one for himself or anyone else.

In the consuming ambition to get ahead and make up for the disconsolate marking time as laboratory assistant at Newton's, he burnt up tremendous energy. Would he have the stamina to persevere at that pace? He rarely thought of eating and for his first year at college said that if he did think of it he could not afford it and still buy a nightly pint of beer, which he preferred and judged sufficiently nutritious. The eventual consequence was severe loss of weight. His tall frame was skeletal; it was not difficult to diagnose pernicious anaemia, which had only just ceased to be a killing disease. The remedy, just discovered, was raw liver: perhaps this affected his attitude in later years (except in his Cambridge phase) to food, about which he was seldom more than indifferent. He also had to find sunshine. Only a few months in Sicily, which with examinations behind him he could now afford, saved his life.

I recall how impressed I was, on his return from Sicily, by his bronzed appearance in a light-grey flannel suit. He had thickened out a little and I was proud to walk with him to the tram for one of his rare homecomings to Richmond Road.

Mother's deep-set eyes shone with elation both with the realisation that Charles was at the start of a fine career and with relief over his physical transformation. She knew she would see even less of him at Cambridge than in these last Leicester years; but Cambridge was to her like elevation to the Lords. Father was less easily impressed, but equally glad to see Charles looking so well and proud of his achievements; his happy relationship with his sons had if anything increased.

Father kept his hair, first grey then white, as luxuriantly as Lloyd George, attributing its profusion to the use of Bay Rhum which added an astringent flavour to the house. When I was the only son left at Richmond Road – I was about fifteen – he would at weekends carry up the precipitous stairs to my attic bedroom a cooked breakfast. 'Rise and shine, young man,' he would call out in his high voice. On weekdays the daily help, Naomi, a blue-eyed married blonde, twice my age, would bring the tray up. She would knock on the door and slip into bed for as long as she dared, while mother was resting in her bedroom directly underneath – she could never climb to the attic. When I told Charles this many years later he said that there were parts of my life that he envied. When I pressed him for an explanation, finding his envy hard to account for, he listed my greater ability at cricket which he considered to be almost entirely due to my having better eyesight, my having captained a cricket tour overseas with all its social and other opportunities, and the ease with which I had reached Cambridge. He never forgot that his own transmigration from Leicester to Cambridge had been a close run thing.

5. Election of a Fellow

The wider world now opened up to Charles; in October 1928, aged 23, he went up to Cambridge. Christ's College was selected because his Physics professor at Leicester, A. C. Menzies, had been there. He lost no time in acquiring what was then a relatively exclusive status, that of Ph.D. Cambridge.

Although I'm not entirely clear on this point I assume that he did not lose his Leicester accent until he'd been at Cambridge for a year or so. I know that it had disappeared by the time I used to accept his invitations to join him for cricket in the 1931–3 Long Vacations. The discerning could always detect an ineradicable Midlands trace in the long 'a' in words like 'faailure' and 'Austraalia'.

His Keddey-Fletcher-Warr Studentship ran from 1928 to 1930 when it was replaced for the next three years by the Senior Student-ship of the Exhibition of 1851. Like other Cambridge post-gradu-ates, he lived outside college – in rooms at 9 Green Street. He had lunches and dinners in Hall with the graduates. Eating was now of a standard and regularity that he had never experienced. He soon filled out. The intolerable pressure was now off him although, to start with, still anxious to make his mark at the highest level, he threw himself into research. His earliest published papers included these formidable titles: 'Band spectra of molecules without unused valency electrons' (*Réunion Internationale de Chimie Physique*, 1928), 'The relation between Raman lines and infra-red bands' (*The Philo-sophical Magazine*, 1929), 'Infra-red investigations on molecular structure' (with collaborators, Royal Society, 1930). His research on infra-red spectroscopy was centred in the Cavendish Laboratories where Lord Rutherford and Sir J. J. Thomson were the giants. As emphasised in *The Physicists*, published posthumously in 1981, it was a time of hitherto unparallelled richness of scientific ability and of vast stretches of exploration in many directions. Cockroft and Walton were working on the atom; Blackett, Dirac, Bernal, Kapitza – these were some of the names that were to startle the scientific world very soon. Cambridge at the end of the 1920s and through the 1930s was one of the most stimulating environments England could offer.

By 1930 he was a fellow of Christ's; no previous student had been elected in such a short space of time. Sydney Grose, the most avuncular of tutors (he was soon to be mine), had immediately seen in Charles a man the college wanted. Arthur Brown in the *Strangers and Brothers* series is a faithful representation of Grose who was always pleased with any book in the sequence depicting him. He was entirely content within the narrow walls of the college. College politics and the intrigue of academics were his whole life which he led most serenely into his 90s, savouring the port and claret and occasionally deputising for the Master. He had no ambitions, except perhaps the Mastership for himself; he was just as happy manoeuvring his candidates around the college's courts to the few offices the institution offered. It was he who, with difficulty, talked an extremely conservative company of fifteen fellows into electing Charles.

Charles's life was transformed. Now he was assured of real physical comfort and peace of mind which changed him from the occasionally angry, always hungry and openly aspiring young man in Leicester to an amiable, rounded and steadily contemplative don. The fellowship gave him financial security: it provided almost luxurious rent-free living. With little, except holidays in Europe, on which to spend a reasonable stipend, he could dismiss many earlier worries from his mind. But his hair, golden and thin-stranded, was receding fast, encouraged perhaps by a habit of constantly twisting a forelock. He had discarded gold-framed glasses for the American-style tortoiseshell frames, as they were then known, and had adopted thick lenses which he was to wear permanently. His rooms were M3 – an oak-panelled study and bedroom. In the corner of the First Court they looked down one way over the immaculate, striped, circular lawn of the court towards the Master's Lodge and the other way up Petty Cury. They had been Milton's rooms and were traditionally for fellows. When I came into residence towards the mid-1930s they were conveniently downgraded as fit only for undergraduates and I was able to enjoy them for two years. There were no bathrooms or lavatories attached; these were hidden away at the back of the courts. Indeed, it was a walk and a half, as one of the characters in *Strangers and Brothers* would say, to the nearest lavatories which were in the Second Court.

Charles enjoyed everything – the High Table with its excellent food, lovingly cherished wines, eclectic conversation and its God-given phrases for a novelist's ear; the Senior Combination Room, reserved for fellows, with its aroma of centuries of wine and cigars; the stately Fellows' Garden, where his memorial was to stand. The effect of all this is evident from *The Masters, The Light and the Dark*, and *The Affair*. The Christ's depicted there is as I knew it.

In addition to all this truly historical, indeed somewhat precious, background there was the excitement of the science to which his early training had led. One of his earliest friends and colleagues was Philip Bowden of Caius College. A taciturn Tasmanian, he was to become a FRS and world expert on problems of friction. He was Sir Francis and, later, Lord Getliffe in all but three of the *Strangers and Brothers* books, and Finbow in *Death Under Sail*, Charles's first published book. Bowden and Charles at the Department of Physical Chemistry believed that they had discovered how to produce Vitamin A by artificial methods. They were so elated after making all possible tests that they communicated their research to *Nature* in May 1932. The national press reported on 13 May: '. . . Sir Frederick Hopkins, who is the President of the Royal Society, and the chief authority on vitamins, tells me that the technical methods of investigation which Dr Bowden and Dr Snow have developed offer the prospect of an immediate and extensive increase of knowledge concerning the exact chemical constitution of vitamins. He believes that their technique . . . is a major contribution to vitamin research. . . .' (*Manchester Guardian*). 'Vitamin A (the general health vitamin) has been prepared for the first time by artificial means . . . Sir Frederick Hopkins, the pioneer of vitamin research, stated . . . Vitamin A has been prepared from carotene – a widely occurring substance which derives its name from being the colouring matter of carrots . . . and the final confirmation from its effect on debilitated rats will only be a matter of weeks . . . Dr Snow tells me that they started on the research quite recently and the work has proved so fascinating that for some time they have been working continuously during the waking hours. . . .' (*Morning Post*). '. . . Bowden and Snow have been able to make important improvements by means of an instrument which is really a spectroscope, constructed with very large prisms and lenses, cut from massive crystals of

34

quartz. . . .' (*The Times*). *The Search* tells what eventually happened. A calculation was faulty, and a new method of producing Vitamin A artificially had not been found.

The trauma after all that publicity put Charles off scientific research irrevocably, arguably to his advantage. He might have recovered his nerve and gone on to make his name through molecular research but, in retrospect, one can feel more confident that literature, combined with his liaison with science, was his métier.

His writing, previously in the background, now came to the fore. At Leicester, possibly in his last years at Newton's, he had written a novel. He would never be drawn by me – nor I think by anyone else – on its nature. All he told me was that it was called *Youth Searching*. Apparently he soon decided that it would not do. If he absentmindedly forgot to destroy it, it is unlikely that it survived because all his pre-1945 papers were destroyed by another hand. A play, *Nights Ahead*, written in his earliest Cambridge years, still exists.

In 1932 he published *Death Under Sail* (Heinemann). It had been conceived the previous year when he had been seduced by Bert Howard and his brother Cecil into taking a yachting holiday on the Norfolk Broads. Sailing, with its discomforts and association with water, was anathema to him; but the locale gave him the theme for what was so successful a detective story that it has been reprinted many times – most recently in America in 1980. He also had published (with Gollancz) in 1933 *New Lives for Old*, an account, as the cover stated, by 'one of the cleverest of our younger scientists' of rejuvenation, which in those days was a talking point. H. G. Wells has written about the process and Maugham was to take it seriously enough to endure the injections that are believed to have prolonged his physical, if not mental, existence. Charles was very reluctant to talk about this book. Dedicated to Stella, a pseudonym for a coal-mine owner's vivacious daughter with whom he had been hopelessly in love at Leicester University College, *New Lives for Old* came out anonymously because, as he said, he was at the time in line for a job which this authorship might have prejudiced. It got mixed reviews, whereas *Death Under Sail* had been pleasantly received in the then comparatively gentle reviewing climate. Efforts by publishers to have *New Lives for Old* reprinted were never sanctioned. Its main value is now as a second-hand find, not easy since it does not carry his name. My copy is inscribed: 'To Philip. This book which will not appear again. C. P. Snow.'

In each long vacation he had been writing steadily. *The Search* was published by Gollancz in 1934. It was here that he recorded autobiographically: 'Mine was a very happy childhood' and 'I enjoyed almost all my time at school'. It reflected some of his agony over his scientific failure, the main character abandoning science to write a political book on the state of Europe. *The Search*, dedicated to Philip Bowden and reviewed glowingly, convinced him that his future lay in writing.

So far he had used only the Leicestershire and Norfolk milieux, a little of London, friends and acquaintances as models for his characters, his school and family experience; but there were the green pastures of Cambridge waiting to be explored. Surprisingly, they had been little written about and certainly not in the form which was taking shape in his mind. Under cover of frequent explosions of laughter – greater than I knew in anyone – his sharp eyes behind the thick lenses were registering an anecdote here, a reaction there, to be incorporated into his Cambridge books. He had at least two in mind, inchoate elements of *The Masters* and *The Affair*.

I joined him at Christ's in 1934 with a History Exhibition of £40 a year augmented by another £40 a year from the Leicester Education Committee and £50 each from the Sir Richard Stapley and Thomas Wall (the ice-cream manufacturer) Benefactions – a precarious enough total on which to live in Cambridge. At first I lived in appallingly dingy lodgings at the back of Petty Cury, demolished – not before time – some years ago. It was the best I could afford, so I spent as much time as I could without disturbing him in Charles's rooms. These were now Darwin's rooms (G3) on the opposite side of the First Court to Milton's. Much larger than Milton's, to which I moved from my lodgings as speedily as possible, they consisted of a superb oak-panelled and beamed dining-room, which had a plaque of Darwin over the fireplace and a coal and log fire burning all through the winter, though it was only used for occasional dinner parties and by undergraduates waiting to see Charles, who was now a tutor; a white-panelled drawing room in Georgian style with large arm chairs clustered round the fire and window-seats overlooking the First Court; a stark bedroom. His rooms were among the best in the college. They were reached by a pair of worn, wooden staircases. Like all college staircases, there were no doors at the bottom and the wind swept triumphantly up as far as the undergraduate attics above. The bedroom, narrow and uncarpeted, with iron bedstead, was directly over one of these staircases and was bitterly cold at any time of year. Cambridge's winds from the Russian steppes, which blew from November to March, made this room singularly uninviting unless one retired to it mellowed by the Senior Combination Room's port. I attribute to it Charles's first attacks of lumbago. On the same floor level were the rooms of J. B. Trend, who could finish sentences in Spanish or Portuguese, of which he was professor, but never in English. You were left groping among his cheerful but unhelpful shrugs of the shoulders for his meanings; it was generally philosophical despair about the way Spain was going. Trend (Eustace Pilbrow in *The Masters*) spent every possible moment away from Cambridge on the Iberian Peninsula until the Franco rebellion, after which he never returned. For him it was like being a chocolate addict with not so much as a glimpse of a bar.

On the first day of 1935 Charles had the idea of a series of novels, certainly four, with a connecting link, himself, as Lewis Eliot. The notion, which was to bring him international fame, came to him on La Canebière in Marseilles. That wide, tree and café-lined boulevard sloping gently up from the lively quayside to the city's parks has an inspiring, dream-creating quality which the noise and bustle does little to diminish; it is one of my favourite places. Charles, who had reached Marseilles by sea from Naples so as to fly to Paris, told me of the *Strangers and Brothers* concept as soon as he saw me in Cambridge a week or so later. 'I think I've a really workable idea that's going to occupy me for the next ten or twenty years. I'm rather excited by it and, given some sanity in the world to enable me to carry it through, I believe it'll make me.' He went on to describe the idea more fully; its appeal was immediately obvious.

It was to take him five years to plan the sequence in general and to produce, as his next book after *The Search* in 1934, the first of the *Strangers and Brothers* series, initially entitled *Strangers and Brothers* and later changed to *George Passant*. This was to be followed by *The Conscience of the Rich, The Masters* and *Time of Hope*. There was to be remarkably little departure from what had formed in his mind on La Canebière.

His programme was naturally interrupted by the war which nevertheless gave him the ideas for *The Light and the Dark* and *The New Men*. Although able to work seriously on the sequence before the war began, his leisure was severely restricted as it developed, and he was virtually prevented from making any progress for five years. But at least *Strangers and Brothers*, dedicated to H. E. Howard and published in 1940, had inaugurated the series: *The Conscience of the Rich* had been virtually completed. Despite his frustration I believe that Charles was for the most part sustained through those gloomy years by the knowledge of his plan.

Certainly his remaining years in Cambridge were enhanced by a private knowledge of the scheme. In the first half of the 1930s, despite the research disaster, he had been happy more often than not. Now, in 1935, his eyes shone, his ears were sharply tuned and his moods jovial, despite his fear that Fascism in Italy and Germany might take a grip in England and of the inevitable showdown. I shared much of these happy times with him; scowling external events have a habit of rolling by and there were entertaining insular ones to absorb us to the exclusion of much else. Admittedly Charles had little to show for it, but he could gather in, like a euphoric harvester, the luxuriant miscellany of material around him.

The fellows encapsulated in *The Light and the Dark, The Masters* and *The Affair* were half-portraits at least of the originals; sometimes rather more than that. We have met Arthur Brown (Grose) and Eustace Pilbrow (Trend), but there were many others.

The youngest fellow was in some ways the most colourful. The character of Roy Calvert, which on its own virtually forms the corpus of *The Light and the Dark* (1947), was based largely on C. R. C. Allberry. He was dazzlingly brilliant. In age he was halfway between me and Charles, whose intimate friend he was. Slender and handsome, Charles Allberry was all elegance. His slightness of build was deceptive for he excelled in sport, particularly at those games, like rackets, fives and cricket, which required wrist-power. His rather close-set eyes belied a general theory Charles and I had that the best games players tended to have them wide-spaced. He and I opened the innings for the college – my brother Charles was one of the spin bowlers – and I would be almost hypnotised by his wealth of talent. He was remarkably agile. He once jumped from the top of a straight-backed chair to the top of a similar one twelve feet away, retaining his upright poise on landing perfectly: all done without a run-up to the leap – pure Nijinsky.

Allberry was as complicated mentally as he was endowed with physical versatility. He was a rare Orientalist specialising in the most obscure Coptic scripts. He and a German professor in Berlin were the world experts on almost transparent fragments of inscribed papyrus that had survived. Standing or sitting for hours on an elongated stool, he would pore over a ragged-edged piece kept in place and from further disintegration between panes of glass. I gathered that he was lucky if he could find a clue to one word as a result of months of sitting, standing, gazing, peering and contemplating. This work was not conducive to dispersing a tendency to depression; it kept him locked away too much within himself. In company, when in the mood – he mixed more with undergraduates than fellows – he could be the wittiest, most entertaining, courtly and irreverent of companions. He enjoyed teasing Charles, whom he called 'Snow' – or 'old boy' if he wanted to be affectionate. He was the most volatile person I ever knew. His enrichment of life in Christ's was incalculable but the black phases were disturbing. They were to grow deeper and more regular as he came to recognise the inevitability of war. He knew that it would mean the end of his work as he and the professor in Berlin would not be able to correspond, which was vital to its continuance. The two Charleses argued endlessly as Munich came and went – Allberry trying to hide from the inevitable, Charles maintaining that war had to come if civilisation was to survive. They were not now on the easiest of terms; Allberry could not bear the thought of war with Germany and Charles wanted it. When war did come Allberry, in utter despair, volunteered for the hazardous job of bomber pilot; he would have to drop bombs over the one man in the world who understood the work to which he was devoting his own life.

C. R. C. Allberry is now merely a name on the War Memorial plaque in Christ's Chapel. I cannot go into that chapel without being chilled to the heart at the recollection of so many friends long dead. Charles told me that after the war he could not walk round the courts of Christ's without seeing ghosts. Perhaps the spectre that lingered longest was CRCA, sometimes jaunty, sometimes wraithlike, seeking anonymity – head perky if his step was springy, head down in a brown study if his step lagged. Charles, he and I spent much time at the Christ's ground at Huntingdon Road playing cricket and commenting on it; my time with them I remember as summer terms full of sun. I was unusual for that period in having an open car; it had cost me £5. It gave Allberry boyish pleasure to travel in it, and Charles was never one to miss a lift in a car if one offered itself. But it was in someone else's open car, that of a rather wild medico, that brother Charles was provoked to comment mildly from the rear: 'Take it a little more steadily, young man. You have one of the most valuable lives in the country in your care – one that, if spared, is going to be quite distinctly valuable.'

By way of epitaph, Charles was reminded of Allberry poignantly enough to say nearly a decade after his death that he was 'the closest friend I ever had. He would certainly have become the most noted Coptic expert that has ever lived. I believe him to be the most remarkable man I have ever known.'

For Charles, Christ's was just the right size; it enabled him to know his colleagues so well. Founded in 1448 and refounded in 1506, it had a perceptible tradition in contrast with more recent establishments like Selwyn and Downing. Although he had friends in Trinity, this would have been too large a setting for the compact and succinct nature of events described by him in *The Masters*.

Charles Allberry was the youngest of the fellows; J. Holland Rose, Professor of Naval History and expert on Napoleon, the oldest. It is principally on his unconsciously entertaining personality that the most likeable, certainly the most amusing, of all Charles's characters, M. H. L. Gay, is based. I never saw him, as on one occasion in the play of *The Masters*, escorted or half-carried by college porters from the Porters' Lodge to the Senior Combination Room; I used to see him, however, once a week progressing, with fast-moving legs but somehow not much velocity, round the court en route with enthusiasm to Hall for his 'meal and a half'. He was eighty when I first saw his handsome head, rubiginous complexion, with white hair and trim spade beard; he looked very much like Field Marshal Smuts. Seeing Smuts, an honorary fellow and a former Christ's undergraduate, at the High Table, with Holland Rose opposite, gave one the illusion of looking in a mirror.

Canon C. E. Raven was like no one else. I used to see that sharp, gloomy, saturnine visage frequently as Raven came into the college from his home for the dinners which were essential for his feel of the college; the Mastership had long been his burning ambition. Jago in *The Masters* is a superbly drawn portrait of him. The details of the election, which is the theme of that book, are not those of Raven's own election but rather based on one in the 1850s at Lincoln College, Oxford, recorded in Mark Pattinson's *Memoirs*, to which G. H. Hardy had drawn Charles's attention. Raven's influence in my time, when he was not Master, was at its most powerful among undergraduates. There had always been a close connection between

Christ's and the clergy; he was active in promoting this among a number of my contemporaries, some of whom, ineluctably drawn to making the church their calling, remained my friends despite my patent irreverence. But Raven had an uneasy relationship with Charles. He was primarily a cleric and secondly a pacifist and ornithologist. The most dolichocephalic of men, with a jutting jaw so black that it looked as though he had not had a close shave for days, he was truly a ravenesque figure.

Another vital figure in *The Masters* was T. C. Wyatt, who may be taken as partly C. P. Chrystal. In the book he was the Dean: in life he was the Bursar. No society was perhaps better designed to encourage eccentricity than that of fellows at Oxbridge. Wyatt was only eccentric in being an exceptionally breezy engineer among colleagues who generally seemed to glide inconspicuously or slip clandestinely around the rhododendron bushes from their rooms to Hall. S. W. P. Steen and A. L. Peck – on whom R. E. A. Nightingale, prominent in *The Masters* and even more important as the Bursar in *The Affair*, is to some extent based – were shadowy figures. Supremely introvert, their undisturbed way of life was ideal for writing books, which they never got round to. They rarely lectured; from comparative youth they idled through life entirely within the college, although Peck supervised enthusiastically the Fellows' Garden for a period and, as librarian, successfully kept out every one of Charles's books. They were also good at taking remarkably obstinate stands, invariably on the unenlightened side, in college issues. It was the exception for undergraduates to know by name any fellows other than their tutor, their supervisor, a lecturer in their subject and, at least by his collar, the chaplain. Seldom were they invited to dons' rooms or brought into conversation with them, despite frequent encounters on the narrow paths of the courts. But Charles kept me in daily touch with what was going on, and later this made my enjoyment of *The Masters* total. My eyes were opened in the clearest possible way to fierce divisions in the smallest of societies and to the never ending variety of men.

It was immediately on joining him residentially at Christ's that Charles and I started to be very close, not least in scrutinising our fellow residents. In a special message to subscribers of the Franklin Library of New York's beautifully bound edition of *The Affair* (1980) Charles writes: '"Me" is the narrator of the story, Lewis Eliot, the centre figure of the whole entire series. Both he and his brother are men with a hard sense of irony who have already by the time of *The Affair* seen a lot of absurdity in their lives, been amused by it and also disenchanted. They have seen, in this decorous background of the College, a great deal more of absurdity (as well as human frailty) during the course of *The Affair*. Their sense of humour and irony is, as with brothers who are very close, much in tune . . .'

Charles brought few Cambridge figures from outside Christ's into his university books. An exception was J. D. Bernal, crystallographer, FRS, half-Irish, half-Jewish communist who became Mountbatten's tame provider of ideas for military devices in the war. Described as 'the most original, the wildest mind in England', he appears as Constantine in *The Search*. Desmond Bernal would come into Charles's rooms at Christ's when I was waiting there for his return; I could never get through to him, but to Charles, who at times found Christ's rather inbred, he was a stimulus. Among dons there was remarkably little inter-college mixing, infinitely less than among undergraduates.

But there was outside Christ's a friend for Charles who, although taking a surprisingly peripheral part in Charles's books as Austin Davidson, an art connoisseur, was outstanding.

Charles would time and again confirm that G. H. Hardy had been one of the three strongest influences in his life; when pressed, he was inclined to identify him as the principal influence. Like Allberry – and he was not unlike a matured version of him – Hardy was, in the years after his death in 1947, one of the ghosts Charles would see on revisiting Cambridge, making returns there a little less easy for him. Godfrey Harold Hardy, always known by his surname, was Professor of Mathematics and a Fellow of Trinity; but he was such a regular visitor to Charles's rooms that in later life on returning to the First Court at Christ's Charles could never escape from his image. Not that he wanted to; he accepted the indelibility of the impression as part of his essential experience of Cambridge. They would meet at Fenner's, the ground where the University cricket team played from the end of April – often in bleak east winds – to mid-June. Every day, for Hardy arranged his summer around cricket with teaching taking second place, his untidy figure would be found at the end of the ground furthest from the pavilion. I was privileged to be with them on occasions both there and in Charles's rooms often enough to savour the interplay of two remarkably sympathetic people. Hardy would invariably at the opening of the season be enveloped in a huge white sweater in Trinity colours (in which he would also give perfectly precise mathematics lectures to undergraduates); over this, an ill-shapen raincoat, with sometimes an extra sweater slung round the neck and shoulders. His fine-drawn, sensitive, retiring face with the brightest of darting hazel eyes, was almost Indian brown, the deep tan accentuated by white-grey hair, short but in some disarray. Charles's essay on Hardy entitled 'The Mathematician on Cricket' is one of the most charming vignettes he ever produced.

Some indication of the measure of their attachment can be gauged from the fact that, after a whole day's watching at Fenner's followed by separate dinners in their respective colleges, I would either see Charles departing in the direction of Trinity or Hardy, head bent down, with a huge scorebook and a large envelope containing the game of *Stumpz* under his arm, coming to Charles's staircase. If the fixture was at home I had a standing invitation to join them. A board would be spread out on a table with special cards alongside. They would draw up sides representing, say, the Go's and the Ha's. Hardy was always captain of the latter, going in first as G. H. Hardy, an amateur, with Hayward T. W., professional, of course. Then Hammond, W. R., with Hadrian as No. 4 and so on, Hannibal at No. 7 combining solidity with enterprise. The sides were represented by men of merit, preference being given to cricketers if they existed under the right letters. The Sn's under C. P. Snow were soon found to be atrociously weak and always beaten by the Ha's, so Charles was allowed to be non-playing captain of a powerful side of Go's, with God, a professional captain, going in No. 1 with J. W. von Goethe as his opening partner: they were invariably successful, as were Gorki, M., and Gogol, N. V. at Nos. 3 and 4. Göring and Goebbels were excluded for reasons of taste; they would certainly have been failures anyway. The field could be set as in a real match, and the bowling cards, with some special rules naturally introduced by Hardy, could prearrange spin, speed or lack of it to which, if a false shot was made, one would rightly be dismissed. God was a formidable bowler of off-breaks, with an occasional top-spinner that would go straight through. Hardy kept the score and every detail in the huge score books in his meticulous writing. The matches would go on over a series of nights, each evening's play starting at 8.30 and ending at 11.30 – with next day's cricket-watching at Fenner's to follow. As regards the world's Greatest XI, Hardy would say that the first half-dozen picked themselves but then it became difficult, most of all for the eleventh place. His selection lay between Charles Chaplin and Jesus Christ, one of whom would have to be twelfth man. On the arguable grounds that more people round the world had heard or seen Chaplin than his rival, Hardy gave the place to Chaplin.

Hardy had been at Cambridge from 1896 to 1919; then at Oxford as Professor of Geometry until 1931 when he returned to Cambridge as Professor of Pure Mathematics. He was a bachelor with a delicately acid perspicacity. His historical sense was a formidable addition to the exquisitely crystalline logical side of the mathematical man. Cricket apart, the academic world of Cambridge went under his and Charles's microscope. It was not easy for me to make comments on anything, except on cricket. Then Hardy would give his quick, shy glance of approval in recognition of my contribution of some experience of the game at a higher level than he had actually played, or of some intuitive judgement that I felt confident to proffer. Charles would encourage me with my limited contributions for Hardy was a stern critic of the irrelevant, the ignorant, the brash. He had not the slightest element of small talk. His communications to Charles when they were separated were by means of the postcard and in the most concise style imaginable. He was the most private of men. It was only when they had been close friends for the greater part of fifteen years that he told Charles that he had once attempted suicide (he was to try again not long before he died). He cannot be understood if his fanatical love of cricket is not accepted. The political events of the 1930s could not be kept entirely out of their conversations, but I had the impression that Hardy was quicker than Charles in wishing to shut them out of his mind. I believe that he sensed that his world of calm, Fenner's cricket, Trinity bowls, his one or two friends, had a short time to run. With war there would be none of these things – well, perhaps Trinity bowls – and there would be nothing to live for. As it was, he stayed at a disrupted Trinity throughout, all his sources of enjoyment gone and unable to recover the will to live when it was over. Charles was with him, as often as he could be, in his last days.

Hardy was entirely original in his judgement of people, his expressions, his avoidance of repetition; the sole exception was one repeated phrase. After he died Charles and I adopted his saying 'That's real old brandy' to describe something particularly esoteric. There is a discerning evaluation of him in Charles's introduction to Hardy's book *A Mathematician's Apology*, published in 1967. Charles used to attribute aspects of his own worldly wisdom to Hardy's precise, penetrating assessments of people. Hardy might have been the epitome of the eccentric; he was also in his supremely introverted detachment extra shrewd, allowing Charles to test his own observations and judgements as well as supplying him with an immense repertoire of conversational aides beginning with 'As Hardy used to say . . .' Yes, Hardy's influence on Charles was deep. He had no need to tell me so; I saw and heard it first-hand for nearly fifty years.

Three books in three successive years, culminating in *The Search* in 1934, had brought Charles to the favourable notice of fellow writers, including some senior ones. He told me later that both he and J. B. Priestley judged the literary climate then as one of better manners and natural patronage, the occasional kind gesture from established towards rising authors contrasting sharply with that which prevailed after the Second War.

Charles invariably arranged for me to meet his visitors – once literally. Richard Aldington, who had followed up *Death of a Hero* (1929) with *All Men are Enemies* (1933), was coming to Cambridge. Charles, engaged that morning, deputed me to meet Aldington at the station as it was his first visit. I had not seen a picture of him, Charles had never met him, and I did not know what to expect, though it was said that he looked distinguished. In the event it was quite easy. He was outstandingly handsome, the most impressive-looking writer I was ever to know. He resembled Herbert Marshall, currently one of the romantic film actors, but with much better features. During the weekend he stayed with Charles his stock grew with us. He was gentlemanly; this need not have followed from his rough war experiences starkly described in *Death of a Hero*, which had made his reputation as one of the most powerful writers on the First War. Mostly he entertained us with refreshing stories of his eccentric friends, D. H. and Frieda Lawrence. When Aldington went to live in the south of France and then, during the Second War, in America, he and Charles maintained their friendship and warm admiration for each other's works. Charles and I shared a by no means accepted view in the 1930s that Aldington was a magnificent poet. Later, with *Wellington, Lawrence of Arabia: A Biographical Enquiry, R. L. Stevenson: Portrait of a Rebel* (in which, never having visited the South Seas, he absorbed the Samoan atmosphere so skilfully) and *D. H. Lawrence: Portrait of a Genius but . . .*, he showed himself a vigorous, often splendidly provocative biographer. For a while after the war there was a break in relations between Charles and Aldington, and their paths never actually crossed after those Cambridge visits; but they resumed their friendship until Aldington's death in France in 1962.

Charles told me that Aldington, who always addressed him as Snow, had said he thought that Charles was Jewish because he seemed to be preoccupied with non-Gentiles. This was when Charles was writing what was finally called *The Conscience of the Rich*, which centres round an Anglo-Jewish family. Charles put it to me that Aldington thought 'such an imaginative exercise was completely outside human power and became fully convinced that I was a Jew myself'. Charles added, 'Having seen me, having seen you, he might as well conclude that Willie Maugham had a club foot. How could he be so naïve?' The only valid point that Aldington had was Charles's nose which, like mother's, though not large or hooked, turned down at the end somewhat sharply; it did seem to command notice rather more than its size merited, especially when he tended to look down it with strongly contrasting expressions of self-deprecation or authoritativeness. Aldington was Charles's first eminent friend from the literary world.

Very different was H. G. Wells, another visitor. His small rounded shape, his squeaky voice, his liveliness, are familiar enough; his comparative self-effacingness when in the company of Charles, whose novel *The Search* he had much praised, was less to be expected. Critics had said of this book that it marked the arrival of another Wells, and Wells seemed fascinated in the presence of a successor. Perhaps he could see beyond the horizons that limited Charles's own vision in the 1930s. Charles was genuinely fond of Wells (who, like Hardy, surprised him by revealing that he had once contemplated suicide) and all that went to make up his personality, as well as warmly admiring his inventiveness coupled with his realistic pessimism.

But the outside world impinged more and more. The Spanish Civil War started in July 1936. The success of the rebel Franco, aided by Hitler and Mussolini, brought to Charles and me periods of impenetrable gloom. I joined Charles in the 1936 Long Vacation at Loxley in Warwickshire where he had taken a house and was looked after by a college servant. At the end of a day in which Charles would sit in the garden working on *Strangers and Brothers*, we compulsively listened to the news, followed by a lugubrious drink in the village pub. We would try in the daytime to put Spain and what it meant out of mind, but in the evening the pessimism returned. There was no doubt about the ferocity of the conflict – nor of the inevitability of world involvement. One of my close friends, who was a pupil of Charles's and perhaps rather anomalously a member of the ultra-conservative College Rowing Club, took this war so much to heart as to leave Christ's prematurely, as had undergraduates in other colleges, and join the International Brigade. Ivor Hickman, whose hair and profile reminded me of Rupert Brooke's, was impetuous and normally light-hearted. Nobody could dissuade him. Ironically, he survived front-line fighting until the withdrawal of the Brigade when he was killed.

1936 was the least enjoyable of our series of Long Vacations together since 1932. That period had seen Charles at his happiest, his gusts and bellows of mirth reverberating round the court as he chatted below his staircase with Allberry, Grose, Wyatt and other fellows of whom he was fond.

6. End of an Epoch

After the Long Vacation there was a new voice in the college – at the top in every sense. One would hear in First Court a great booming voice conducting what was in fact a normal conversation outside the Master's Lodge. We called Sir Charles Darwin, namesake of that Darwin who had been an undergraduate at Christ's before his monumental circumnavigation, the Chief Sea Lion. Charles thought that Darwin, larger than life as he was, more than fitted the Mastership. Charles himself was now tutor to undergraduates reading science and medicine. They could call on him for permission to stay on after midnight and for emergencies; he was virtually *in loco parentis* during term. His quota out of 400 undergraduates was high spirited. It did not include Wilfred Wooller, one of the most eminent double Blues in the University's history and renowned for his massive strength, especially when fortified by beer. He appeared before his tutor for dislodging a telephone box out of its concrete base and, with the Oxford match coming along, Charles interceded with the tutor and was principally responsible for the Solomon-like judgement to rusticate him after the Oxford match when there were only a few days to go before the end of term. Wilf Wooller, on another occasion, created havoc within the college by dislocating the rows of cast-iron cisterns, seven on each side, in the only lavatory block the college possessed. Charles's intercession on his behalf limited rustication to a month or so in a term which did not culminate in a meeting with Oxford. The giant was otherwise remarkable for his mildness.

Being in the same court as Charles was on occasions rather inhibiting, but on balance the advantages outweighed the disadvantages. As a member of the provincial lower middle class I had come up to Cambridge as radical as a Labour supporter could be. Poor in relation to my public school friends, I had difficulty in keeping up with them; the effect was to drive me further to the left. In particular I was incensed by the British Fascist movement and Mosley's brutality which I saw first-hand when attending their meeting at the Cambridge Guildhall. The sight of the black-shirted, arrogant Mosley, escorted by his thugs armed with coshes, was too much for me, as it was for many others. This made us potential material for the opposite pole, the Communist Party. Every college had a member or two, and I was approached. It was the greatest comfort to discuss such problems with Charles. In this instance, he had not the slightest doubt that, whatever my conviction and fears, it would be imprudent to join the Communist Party. Its members were listed, he said, and known to 'the Authorities'. If I joined it would be very difficult to find a job on leaving Cambridge – or at least one's choice would be highly circumscribed. Nevertheless I wanted to make a dramatic gesture; had the invitation to join come from a personable fellow in a different age-group, and had I not been able to consult Charles, perhaps the result would have been different.

In 1937, I organised a dinner at Christ's in honour of Bert Howard at which Newtonians at Oxford and Cambridge were present. There were four speeches, one by J. H. Plumb and another, inevitably, by Bert. The other two were by Charles and myself; the only occasion on which we spoke together in public as far as I can recall.

Jack Plumb, who had followed Charles to Leicester University College, was another protégé of Bert Howard's. He was researching at Cambridge until the war which he spent mainly at Bletchley. After the war he became a Fellow of King's, then of Christ's, Professor of Modern English History and eventually Master of Christ's. He corresponded with Charles to the end of his life, and Jack gave dinners at Christ's for Charles's fiftieth and seventieth birthdays. They were memorable epicurean occasions, spiced with a fair display of lively cynicism and a complete absence of nostalgia. Plumb, with his historian's eye for the past, had also a keen one for the future. Charles told me that there were elements of Jack Plumb (and Lord Beaverbrook and others) in the composite character, Reginald Swaffield, in *In Their Wisdom*.

Harry Hoff, a teacher at Newton's, had been an undergraduate reading spectroscopy at Christ's in Charles's first post-graduate years. Charles found him effervescently bright and sharp. They continued their friendship when Hoff joined the science staff at

Newton's where I was head prefect, though I had met him earlier in Cambridge Long Vacations. Early in 1939, when Charles and Harry Hoff were staying at the Cap d'Antibes Hotel, they met the Brett Youngs for the first time. Francis was, after Aldington and Wells, one of the first successful writers whom Charles came to know well. He and Jessica Brett Young were Lawrence and Mrs Knight in *Time of Hope* and *Homecomings*. During the war Charles and Hoff, who had left Newton's for the administrative side of the RAF, kept up their friendship and their careers ran parallel. After Charles left the Civil Service Commission Hoff was Personnel Consultant to the Atomic Energy Authority and Central Electricity Board. A prolific novelist under the name of William Cooper, his style somewhat resembles Charles's. Charles is Robert in *Scenes from Provincial Life* and *Scenes from Married Life*, Swan in *Young People* and Frederick in other works now about to be published. As a close friend and confidant for nearly fifty years, Harry was unmistakeably influential in keeping Charles informed, encouraged and entertained with a vivacity which the passing years have only faintly sapped.

In 1937 Charles became editor of *Discovery*. Its sub-title was 'The Popular Journal of Knowledge' and he expressed to me his delight that he had been given this chance to popularise science; his writing of general scientific articles (for *Nature* in 1934–5 and for *The Spectator* in 1936) to that time had been only sporadic. Founded in 1920, *Discovery* was taken over by the Cambridge University Press which produced its first issue in April 1938. Charles, in his opening editorial, 'Discovery Comes to Cambridge', wrote: 'The present time is not a peaceful one but for those who are occupied by the search for knowledge it is full of exhilaration. This century has been lit up with the glow of successful discovery. In science, in particular, it has been a golden age. Unless we understand these achievements of our day we miss one of the greatest rewards of being alive in the twentieth century. Every means ought to be used to explain these results. They ought to be within the reach of the interested layman, if he does not possess the time or the training or the technical details . . .'

Predominantly scientific, the first issue nevertheless contained one article entitled 'Inquest on Detective Stories' by two authors, one of whom was R. Philmore, H. E. Howard's writing name. In the same issue were reviews of *The New Vision of Man* over the initials HEH, and of a travel book (*South Latitude* by F. D. Ommaney) over the initials CPS – his first of many nationally published reviews (if one excludes his 1934 articles in the *Cambridge Review*). Among distinguished contributors to *Discovery* was, rather surprisingly, Aldington on 'Science and Conscience'. In response to Aldington's interest in *Discovery*, Charles wrote a pamphlet, *Richard Aldington: An Appreciation* published by Heinemann in 1938. *Discovery* brought science nearer to my understanding than any other publication before or since, and I shared Charles's enthusiasm over what he had taken on. When I was reading through the early numbers I was interested to see that the third issue contained new and expert opinion on possible connections between pernicious anaemia, from which Charles had so nearly died a decade earlier, and a gastric ulcer, which was to be the cause of Charles's death forty-two years later.

Discovery, the perfect medium for Charles's messages and predictions, was to end under Charles's editorship in March 1940. It would be many years before he found another vehicle, and then a much wider one, for his reviews, briefly in *The Sunday Times*, and then for a long period in *The Financial Times*.

Throughout my four years at Christ's Charles and I played table tennis every winter for two hours each weekday afternoon. We had only to walk to the YMCA two minutes from Christ's Gateway; the whole of a large hall was entirely ours. The scene would be set for ferocious encounters, no holds barred, no quarter given. Ten years younger and altogether fitter, I was merciless, even though there were times when Charles insisted on playing after spasms of lumbago. I could not afford to let up without running the risk of falling behind in the scores which we religiously kept; we were very well-matched.

Our styles too were not dissimilar, although Charles's racket grip was a backhand one while mine was the pen-holder type. With much slice or top-spin on the serve returned with contrary spin, the next shot would be a work-up to a flat-out smash with a fully extended arm. In the meantime, the one put on the defensive would be twelve feet or more back from the table, returning the ball with a heavy cut or over-drive. Rallies would often run to a score or more shots, of a standard drawing applause from any spectators. We were both selected to play for the university and for Cambridgeshire.

In 1938, when the World Championships were held at Wembley, I was selected to play in the preliminary round where I was knocked out. Charles conceded that I had done creditably to have been selected at all; this was real praise for we were critical, as only brothers could be, of each other's game. Dressed in red silk short-sleeved shirts and our rackets thick with pimpled rubber, we were near-professionals – not surprisingly when we played so regularly with such serious intent. Charles would fill the hall with elephantine bellows of agony when he missed an outright smash; I would wince as I bungled a sham drop-shot over the net when he was yards away. Tension was always high; our rubber shoes would screech on the wooden floor. The most astonishing feature of these unyielding struggles of spin, smash and slice was Charles's nimbleness. At just over six feet, he weighed two stone more than I did; nevertheless he could move with the agility of a gymnast. This will surprise those who only knew him after the war. After our four winters' playing the score was, I think, something like 1,795 games to me and 1,601 to him. Charles considered that luck was not on his side and that I was overendowed with it, for I was regularly selected to play for Cambridgeshire whereas he was chosen only occasionally. If he believed that he had played particularly well but still lost the balance of the games in an afternoon's play we would walk back to Christ's without a word – only to meet the following afternoon when I would ritually call for him. This was the only cause of disgruntlement between us that I can remember.

In 1937 I joined the Colonial Service. This enabled me to have a fourth year at Cambridge on that service's idiosyncratic course, preparing myself to be an administrator in Fiji and the Western Pacific. Charles and I became closer still as we realised that this would inevitably lead to a separation broken only by periodical leaves. We both recognised that in Fiji I would be out of the war unless, or until, Japan came in, in which case things in the Pacific would probably be hotter than in England. My going to the South Seas produced several family complications, the most serious of which involved my financée, Anne. (On the announcement of our engagement Charles, with characteristic generosity, had given us a large party in Darwin's rooms.) Anne could not follow me to Fiji until I had passed my examinations there in Law, Fijian, Hindi and other subjects without which my appointment could not be confirmed. This was a hard and fast rule and, since it seemed increasingly obvious that Germany would start its war before I could complete my examinations, it was a bleak prospect.

Another cause for sadness was that just before leaving England I

52

missed an opportunity almost as dear to Charles's heart as to my own. I had been doing well for Leicestershire 2nd XI in 1938, captaining them with success. But, partly because it was known that I was to leave England for a long period, others were preferred for the county side. The one compensation was that a month before my departure, when I had just had my anti-typhoid injection, Ewart Astill, captain of Leicestershire, asked me to be twelfth man for the game with Somerset. I explained that my arm was stiff and painful but he replied that I would have very little, if anything, to do. In fact, after the opening two or three overs Ewart signalled to me and I went on the field, passing Haydon Smith who winked and said, 'I'm feeling sick'; it was a kindly professional gesture towards an amateur. I was able to stay on the field all day, enjoying even the peppering I received from the immensely hard-hitting Somerset batsmen. At least before leaving England I had realised an ambition in part.

We discussed the possibility of Charles joining me in Fiji once I'd done an initial reconnaissance so that he could get on with what he recognised as his life's work – the *Strangers and Brothers* sequence. As things turned out, this proved a pipe-dream. As for mother and father and Eric in Leicester (Anne was there too), the best that one could hope for was to see them on every four-year leave. What effect a war with Germany would have, particularly on mother who was not strong, could not be foreseen. In fact I never saw her again.

7. Two Kinds of Danger

As soon as I reached Fiji I sent Charles my first impression. The following excerpts from his letters – square brackets indicate insertions by me – tell us a lot about him in this critical phase of his life.

Christ's College
Cambridge

Oct. 13 [1938]

My dear Philip,

Your letter lit up a particularly unpleasant and windy October morning . . . I was enlivened [by it] and chuckled hollowly – in all the circumstances, and the world what it is, it takes a pretty good joke to make one laugh much. You must write more. I'm sure, from your letter, that you'll entertain Americans with your points about the South Seas; and I expect we shall need to entertain Americans before very long. As for the world, I don't believe there was ever the slightest danger of war. I didn't at the time, and said so continually. I refused to dig a trench in the College garden, though all other Colleges were submerging themselves. Almost as soon as you had gone, it was plain from the English and French Conservative press (and also from what ministers did and did not say) that the fear of the *effects* of war (i.e. a revolution certainly in Germany and Italy, possibly elsewhere) was too great for them to face. They have become genuinely pacifist now, except for a German war with Russia; and they would rather give Hitler Alsace, Kenya and Bournemouth, and appoint Londonderry Gauleiter, than fight him on any pretext whatever. Unconsciously, they are better internationalists than the left, as we've often said; and, as well as the class-sympathy, there were other reasons which made it easy for them to let Hitler have his way – though, even if they had been differently placed, they would still have felt obscurely that he was right and given him his head in the end . . . I don't think there is now any chance of a major war in Europe for years – except possibly a German conquest of the Ukraine, which people now think would be fairly easy. There may easily be a repetition of the Franco affair in France. But it is more likely that Fascism will spread, quickly and fairly quietly, over France and England: beginning with an increase of censorship and ending with anti-Semitism and the whole bag of tricks. It will probably happen without much fuss, inside the next three years. It must be a long time since the world looked so black to liberal-minded men. But there are no two ways. Fascism has won, in Europe at least: I am inclined to think that it had already won in 1933. It will last our life-times. There is no one to fight against it, and nothing to fight with. So it remains to see what we are to do as individuals. I think your course is fairly obvious: you've cunningly embedded yourself in one of the safer places. Presumably you carry on as impassively as you can . . . .

Meanwhile you proceed to write as observantly and amusingly as you can . . . . The idea being to end up in the US, which with luck will stay out of the Fascist bloc, or at least will be so different that we could live there without too much loss of self-respect. As for Fiji being defenceless, I fancy that's lucky. It means that if it's lost, there's no fighting and you're probably taken off in dignity in an English or American warship; while the actual fighting will take place round Singapore. Surely the really dangerous places to be in are the fairly heavily defended, like Hong Kong? My own course is entirely a matter of timing. I must get the first book (now 2/3rds finished and I think you'll like it) out early next year in the US. [This was *Strangers and Brothers*, later retitled *George Passant*.] And after that I retire to California as late as I can in good order. If the first book goes pretty well, I shall go across to California next summer and stay more or less by accident . . . . The chief news in the College is that Darwin is going. He is becoming Director of the National Physical Laboratory, and announces it with quite indecent gratification. The Lodge has cost the College £5000, and he will have been in actual residence rather under two years: which is the most expensive Mastership in the history of the College. His departure is a loss to the College, as Darwin himself will probably say. It isn't known who'll be the next: Raven is digging us all very hard in the ribs. I'm not taking an active part . . . . Charles [Allberry] appears mysteriously from Berlin now and again . . . . I spent a pleasant month at Bandol with . . . Bert [Howard] . . . . We played Provencal bowls by the sea, an admirable game which I shall introduce to the Pacific. Bert seems to be going down the hill, getting more self-indulgent under one's eyes . . . . H.G.W. [Wells] appeared for the British Association at Cambridge in late August, and was in admirable form. He is a man whom one admires more as some of the superficial impressions wear off: he seems bouncy and bristly and self-centred, and all that's true but nothing like all. There is a kind of resignation and stoicism buried beneath it which I find very attractive: he thinks he's a complete failure. He didn't set out to perform works of art, but to add to the wisdom and powers of mankind – and the world hasn't taken any notice in that way. 'Life is a very disappointing business,' he said in his squeaky voice. 'When we're young we think we're Lords of the Universe. It takes a long time to realise all that we shall never do. And all that we shall never get' . . . He was very angry because Hitler is reputed to have platonic passions for young girls. '*Dwarfish*,' says H. G. 'It's dwarf- ish, isn't it? I shouldn't mind if he paired off with a woman of his own age and had a *good do*' . . . . The Windsors invited themselves to lunch there recently [with Willie Maugham]. Raymond Mortimer was also present and slightly surprised to hear Windsor say that he approved of the *New Statesman* – 'it was on our side during our trouble'. I like the phrase 'our trouble'.

Yours ever
CPS

The fight for the Mastership is on again; much of Charles's next letter is taken up with it.

Christ's College
Cambridge
Dec 18 1938

My dear Philip,
   Your letter was extremely amusing, and I shall preserve these communications from Fiji. You may find it a convenient way of putting down notes that you would otherwise forget (it's surprising how the most vivid things fade, unless they've been of central emotional experience). It would be a pity to lose such letters. Will you also keep mine? For I shall use them in the same way, for things that I might otherwise forget. I wish now that I had written down my talks with L.G. [Lloyd George] last winter when they were fresh. I hope to meet him at Antibes again next week. I don't regard your life as escapist in the least. I think it is extraordinarily lucky that someone with your detachment and perception should have taken to such a life. I mean, lucky both for you and everyone else. I doubt whether anyone of real perception and particularly of your ability *not to take anything for granted* has ever lived among people of such a widely different culture before Forster wrote *A Passage to India*. I receive your observations with complete confidence because you've got no prejudices . . . . There is little to report on my per-

56

sonal life. I had lumbago badly from September to November: have been writing hard and pretty well; and met a Jewish refugee who attracted me enough to make me wonder whether I ought to pursue her (she is called Rachel N . . . . and I suspect is coolly self-centred like most women that I fall for). That's all. The main interest here has, of course, been the high jinks over the Mastership. As soon as Raven knew that Darwin was going, he set to work single-mindedly and rather naively to get it for himself . . . . Grose, who supported R. warmly in 1936, of course, looked very pink when Raven approached him and said that, though his own opinion of Raven was unchanged, the opinion of important sections of the College, namely Wyatt, had changed drastically: and so Grose couldn't vote for Raven if it meant a complete lack of harmony between Raven and Wyatt. So Raven went off irresponsibly to see Wyatt, and asked him whether he could explain why his (Wyatt's) opinion of him (Raven) had changed. Wyatt told him. Raven asked for his frank opinion. Wyatt gave it. He thought R. dishonest in College politics, of negative judgement, and personally unscrupulous. 'I gave him chapter and verse,' said Wyatt afterwards. 'It made him think.' R. went away and immediately wrote the following letter: 'My dear Wyatt, I was extremely grateful for our talk this afternoon. When a relation like ours, personally so friendly, is interrupted by misunderstandings about outside affairs, there is nothing like an intimate talk. I believe that some of the faults you point out in my behaviour I shall be able to remedy, and I owe you much for your help. Not, however, that I admit that all the faults are on one side. Of all the men I have ever met, you are the most impossible to carry on a controversy with. You become hot and violent at the slightest sign of opposition. You think anyone who disagrees with you is either a fool or a knave. You are a born dictator: and I don't like dictators. Let me say that this difference of opinion will make no difference in my mind to our personal friendship.

Yours ever
C.E. Raven.'

To which Wyatt replied:
'My dear Raven, When I agreed to talk to you yesterday I had no idea or intention of letting myself in for a correspondence. And I might point out that, though you asked for my frank opinion of you, I did not for a moment ask for your opinion of me. I can only repeat what I told you yesterday. You are a dishonest man in College politics. Our standards are not the same. We do not talk the same language. You may persuade yourself that this is another case of my becoming "hot and violent". You are capable of persuading yourself of anything. All this makes it only more certain that we

could not work smoothly in double harness. Like you, I have not the slightest intention of letting this interfere with our personal friendship.

Yours ever
TCW

P.S. Have you seen Vol. 2 of Witherby's *British Birds?'*
. . . . Darwin had meanwhile circulated a superb document in favour of the abolition of Masterships: 'the idea is presumably that Masters of Colleges should be distinguished men. When you look round Cambridge, you see this is very far from being true. Almost universally the Masters are a set of promoted tutors and bursars . . .' and so on: very much the best and rudest attack on an office ever written by a present holder of that office. So we had a full College meeting with Darwin in the chair. He made a brisk and cheerful speech saying that he knew more about the Mastership than anyone else and thought it ought to be done away with. The voting was finally 9 each, which didn't carry it by a long way, of course . . . .

Yours ever
CPS

In May 1939 Charles has no more hope that Britain would shake itself out of lethargy than he had at the time of Munich. And there's more about Raven who has been elected Master.

Christ's College
Cambridge
May 26 1939

My dear Philip,
. . . Politics have a grim fascination these days. It's surprising how one is still shocked to see something occur even though one's prophesied it for long enough. It was like that when Prague went last week; and it's morbidly amusing to find each new example of how Conservatives are ready to give everything to Hitler, including London, and are only anxious because they can't throw in Moscow and New York. To be fair, this is only true of the Chamberlain-Simon Conservatives, the typical men of property. But they appear to form 80% of the party. The Churchills, the old-fashioned imperialists, are as bitter as I am; that seems to be true of the Foreign Office also, and I should expect it to be true of the Civil Service. The rumour goes about that Halifax leads the anti-Chamberlain party now in the Cabinet, and wants a Russian alliance, a specific guarantee of war if there is any more aggression, and conscription in England. But we shall get none of these things. You've no idea what it feels like to be living in England this Spring, particularly in the last

58

few days. All the old rhetorical clichés go whirling round one's head – the lights are going out, the twilight is deepening, the sands are running out (and incidentally someone uses them in a speech at least once a day) . . . . R.—and his wife talk of suicide. But wouldn't you, if you were a Jew living in Europe today? Talking of Jews, Houghton Mifflin, who are about the best publishers in the US, like the book quite a lot. [Its working title was *The Disowned*; it was eventually published as *The Conscience of the Rich*.] They want me to revise the last quarter which, since they are intelligent and friendly, I am quite prepared to do. It means you won't have proofs before the summer but probably ought to get me fairly started in America.

Apart from literature, studying politics and playing ping-pong, my life has been pretty grey this term. I deliberately didn't see Rachel again: I daren't get entangled with a woman just now: it's better to travel light. If I make any money in America, and there seems no immediate chance of the US going the same way as England, then I may look round for a wife. One Saturday night, when things looked particularly black and I was waiting for Mifflin's verdict on the book, I sent for Rosie from Nottingham and had a distinctly satisfactory champagnerous Edwardian sort of night. Jack [Plumb] can't understand this, but I like vulgar people and he doesn't. And I've decided that I prefer women that I don't have to respect . . . .

I think if I had gone all out I could probably have kept him (Raven) out . . . . . You should have seen him on the morning of his election, when it was fairly certain that he would get it. He kept walking round the Court, only keeping himself from smiling by an effort: and, though he kept his mouth from smiling, he couldn't control his eyes . . . .

He (Raven) immediately went off to America on a lecture tour, fixed up before he was elected, to be fair. Over there, his major exploit has been to tell Americans, quite truthfully, but hardly tactfully, that the English are afraid to fight in any circumstances. By the way, he appears to have departed from integral pacifism: which spoils the pleasant prospect, if the 1 in 10 chance of war came off, of Nicholson [head porter] coming into a College meeting and announcing impassively that a Black Maria had arrived for the Master.

It is sad that he should preside over the College of ourselves and other good men . . . . But so much is going to happen to the world that I can't find it in me to be deeply moved. Our period ended in 1938, after all: and probably we shan't see those days again in our life-time . . . the triumph of reaction was bound to come . . . .

Minor news . . . . So far as I know, no captain [for Leicestershire] has yet been appointed: I should think you would probably have been offered the job . . . .

Ever
CPS

Having finished the revision of the novel that came to be called *The Conscience of the Rich*, Charles's clear preoccupation is whether he can go on living in England which he sees as drifting quietly into Fascism.

Christ's College
Cambridge
June 1 [1939]

My dear Philip,

. . . . Schaeder, the Professor of Oriental Languages at Berlin, wrote on Tuesday to say that CRCA [Allberry] at the age of 27 was one of the most eminent Orientalists in Europe . . . he [Allberry] has deeper fits of depression than ever, despite his success, which indeed seems quite irrelevant . . . . I have been frantically busy this term, which is the reason that I haven't written before. I've spent every available scrap of energy in revising *The Disowned*, now just about to be sent to USA. I shall be glad when the proofs arrive and I can send you a set: if the world breaks up (and, despite all appearances, I am still sure that Chamberlain will hand Europe over to Adolf), it would be some comfort to know that a largish fraction of one's work stood a chance of being read. *The Disowned* will be followed by a revised *Devoted* [published as *Strangers and Brothers*], then by a College book [*The Masters*], then by Lewis Eliot's personal story [*Time of Hope*]. I think I can finish the whole lot within two years: after which I shall have to look for another field to write about . . . . These literary plans are of course the things that are occupying me most. Whether the world will let me do them I don't know. I'm going over to Boston in July to talk them over with Houghton Mifflin. Perhaps I shan't return to this country: obviously if there's a fascist England following another Munich, I shan't. I sent £500 to the USA last month, and hope to have another £500 there by the end of the year. This is a sort of last trench naturally: what I should like is for *The Disowned* to do well enough for me to appear in Fiji and finish off the series. If, on the other hand, you are hounded out of Fiji by Chamberlain plus the Japanese, you will presumably come to America and we can live there somehow. If my reading public remains at all, I can make some sort of subsistence: though probably I may not be able to write the things I most want to write. On the whole, your chance of staying undisturbed is greater than most of ours. And if by any miracle the world recovers and we survive, they will have been remarkable years to have lived through. You would find it hard to imagine the panic-stricken atmosphere of England in September and March; now many people have settled down to a sort of fatalistic acceptance which is more commendable than the state they were in before . . . .

The year after this I expect to have been removed from Cambridge, either by Hitler or my own free will. At the moment it is not unamusing: Raven extracts every ounce of drama out of being Master and dines nearly every night, saying to himself: 'this is *my* high table: these are *my* fellows' . . . . I must finish this letter comparatively soon as I am busy with a lot of trivial things (conscription means a good deal of tutorial work) . . . . Your account of the Governor's visit to Bau has caused helpless laughter to most of our friends . . . . The JC [Sir Julien Cahn] encounters are good fun . . . . JC himself, rejuvenated by meeting you, scored 39 and 18 in consecutive matches . . . . I should beat you easily at table tennis nowadays . . . .

> Ever
> CPS

The Nazi-Soviet pact convinced Charles that Britain and France would fight after all; it is interesting to find him saying that our world died in the summer of 1936.

> Christ's College
> Cambridge
> Aug 23 1939

My dear Philip,
. . . I am scheming to take the Lent term off. But of course all the moves depend on politics which are gyrating anarchically at a tremendous pace. One of my motives in staying here this summer was to watch things happen: it will be interesting material some day, though I hope I haven't left it too late.

Yesterday the Russian–German pact came out in the newspapers. It has, of course, altered politics at the root, certainly for the moment, possibly for years. I think everyone was surprised that it came at this particular moment. I myself had prophesied and bet on another Munich, probably brought off via the Pope and with Russia preserving the somewhat anomalous attitude that they took up last September. But I've long thought a German–Russian rapprochement was in some ways a natural thing to happen and might very well do so: I think I remember shocking you with the proposal in days when you accepted human frailty less completely than you now do: I certainly shocked Jack [Plumb] in his zealous period since. It always has seemed to me that liberal-minded people were astonishingly unrealistic about the Stalinist state: probably because it's hard for anyone to give up hope bleakly; whereas it should have been clear since 1927 (probably before) that there is no shadow of hope for our world, except by accident – and that one just can't see *at all* how society is going to organise itself in a way that's both enduring and tolerable. I don't see any important factor that gives liberal-minded men more chance now than they had in the Roman Empire, and a good many factors that give them less. Free intelligence has only struggled clear in a few privileged jumps, in a few exceptionally stable epochs in the world's history: ours was the hangover of one of them, probably the last for a long time.

I haven't had time to analyse the effect of the German–Russian pact, but here are a few impressions. (1) It makes war over Poland extremely likely. England and France may fight nominally: or they may go all in. (2) The possibility that England and France will go all in is greater than at any time since the War. Conservatives feel (a) that Hitler is letting their class down, so to speak, (b) that they have got rid of a dreadful danger in fighting with Russia, & having a 'Communist' power on the winning side. Grose was happy last night: 'Now we know where we are,' he said. (3) In a sense, it masks the class separation which had become naked during the Spanish war. I suspect a first assault will be to sharpen *nationalist* feeling in England, France, the US. But it seems to me quite conceivable that working-class sympathy may drift to the German–Russian bloc: & inevitably will with an economic collapse. (4) If there is a serious war I shan't know enough of the military position to be certain. But it would leave the US and Russia the greatest powers on earth: China would win, and there would be a revolution in Japan. In fact there would be chaos. And at the moment chaos is preferable to any realisable order. So that, for the survival of any decencies in the world, a war *à l'outrance* – even if the democracies lose – is probably better than any settlement. The real danger is a Hitler Europe achieved peacefully and that is definitely *far farther away* than it seemed on Monday night. (5) Marxism is an invaluable analytical method, 90% true at least, and without it history is nonsense. But I now see that the mistake of Communism is to think that an analytical method automatically prescribes a course of political action. It is strictly comparable with psycho-analysis: you can't understand human beings intellectually without it: but to think it prescribes a course of personal action is fatal. That, of course, was Bert's [Howard] crowning mistake & all from educationalists. Stalin and Bert are the active results of Marx and Freud & the two chief lessons

62

of the two great misunderstandings of our time. We shall have to do some more thinking before we assimilate our analytical results into a possible programme of life, public or private. Fortunately in life, instinct does it for one. I shall probably think some more about it: if indeed I have time to think in the next few weeks. I ought to knock some of these reflections into a publishable form, because it's going to be an anarchic future and the orthodoxies will all be tottering. But of course I probably shan't have time: which reminds me that I ought to give you some instructions in case of a sudden death (obviously the chances are small for any single individual but they ought to be allowed for) . . . .

There is little personal news. I have been busy writing & observing the political situation. The College is full of its usual feuds . . . . It's curious how these things do irritate one, even when one knows that a war will have begun before Grose resigns [as Librarian] and that, whatever happens, one's world will never be the same again. This last is true, of course, war or no war. Our world really died for good in the summer of 1936. But I am beginning to have a faint flicker of irrational hope, for the first time almost since that summer, that those of us who survive the next three years are going to have some fun . . . .

Ever
CPS

I had not been in Fiji for a year before Philip Bowden, passing through on a liner from England to Australia where he was to remain for the duration of the war, visited my out-station in the bush. He brought me a nostalgic whiff of Cambridge and Charles. At first my own life in the totally strange environment of the South Seas absorbed me. Then on the declaration of war I was recalled to the capital, Suva, where I was appointed Extra Aide-de-Camp, decoder of secret cables in cypher, and private secretary to the Governor and Commander-in-Chief. Charles's apocalyptic letter of 23 August did not reach me until about two months later. His next letter, written in the last week of October, shows him as baffled as anybody by the phoney war.

Christ's College
Cambridge
Oct. 23 1939

My dear Philip,
Your letter arrived three or four days ago. I don't think you ought to worry, at least not yet: if there are air raids on English towns, you'll

hear of them soon enough (they will be so important as propaganda that the first bomb will probably be recorded by the BBC: and, of course, the chances of any of us being eliminated even if they happen are reasonably slight). The proper attitude – I know it is easy to say – is to be as stoical as one can, and keep interested in the human scene . . . . From my last letter you will have gathered that the war ultimatum did not come as a surprise: the Soviet–German pact really settled that: but the way it has developed *was* rather a surprise. I was puzzled on the first night of the war, and more puzzled now, much more than I have ever been on political things. I remember (it seems a long time ago) walking with Hoff – who was in Cambridge for no particular reason – on to King's Bridge on the night of Sep 3. In a way I was rather relieved, for there had been the extraordinary two days' delay which we assumed to be a last minute attempt at another Munich: but I was really pretty gloomy. Whatever happens, we were saying, our world has gone for ever; it went, of course, years ago, in 1936 or before: it doesn't seem possible that the things one most wants to do, or a world one is content to live in, will return in our time. It was a lovely hot September night. I was certain that air raids would not begin at once and I went to bed and slept soundly: and was somewhat disconcerted at 3 o'clock to be woken by a mixture of Hoff, Nicholson and sirens. I wondered if my intellectual analysis had been so right after all: we were all frightened, wondering what we were in for. Performing my air warden's duties under the moon, however, I soon decided that I must have been right: meanwhile the Groses, the Ravens (with an atmosphere of drama), Peck, Charles [Allberry] arrived at the trench in the garden. There was a full moon, and I watched the English fighters with their lights on, whirling at terrific pace round the sky. There was a certain sinister beauty about the whole business. It kept us up about an hour: we suspected that it was a practice affair, but it is more likely to have been a single reconnaissance plane. We have had one or two warnings since, chiefly in the early mornings (7–8 o'clock) of that week: both these we took as a matter of course. Cambridge, being near the east coast, is liable to a lot of abortive warnings: I believe that Leicester has so far not had one. Meanwhile, the war went on getting more mysterious. I think most people felt unconsciously let down that it had not opened with a cataclysm. All the preparations (evacuation, black-outs – which impinges on ordinary life more than you'd think, unless you have them in Fiji, which I am quite prepared to believe – trenches) had made people expect great air raids at once, and they had a sense of anti-climax when they didn't come. Now they tend to believe that they will never come: which is quite unrealistic. Among our friends, as this curious nominal war went on, one found everyone driven, rather unexpectedly, on to the driving passion in their private lives. Very few had war jobs or the like-lihood of jobs (I was busy with tutorial work (a) to advise young men about their joining up (b) because it was soon clear that the University would be going on with some pretence at normality . . . . But other-wise no one has yet felt that I was necessary to the war. There was a half-conceived attempt to send me to the Balkans on some myster-ious manoeuvre but that appears to have fallen through, and since then nothing). Well, we are all driven to our private passions: I felt my books more important than ever before and at once arranged with Faber (FABER, 24 Russell Square in case of accidents) to publish *Mr March Loses his World* [*The Conscience of the Rich*] next Spring or at any other time that seems better. He likes the book very much: *The Devoted* will succeed it. Hoff was also driven on to his writing . . . . Raven to drama about prostitutes in Cambridge . . . . Trend to hide the view of the washed Chapel by means of window boxes. It would have amused you to see. It was like one of the great scenes in Dostoevski where you suddenly see, under the impact of some melo-dramatic shock, exactly what matters to the characters.

It may not last when the war becomes serious. What will become of the war I find it very hard to prophesy: there seem three alternatives. (i) a sort of armistice under arms after a 'peace' conference (ii) a nom-inal war like the present (iii) a real Blitzkreig beginning with air at-tacks on a big scale against English ports. My guess – not worth very much – is a mixture of (ii) and (iii) gradually leading to an immensely long war in which finally the great land mass (Germany, Russia, China) fights the rest of the world. This, if I am right, will go on for years. More and more, I believe, this is one of the major upheavals of civilisation: and I see nothing for it but stoically and hopelessly to fight it out. The Communist line seems to me entirely discreditable: they mustn't call on simple people to fight against Hitlerism for years and then suddenly discover that it is a wicked thing to do. I have not much use for them: they have the same mixture of childish optimism and self-centred cynicism as Bert, and he in himself represents all the hope and inevitable decay of the Left in our time.

I am, despite all my lack of hope (I never had much: not really by temperament, for I am as you know a comparatively optimistic man, but simply by the impact of brute facts), very cheerful and interested in things. I hope you are. I agree that you can't send for Ann yet: but next year you might think again, as soon as we get a clear idea of what the war has become. Write as soon as you can.

Ever

CPS

I was naturally worried about Anne in Leicester. I wrote to Charles about her and received the following reply.

Christ's College
Cambridge

Nov 28 1939

My dear Philip,

Your letter asking me to advise Ann [sic: it was some years before Charles discovered that Anne spelt her name with an 'e'] arrived last week: I had actually written to her before: but I wrote again to say that – so far as I can judge, which isn't very far – neither the risk of crossing the Atlantic nor the risk of being bombed in Leicester is great: but that, on the whole, she is safer in Leicester than on the sea. I suggested that she perhaps ought to wait until the Spring, when we could see how the war was shaping: by then, at any rate, the new attack by mines (which had unfortunately just become ferocious in the days that Ann had to decide) will probably have been coped with.

I should feel guilty if a bomb did fall on Leicester: but I am sure that this would be the advice of any informed person at the moment. No bomb has yet been dropped on English soil: the nearest fell in the Shetlands, and did no harm. Why, no one knows. The more expert one is, the more puzzled. But even in bombing convoys the German Air Force has apparently been advised not at any cost to touch the merchant vessels. It is all very peculiar: you can work it out as well as I can. I am still very puzzled. I do not think it means that the war is bogus: I think it is genuine and will go on for years. And so I expect bombing, first of the ports, and then of inland towns, to start in time, but so far as I can judge odds at all, I believe that the chances of a bomb in Leicester before this time next year are pretty remote.

The only thing which made me hesitate in what I said to Ann was the thought for your peace of mind: it is obviously more unpleasant for you than for us. But being in a ship on the east coast just at present is no joke: and though Ann's voyage would be less risky, there is a danger that one can't ignore altogether. I think, if the positions were reversed, you would have given the same advice. The problem of getting her out, even in the Spring, won't be easy. No US boats now come near England: Dutch boats may be stopped by Hitler (and, of course, neutrality is a somewhat absurd comfort if you hit a mine) . . . . . If HM Government in its infinite wisdom decides to send me to Belgrade, I should propose to take Ann to Athens and put her on a boat there: but that is a slim possibility and becoming slimmer. If I could find any war job that took me to the

East, I would likewise take her: but unless you can prove that it is essential to the course of the war that I am sent to the Pacific to organise a fleet of Polynesian canoes I don't see how I can manage it. I would go anywhere and do anything within reason: but, while the war lasts, it would have to be a definite job. As for money, I should be prepared to contribute a fair sum as a wedding present. Incidentally, I enclose a bill that I have been badgered into settling for you. And Grose (who sends his love) says you still owe £9 to the College . . . . As you see, it isn't entirely simple: and, as you rightly say, it isn't every day that a girl of 20 goes 14,000 miles by sea in war-time. As for the actual risk to her in England, that you almost certainly over-estimate. Obviously there may be indirect risks – such as the general collapse of the financial system, which might mean real privation: or military defeat, or an effective blockade: but in all of these she would really be in as much danger in Fiji, or going out to it, as here. So long as our system, and the Empire, lasts she is all right, barring wild accidents: if they don't last, then we still have to be lucky as well as cunning to survive.

I am myself cheerful, though tired . . . . Geoffrey Faber is shortly to receive a revised *Devoted* in order to see whether it or *Mr March* should be published first. He feels the whole work is important enough to deserve a little extra patience: and I don't mind, as the sales of books has sunk to zero, despite black-outs (do you have black-outs in Suva? They do in Halifax, Nova Scotia – which is a remarkable piece of imperial defence. They also do in Dublin). He thinks that No. 3, hereinafter called *The Masters* – about Cambridge, of course – will probably be the one through which I shall establish myself.

It is slightly ironical that I should be just getting through, in the one field that matters to me, too late: but in fact it isn't too late to make me feel unusually tranquil. I have had moments of gloom and distress when I thought that I might have wasted my life; but I have put those more or less aside: not that even in my worst period they were ever very frequent. The Snows have a sort of ultimate fortitude: 'a certain toughness', as Hardy says, being the only virtue of the legendary CPS of Stumpz. And Jack [Plumb] is coming to consider me a rough and insensitive man . . . . Bert is in superb form. A fortnight ago we spent a week-end in Ely in order to talk undisturbed about our books . . . . we walked 14 miles over the fens before lunch, Bert talking most of the while in an enormous voice. Somehow, God knows why, he is back at the top of his world . . . . Hardy and Charles [Allberry] are profoundly dispirited by the war, and for both of them life is nothing but black. Grose bears up, with a sort of realistic stoicism that I admire. 'If we lose, I don't want to live,' he says, in that being much sturdier than most Conservatives (or most left wing people either, for that matter, soft and silly people most of them) .... Raven sees opportunities for drama where no one else would but in general he is lying pretty low. If the war lasts long, it will harm the College having a pacifist Master; and, after some warning, he is apparently sticking to his pacifism ...

Ever
CPS

I have a splendid and very heavy tin hat!

Although I had passed some of the required examinations, with distinction in the Hindi language in the Devanagri script and the Fijian language and customs with credit, before the time of confirmation of my appointment was up, after which I would be free to marry, there remained one or two examinations. But I couldn't wait for that; I had to get Anne out. The Governor was in New Zealand at the time: so I took the law into my own hands and sent for her. On his return he readily agreed that formality could, under the circumstances, be waived. Charles paid her fare, which I could not possibly have managed on my small salary, a magnificent wedding present.

The Cobble
Polperro

Apr 8 1940

My dear Philip,
I have meant to write every week since January but I kept getting busier and busier with (a) books – the MS which you saw as *The Devoted* has been rewritten and is just going to Faber (b) a war job, which I'll mention later (c) extra tutorial work because Grose was ill with phlebitis from which he is slowly recovering. So through last term I was working 14 hours a day: I only went to two entertainments of any kind, I think; and I thought my available energy vis-à-vis you were better spent in despatching Ann than in writing a letter. Ann has been despatched. This morning I had your cable asking for news: I naturally thought she would have cabled you from France. I received a phlegmatic postcard saying that she had arrived on board at Marseilles. She should now be proceeding contemplatively down the Red Sea .... My war job (which I shall presumably hold for a good many years) is to supervise the employment for war purposes of all scientists connected with the physical sciences (physics, academic engineering, physical chemistry & so on). I got it through meeting Bragg [Sir Lawrence, a friend for life

68

afterwards] on Kettering railway station. It is, in fact, something for which I am suitable and which most people wouldn't be, since it needs a knowledge of the men themselves and of physics, about 50–50. To let me do it, they have co-opted me on to the Physics Panel of the Royal Society which is the body that advises the Ministry of Labour and, through the Ministry of Labour, ultimately the Service scientific departments. The figures of the Royal Society all act without pay: and so do I. But as I can keep my Cambridge jobs (I have to be in London 2 days a week), I am no worse off, and no better: & I shall have some time to write, which I shouldn't in a normal war time job.

So I consider myself lucky. It is a curious old brandy side of the war to see from the inside: I can't say more about it now, of course. On the whole, it is impressive and encouraging to see, more so than anything else I've heard of in the war. But my opinion of the regular Civil Service goes down. I should like to compare my judgements there with yours. I expect to gain further light on the Civil Service for the next ten years: for, as I say, I can't for the life of me imagine how the war is going to end . . . .

Anyway, my first bet is on a number of years of indecision – unless the French do something silly. That is a real possibility: they have an enormous proportion of their population mobilised, & pay them nothing. I suspect the standard of living in France will have to rise at our expense if they're going to stand a ten years' stalemate. In a military sense, they seem as sturdy as usual (incidentally, you have noticed the signs that my first guess, the land mass against the rim, does seem to be coming off? They are not the sides by pure chance, of course, but for technical, economic-geographical reasons. I fancy still that those will be the sides – though the military operations need not go beyond their present limits). Our friends here, in the main, settled down to stationary war much as you would expect. Lack of hope is the commonest general emotion: many people find how necessary hope is to them, now they can't rationally hold it. Of course people still hope, irrationally and in patches: but on the whole among intelligent and sensitive people it has never been harder to do so. There is also a pretty obvious sprinkling of anxiety – nerves are frayed and minor personal feuds and irritations are nearer the surface (this isn't true among people, like the scientists I've been concerned with, who are actually taking an active part in the war). I don't know how many people face the fact that their careers are probably gone for ever and that, at best, they will be doing something arduous, dull & meaningless for years (even the decoding & such jobs which dons are given turn out to be intolerably tedious). Charles [Allberry], I'm afraid, is the one of us who is most deeply affected by the war . . . . He is at present still at Christ's, going on

69

with his Egyptian . . . . The [Cambridge cricket] team won't be bad though you would no doubt have found a place. I shall see as much cricket as the scientific war permits me . . . . I have been in Cornwall for 3 weeks, and in the last week have had a fairly complete rest, apart from daily letters from the Royal S. I have walked 10–20 miles a day and feel better for it. I was so busy last term that I couldn't work in any ping pong: so I shouldn't be more than 4 points better than you when next we meet. Write as soon as you can: life here is liable to get bleaker.

Ever
CPS

Love to your wife.

His next letter, dated two days after Hitler opened his offensive in the west, reflects his feeling of relief that the inactivity was over at last.

Christ's College
Cambridge
May 12 1940

My dear Philip,
I got your cable last Monday morning, with great relief and satisfaction, though I imagined Ann was safe enough as soon as she got past the Red Sea. It doesn't seem to have taken her quite as long as I expected; I suppose she didn't have to wait many days in Australia. Good luck to you both. You'll need it, incidentally: just as we all shall. The war has really begun for us now: it began last Friday when I was woken up by a wireless voice booming across the Court that Germany had invaded Holland: it was 8 a.m., but I was sufficiently stirred to get up, and immediately found a letter that the book you read in a first draft as *The Devoted*, but now called *Strangers and Brothers*, has just gone to the printers and will be out in September. It will be one of the last books in England for some time, for there is no paper and the book trade will be extinguished: but Faber hopes to save enough paper to produce *Mr March* in 1941. But by September Germany will either have won the war, or we shall know that they can't win it. I never have a bath in the morning but I decided to celebrate this combination of events by treating myself to one. I lay there and reflected with a certain amusement. Curiously enough, a good many people (myself included) were more cheerful on Friday morning than we had been for weeks. I think we are still, though it looks as though the Germans are going through Belgium as expeditiously as in 1914. I don't really know how to explain this cheerfulness: chiefly perhaps that the waiting is over, and that the crisis is

70

going to be short: and I suppose most people still have a quite irrational and unjustified confidence in victory. Anyway, Brian Downs' [Master after Raven] subfusc exterior broke into a broad smile: Richardson [Charles's gyp] announced his intention of fighting if the Germans landed: people were excited in the streets. The news had even percolated as far as Fenner's . . . . And at night Chamberlain resigned which gave a good many of us a bitter pleasure – very likely too late, for I don't put our chances better than evens. Whereas, with reasonable competence, there should never have been a chance of defeat . . . . This morning I write this in the garden (it is unusually sunny for May in Cambridge) and shortly go to play bowls with Hardy. The feeling that this sort of life may soon end rather peremptorily gives an edge to all sorts of quite ordinary pleasure . . . . As for us, if we lose: I shall try to get to America if they'll let me. And you? I fancy the US would take over our possessions in the Pacific – or rather Canada would, under the protection of the US Navy. So I think you'll be untouched yet for a while . . . . Any unfinished MS will be either at the Bank or in the steel filing cabinet in my rooms. I don't want to give an unnecessary Raven-like note of drama, but I think it's sensible to say as much as I did in August: and now, with 2 of the 4 novels in this series finished to the last word, and No. 3 beginning to be planned, I should be irritated if no one knew where they were. I am also mildly irritated in passing at having to pay the College £9 2s 6d on your last account. Your masterly inactivity about Cambridge bills is the most effective stratagem since the Norwegian batteries were ordered not to fire . . . . The only way for me to keep equable at present is not to look forward at all. As you know, I usually do a lot of planning: but . . . I have scarcely given the future a thought. This isn't conscious, but a sort of automatic defence. Give my love to your wife.

Ever
CPS

In May 1940, I was appointed Provincial Commissioner and Magistrate of the outstandingly beautiful, isolated, Lau Archipelago of fifty islands. Now I was officially on my own. There was no telephone and a boat brought mail once a month at best. I was in charge of 10,000 Fijians and Tongans. It was in this responsible position that I first began to miss Charles's advice; his shrewd judgement of men would have been invaluable, and naturally I was worried about what was happening at home. The following letters were typical of the way Charles attempted to keep me in touch. The sadness was that by the time I received them the news was always out of date, but it was remarkable that the censor let so much through.

Lion Hotel, Bucknell
Leintwardine
Shropshire

Sep 4 1940

My dear Philip

I am writing this on a beautiful sunny morning by the bank of the Teme in one of the spots in inland England that you must see if ever you come back: not being able to go abroad, and a good deal of the sea coast being difficult, has meant that we have discovered the less dreary stretches of the English countryside. Some of them aren't bad: Francis Brett Young has made £8,000 p.a. by writing steadily about this one, & it was he (a more amusing character than his books suggest) who sent me here: and in this most sunny of all summers – apart from the bleak July – the little hills are pleasantly misty in the distance, and the little river runs pleasantly by. It is hard to realise there's a war on this morning: but last night German bombers chugged methodically over at 15 minute intervals (4 of them) – for some obscure purpose best known to themselves – and each night there is a lovely pattern of searchlights and anti-aircraft fire over Hereford in the southern sky. I have got used to this part of the war, I think – though it is perhaps early to speak, as Cambridge has only been bombed twice and then not badly. I woke up a fortnight ago hearing a subdued plop! in the distance: then a sinister whistle and a louder plop: I thought it was time to look round, and groped round for a torch – a considerably more sinister whistle and plop: I had just got trousers and a tin hat on when I heard a reassuring whistle obviously further away. It was a single plane dropping fairly small bombs at 5 second intervals in a straight line. The nearest to Christ's was in Pemberton Terrace, about 600 yards away. No one was killed or injured, rather oddly. And, to show people's curious faith in authority, when I went round the College as air raid warden, people refused to get up because the sirens hadn't sounded. I suggested that the dropping of bombs seemed to me a fairly reliable sign of hostile activity: but some people who would stay in shelters for hours once the sirens go (I firmly depute my warden's duties to Nicholson & go to bed) were very disinclined to stir. Mother has been the nearest to a bomb of anyone I know well: but she is still pretty belligerent. You know that Cavendish Road had been badly knocked about? It was strange to hear the news: I didn't believe somehow that war would come there. Nor apparently did the pilot, for they brought him down in Northamptonshire and asked him why in God's name he had bombed Leicester (a town singularly free of military objectives). He gave the somewhat irrelevant answer that he thought it was Birmingham. Cecil [Bert Howard's younger brother] was also irrelevantly bombed at Eastbourne. Everyone is, I think, taking it stoically. The English are still a tough people at heart and at times (with a sentimentality that I was surprised at) I feel proud of them. I have never felt for a single instant angry with the Germans: but I still feel the coldest and bitterest contempt for our fools who brought us to this. Still, it's not going to be easy to lose the war now . . . .

Personal news: *Strangers and Brothers* is being published this month (this is the book which you read, in an early draft, as *The Devoted*). I have signed a contract with Faber for all 4 books of this series. As soon as I get back from this fortnight's holiday, I start a 3-day a week job at the Ministry of Labour: this is an enlargement of my present job as chief of the Physics section of the Central Register. There is just a chance that I may become scientific liaison officer with the A.A. Command – a most important job at the present moment, and one I should enjoy. But it will probably be thought better to leave me where I am. Hoff has a technical commission in the RAF and is wirelessing bombers home from their night raids . . . .

Your letter was fascinating, and I read the diary several times. You will obviously have to write up all this material: it is too good to be wasted. And I felt an intolerable homesickness for your lagoon. England is too small an island to be cooped up in; and if ever I can travel again, I shan't spend an unnecessary minute in it. I shall come and write books by the Pacific . . . . I duly paid in your £5. Write as soon as you can. Letters are more than ever welcome in these days.

Love to you both

P

Christ's College
Cambridge

Dec 11 1940

My dear Philip,

I have just received a letter from Ann, with a long postscript from you about Fijian intrigue. This pleased me enormously, and there's clearly a unique book in it. If you don't write it, I shall. Incidentally, how well Ann writes – quite naturally and without any affectation of style . . . .

I envy you your happiness. Actually, I myself have had a not uneventful time. The George Passant book appeared under the title of *Strangers and Brothers* (a copy should be bouncing its way on the sea to you) on Oct 17th; two days after my 35th birthday, the midway of this our mortal life, which as you probably don't know is the opening sentence of the Divine Comedy. For a fortnight the only reviews were bad beyond belief: some anonymous pipsqueak in the *Times Literary Supplement* was just abusive, Frank Swinnerton in the *Observer* was not much better, some irascible Scotsman in the *Glasgow Herald* was even worse. Then Richard Church in *John o'London* decided that 'my achievement was comparable to Dostoevski'. For the next three weeks the reception continued in this bizarre way: a good deal of abuse, even more puzzlement, and a few sturdy voices proclaiming that I was a good writer. Pamela Hansford Johnson, herself a good novelist, said 'the portrait of George was as good as anything in modern fiction'. Then on Dec 1st Desmond MacCarthy, although the book had already been reviewed rather dimly in *The Sunday Times*, exerted himself and did me proud. He very rarely reviews novels, and how he got hold of mine is a mystery: but it is a definite landmark. The sales have not been as good as *The Search* but by no means bad considering the war; and Faber feels, and I feel, that I am just about to arrive. It is the typical reception of a writer's first major work; and if I survive and there is anything of our world left, I am confident now of the only sort of success that I ever wanted. If I die now I shall die pretty cheerful. Which is as much as one has a right to hope for. If God had offered me 5 years ago as much certainty of my achievement as I feel today I should have accepted without a moment's hestitation. Of course, any of us may die. But I expect in Fiji things must seem more lurid than they actually are. I have been in London half of each week since September (they are not to know this at home because it might worry them): I don't pretend that I particularly like it, but it's surprising what one gets used to: it is quite endurable and has a curious sort of fascination that is difficult to communicate. The first night I spent in London I was frightened: this was on Sep. 15, at the height of the first attack: the whole day was slightly like a Kafka nightmare. I arrived to take over my new job (Head of the Scientific Section of the Central Register, a natural extension of my previous work): I arrived at midday during a daylight air raid (which have now gone out of fashion). The taxi charged along amid gunfire; when I reached the office, I was promptly taken underground to the shelter and was instructed in my duties. After staying there about 2 hours (everyone is hardened to these proceedings now, & we don't go to the shelter even when the emergency signals go), I was allowed to visit my staff. I should have had 10 people there; I could only see one wretched woman. She promptly resigned. Then I went into my office, which was completely unfurnished apart from a gigantic file of Government instructions. I plodded through these all the after-

74

noon, with gunfire in the distance, and went off about 7 p.m. to some rooms in Earls' Court. I had dinner and the raid began at 9 p.m. . . . . I decided to go to my bedroom at 10 p.m. I had been in bed about an hour when there was a sinister rushing noise and my window was blown in. I didn't get much sleep until the aeroplanes went away, about 5 a.m. Since then, I have slept pretty well in various places, quite often at Bushy House, Teddington, with Darwin. You would enjoy seeing us at dinner in the very palatial dining room, the Chief Sea Lion booming away above the guns: once or twice there has been a bomb near, the house rocked like a ship in a slight sea, and the CSL looked rather thoughtful. There we sleep in the cellars which are very solid: the CSL reads Gibbon in an enormous cellar bedroom; from mine one sees anti-aircraft shells breaking in beautiful red sparks above the mist.

After Hall, same night. . . . . . You can probably imagine my sort of life just now: busy, doing a rather important job which takes me behind the scenes in various ministries and sometimes to the outskirts of the War Ministry: rushing about in trains, interviewing vice-chancellors, reading *War and Peace* and the lesser Doestoevski novels in interminable journeys through the blackout: occupied, harassed, overworked and fairly cheerful.

As to the war itself, I still can't say more than I did in September. My feeling is that we have a good chance of at any rate avoiding defeat. I don't think we shall lose by bombing, even if night bombing is not mastered, as it may be (scientifically, there is an even chance that by next autumn night bombing will be getting a lot less profitable). The most serious danger is, of course, the submarine blockade; but everyone agrees that we could at least make this bearable if we occupied the west of Ireland: & I simply can't believe that we shall lose the war through not daring to take bases in Ireland. On the other hand, I can't see our aeroplane production ever catching up with Germany's; & it will be a long time before the American contribution makes us anything like equal. So I don't see how we can seriously touch the Germans; and I don't believe they can finish us.

The spirit here is, on the whole, very good. We are a singular people; I have more affection for England and the English, more even for London, which I previously did not like, than I have ever had.

Personal news: Charles [Allberry] is going into the RAF to become a pilot. Bert refuses to let the war interrupt any of his activities . . . . Write whenever you can. I always get an hour's pleasure when I see a letter from you on my breakfast table.

Love to Ann and yourself
CPS

Apr 13 1941

My dear Philip,

Last week I received a long and amusing letter from you (together with your January diary) and also complaints that *Strangers and Brothers* hadn't appeared. I was just going to send you another copy when a telegram arrived: thank you very much. I thought you would like the book. Most people of any human insight do: most people without insight dislike it profoundly. There are two exceptions to the latter statement; H.G. [Wells] (who, after all, isn't a man of insight) wrote me a warm and flattering letter and old Richard A. [Aldington] (who has what you might call negative insight) wrote from America that I was the greatest writer since Proust. The sales haven't been large but all sales are down, of course, and mine might have been worse in the circumstances. If I survive and if any of our world survives, then I shall make my niche. But will any of our world survive? I am writing at a time when most people are as reasonably pessimistic as they were unreasonably optimistic after our victories over the Italians. The Germans are just rushing at Tobruk; they have wiped out the Serbs: they are ready to attack us in Northern Greece: and they are sinking a large number of ships in the Atlantic. It's difficult to judge all these events, but my present opinion is (by the time this letter reaches you, you will know whether I was right): (a) I don't see how the US can let us lose the Atlantic: I suspect the Japanese–Russian–USA triangle will stay in uneasy equilibrium this summer, except that, somehow or other, American ships will help us keep the shipping losses down to a manageable figure – say 60,000 tons per week (b) the German tanks will push us firmly into the Aegean and will go on to Iraq (c) they will also push us out of Libya, but we shall just hold Egypt from the West.

If these are correct judgements, I can't see the war ever ending. We can as good as lose it this year: but if we don't (and I think it's 6–4 that we shall escape) then it becomes an infinite siege, England + America v. the European Continent + the Near East.

It seems to me quite possible (as it did at the beginning of the war) that such a siege could go on indefinitely. I don't believe either side will win by bombing towns: both air forces will stay approximately equal for years, and defence will perceptibly improve. Part of my journeys round the country this spring has been to find scientific officers for the new devices. I went to every University from Aberdeen to Exeter and this part of the organisation is now quick and competent. So will the devices be, in time, perhaps before the end of the summer. My picture of the spring, by the way, is of arriving in some unknown provincial town in the dark: conferences with vice-chancellors, professors of physics and engineering, and other characters: getting up in the dark next morning, and immense numbers of interviews with pale unknown faces: then off again, to arrive at yet another provincial town in the dark. They nearly all look better in total darkness than they do by day: I didn't sleep more than twice in the same bed between Jan 4 and Mar 10.

Getting back to my point, I don't believe either side will win by bombing towns. Much of my inside news, which I cannot tell you, is encouraging: we are a gifted people and we are gradually becoming competent. But the Germans, not so gifted, are more competent than we shall ever be. It is as though people like you & me have thought of nothing but war for 10 years. If the war between two such combinations ever becomes stable, I can't for the life of me see either of them losing. This permanent war won't be comfortable to publish books in, or even to live in: but it would, of course, be incomparably better than defeat. I'm prepared for it with comparative equanimity . . . . Hoff is now attached to me at the Central Register, where he is extremely efficient (competent administrators are pretty rare, as you know: after a slow start, he is making a real success of being my understudy) . . . .

Write as often as you can. Love to Anne
CPS

The following letter arrived from him three months after despatch as the Japanese were starting to rampage through the Far East. It was in this period that Charles began to establish himself in public life.

Boscawen Hotel
Looe

Sep 16 [1941]

My dear Philip,

I haven't written to you for over three months. This is partly the result of excessive work: I have been rushing all over the country to chase young men into being officers for what you know of as 'radio location' apparatus; and this, my part of which has been done efficiently, and others – shall I say, less efficiently, hasn't left me much time. (Incidentally, it has brought me into contact with the high official world which I find amiable but unimpressive . . . .) I have been almost insanely busy: then God took a hand and my lumbago, which I had had intermittently since last December, suddenly flared up so sharply that I was sent to the Evelyn [nursing home in Cambridge] for a fortnight, and even here afterwards to convalesce. I am feeling better, but tired and unusually depressed.

But being busy and lumbagic wasn't the only reason for not writing. I have been waiting from one week to another, almost from one day to another, to see which way the Russian war was going, in moods fluctuating between extravagant hope and black anxiety. I wanted to write to you when we could make a judgement about our fate. I don't know whether this sounds overstrained when you read it in the Pacific: but I don't think it will. To any intelligent person here, the Russian war has been more of a strain than the summer of 1940, partly because we are spectators, but mainly because so incomparably more hangs on it. If the Russians can hold without losing too much (without being driven, say, to the Volga) then I think the war will be over in 12–18 months, with a fair chance of a world at any rate better than the one we've lived in since 1931. If they don't, then the best hope would be a war going on for ever. One has got to watch this being decided: and it's obvious that the balance is pretty even, and it will be a long time before one knows which way it has dropped.

It is a curious irony that events have forced us and the Russians (and generally the people one would like to be fighting with) on to the same side at last. I'm glad to say that feeling here is extraordinarily strongly for Russia – not only because of the reprieve, but a genuine admiration that is as lively among the solid classes as in the intelligentsia and the proletariat . . . .

Just as I am writing, the battle for Leningrad is getting fiercer, and the Germans are charging through between the Dneiper and the Donitz. I don't know about Leningrad. Many people have a sort of mystical faith that it will hold out. I doubt it, but I think it will cost the Germans another 3 weeks and another 200,000 men. In the Ukraine, I am afraid the Germans will get in up to the Don before the winter. What no one knows is how much difference the winter makes to mechanised war. Budenny, in addition to his moustaches, has lots of horses for winter wars. I am not sure that I believe much in horses.

All of this will be tedious for you, for these problems will most of them be solved by the time the letter reaches you .. . .

Love to Ann
CPS

But soon his thoughts were diverted. As the winter closed in the Russian army hit back; it was the initial Japanese success that was the worry now. We had exchanged roles as against the summer of 1940; now it was Charles's turn to worry about Anne and me, directly in the line of fire should the Japanese continue their advance towards Australia. In mid-March he wrote to our mother: '. . . I am naturally worried about Fiji. It is possible the Japanese will attack it, to cut the Americans' route to Australia . . . . If they don't attack it before they go for Australia then our worries may be suspended for some months at least . . . .'

Now in charge of the most strategically important district in Fiji – Nadi, where the country's first aerodrome was being developed – I was deeply involved in slim but diffuse gestures of defence and there was no time to write to Charles, so far as I can recall, throughout 1942. That year, as Director of Personnel, Ministry of Labour, he too was clearly stretched to the full. On 17 December 1942, he wrote to mother: 'Try to get hold of a *Times* or *Telegraph* on Jan. 1 and study the Honours List. Winston has offered me a CBE. I hesitated about accepting (it hasn't any bearing on my real ambition) but decided to . . . .'

I wrote immediately, though the letter may never have reached him, saying prophetically 'not even your elevation to the Lords would surprise me after this'. But there were other involvements in his life and the following letter reached me on 12 October 1943.

> 95, St. George's Sq., S.W.1.
> Aug. 13, '43
> (You'd better send letters to Christ's: this is Hardy's flat which I've been living in for 18 months)

My dear Philip,
I have been feeling extremely guilty about not writing to you. It isn't, as of course you know, that you've gone out of my mind: that is the opposite of the truth. I've thought of you very often, & we talk of you a good many times a week. My excuse, such as it is, is a very private one. There were certain other things which made it very difficult to write. I was extremely busy between Sep. '41 and this summer, travelling a great deal on over-crowded railway trains, arriving at strange towns in the dark & getting excessively inadequate food in all the larger hotels of the dingier provincial towns. And also it was curiously difficult to write while Fiji seemed likely to be attacked by the Japanese. I watched the Japanese offensive with the same anxiety that you must have felt in '40. I thought the chances were perceptibly on the Japanese arriving in Fiji about the middle of '42. That wasn't a pleasant thought . . . . Somehow writing a letter which couldn't reach you for 3 months, at a time

when 3 months might mean you were a prisoner, seemed an almost impossible ordeal. But I should certainly have made myself do it, if I hadn't been going through perhaps the most acute experience I've ever known. I found I couldn't write honestly until I knew where I stood. I do know now: it's ended in disaster, and I'm desperately miserable. But I shall recover in time, & I am more responsible for my actions now than for some time past, which means that you can expect letters fairly regularly.

In July '41, I met a girl called S. . . . Harry thought I might like her, & brought her to Cambridge one weekend. Both she & I were attracted from the beginning. I remember saying goodbye to her on the Sunday night, holding her hand for a long time (with Harry, himself slightly wrapped up in her, standing by in a state of not unnatural irritation) while she said that she'd soon come & visit me. I had an apprehension of danger, & shouldn't have taken any steps myself. She did come & visit me three weeks later: for months after she made all the running; we never met except at her suggestion. She was in the WRNS and used to come to London or Cambridge when she could get off & when the mood seized her. I knew from the beginning she was eccentric . . . . But I was extraordinarily exhilarated with her; life took on a brightness & intensity that I'd never known before, not even with Stella [a previous girlfriend]; I can still remember every word we said to each other & I think she could too. Then a day or so after Christmas in '41 she came to London in a state of hysterical strain. She wanted to desert from WRNS & for two days I had to look after her & persuade her to go back. She cried in my arms in a mad, cruel way all one afternoon in a room in the Regent Palace Hotel [Piccadilly Circus, London]. Up to then I think the relationship had mattered more to her than to me. I had managed to keep myself from being utterly captured. But that afternoon I fell in love; and, though I knew that it must inevitably mean bitter unhappiness, for there was no chance of settled love with her, I walked from Waterloo, after putting her into the train to Winchester, through the dark streets to Victoria & my flat, in a state of pure & lunatic ecstasy.

I ought to say that she was a remarkable young woman, more remarkable than any young woman I've known well. She was 22 when I met her . . . very handsome in a slightly more featured way than I generally look for – with a somewhat beaky nose and bright distant-looking grey eyes. She was pretty strong physically & distinctly broad about the beam. Theoretically she shouldn't have been my physical cup of tea; in fact she was. I've never been intoxicated by the senses so completely. I was not alone in finding her very beautiful, though it was somewhat surprising when one studied her; she was a girl whom every man in a restaurant looked at as she

80

walked in. She was also very intelligent with a generally deep taste for literature, & some talent herself. She might quite reasonably have written something odd but gifted in the Rimbaud line, straight from her fantastic inner world .... She lived in a queer remote inner sensitivity, intense, sharply self-centred, morbidly self-conscious. She couldn't bring herself to begin a letter in the conventional way 'Dear –': her letters (to anyone, including her parents) just started straight off, usually with the word 'I'. She had a dismaying habit of chuckling quietly at her own thoughts in the middle of a conversation. She was sensuous, spiritual aesthetically sensitive, but either below the ordinary level of emotion or was frozen emotionally (I was never sure which, but I think the first: you know how extremely *cold* old Bert seems, for all his vitality? ...) She only really felt acutely – as you or I or a normally emotional person feels during part of every day – when she had worked up some kind of ... scene .... She was in many aspects of a relationship exceptionally goodnatured & magnanimous. Like most really beautiful women, she didn't trouble about petty attentions. She had wit, originality and great distinction. Her inner vision was uniquely her own & it meant that I saw the world as though it had suddenly turned quite fresh overnight. All through I felt (a) this could only end in catastrophe (b) I should never meet a girl of this quality again.

Well, it went as it was bound to go. Through the grim winter of '41–'42 ... I was precariously happier than ever before. When I fell in love, her side of the struggle for power began to sharpen; we had a mad harrowing scene the last week-end in Cambridge before I left the College altogether for the duration of the war. Then we were reconciled a month later, in April '42, in an evening of pure joy that has tormented me ever since. We had an apparently final parting in May '42, not exactly a quarrel because I refused to play. I felt a mixture of desolation & insane relief.

Then I did a silly & unforgivable thing. I was frantically occupied from Mar–Dec '42, charging round to big firms & industrial towns extracting a number of qualified engineers to become technical officers in the Services. In the course of all this hectic travelling and interviewing I came across another young woman called J ..., and I felt desperately in need of uncomplicated companionship. But I'm afraid that I had already given half a thought to the possibility that she might be a consolation for S ...

She was an attractive, intelligent girl with a bleak manner (but soft underneath, too soft, unless one loved her). I knew she was ready to fall in love with someone & I thought it might easily be me. And I thought too before I started that I could conceivably enjoy myself enough to forget S..., & I wanted to marry, & in all theoretical respects J... would be a most suitable wife.

By and by she fell in love with me, & I simulated love for her, hoping that some flicker of magic would grow. Naturally it didn't, & my spirits grew heavier every week. She was possessive beyond the normal, & I can't bear being possessed: she had great strength of character, but her everyday level of interest was low, & it was hard work to get her inspired to anything except her single-minded pre-occupation (which was, quite simply, to marry me). I should say, in fairness to myself, that her level of spirits & interest is low with people for whom she has no feeling at all. Being loved when one doesn't love makes almost anyone behave badly: I couldn't forgive myself for the pain I was bound to cause her, I felt cheap, low-spirited, mean, bored; I don't like continuous lying; & at times I was angry with her because I was behaving badly to her. I don't think anything else I've ever done made me think worse of myself; & all the time I was sick at heart because of S. . . .

Then in Aug, '42 S. . . reappeared as though nothing had happened, beautiful, complacent, charming, flattering (I always felt slightly larger than life-size when she was about; she thought, I believe sincerely, that I was probably a writer of genius. J. . ., who would have worked herself to the bone to make me successful, none the less had considerable doubt of my real powers. Or at least she never could express her faith in them – which is very hard for a man of ultimate confidence). For about 8 months an absurd Box-and-Cox act proceeded. S. . . came to see me much less often than in the past, but when together we were usually happier & more placid – which was really a bad sign. I could not bring myself to tell J. . ., & I still hoped that things could get better between her and me.

During all those 8 months I was miserable. I used, as you'll remember, to be fairly gay in the middle of my gloom. That had gone altogether. I was harassed to the roots of my nature, actively unhappy and ashamed, unable to see any solution; I went from committee to committee, going through all the motions of my comparatively lively self of a year before, & I could hear myself making [illegible] speeches with a kind of hopeless distrust. In March '43 I saw S. . . for the last time. Neither of us knew that it was the last time, & we were extremely cheerful. The only illuminated moments in those months had been her visits: there was one November afternoon when we walked through pouring rain, & this last day when we strolled by a river & made up poems in the Japanese style.

Late in May, a few days after I heard the definite news of Charles's [Allberry] death, I received a postcard from her saying that she was in love with someone else . . . . The postcard also said that she wanted to see me again. After a few days she sent a telegram (& this is the feature of the story in which she seemed to me petty) 'Am usually fairly perceptive but don't understand your last letter'. I shan't see her again. That is the only way to recover. I am left with an intolerable sense of loss . . . . There are a fair number of women of deep personality & lofty spirit, but usually they don't capture one's imagination and drug one's senses. This one did, & I'm sure I shan't find anyone like her again. I also feel that somehow I've been inadequate to the most important situation that has come upon me.

When I told S. . . that I had finished, I also told J. . . the truth. She took it with dignity and understanding at the time, and treated me better than I deserved. But I suspect that she hoped, perhaps believed, that I would change my mind. I found it very sad to part with her, & liked her more than at any previous time. But I shan't change my mind about either of them. I expect I shall recover in time, but at present I'm pretty exhausted. As one gets older, these things happen more seldom & one is more cautious about going into them; but when they do come they are more shattering than in youth. Ideally, I should like to marry someone who didn't either drive me to despair or leave me [illegible] and depressed.

Charles's death affected me with another kind of grief. I heard that he was missing from the raid of Essen on the night of Apr. 3–4. I never had any hope from that moment, & in May the Red Cross reported that he was killed. For nights I dreamed nightmares of the sort of death that he must have found. I saw him last in February when he came into my office one afternoon. He was rather highly strung but quite cheerful – very pleased about his child which was due in July. 'We Allberrys do our bit,' he said with his prim, mischievous smile . . . . 'It's clear to me, dear old boy,' he said, 'that you ought to be the next Master. I only hope it's equally clear to our colleagues.' But I think he often knew that he was going to die. I feared it from the night I heard that he had joined the Air Force. I should have feared it for anyone, of course: but with Charles it seemed fated . . . . His loss is harder to bear than that of any other of my friends would be. I learned from him more of the adventures and solitariness of the spirit than from anyone else; in some ways he was the most gifted & the most remarkable of all of us, and the most unhappy.

It's the first time I've known loss through death. I've only visited Cambridge twice since this news, & each time quite ordinary things brought back some fragments of the past and revived the grief as though it were a physical wound. Once or twice it seemed incredible that he could be dead: I expected to see him come with quick light steps through the Court ready to make some mischievous joke at the expense of some puzzled solemn clod. His child, a boy, was born on July 31. I am glad: & I'm glad that his Psalm book and other work is accepted as the best scholarship in his field for a generation. Somehow it's a comfort that he should have left that curious memorial behind him. Going through these two losses, the tragic one of

Charles and the harrowing one of S. . ., so close together, I could distinguish the sorrow of death from that of love. The sorrow about death is perhaps the only sorrow that has no element of wounded self-esteem. It is utterly different from the sorrow of love in that aspect, for even in the deepest love one's hurt pride and self-respect give an added corrupting pain to what one has lost. The sorrow about death is purer; one is grieving because of the loss to oneself, of course, but it is a grief that isn't tied up with one's vanity & there is no petty shame to fester among the grief. But, just because the petty side of one's nature isn't touched, I doubt if the deepest sorrow due to death can last as long as that due to love . . . . I'm ashamed that that should be true; but, though after Charles's death I couldn't eat or sleep for days, I'm afraid it is.

Aug. 22

I began this letter over a week ago. I've been busy most of the working week and haven't been able to go on. I think I've now told you the important things about my personal disasters. In the war I've had a comparatively interesting time, met a lot of people I otherwise shouldn't, & seen a good deal of the inside of affairs. I've made a bit of a reputation, & I suppose I could stay in this kind of life & have a success as an administrator. But for that kind of success, as you know, I should care nothing. I haven't been able to do much writing, & it's a fairly serious break. But that still is the only steady consolation I've got, & it's possible that I shall write better when I return to it.

I shall hope to begin writing with some passion as soon as the German war is over. When this will be I don't know, but the usual guess is sometime in '44. We've been very lucky: the Russians have done miracles of large-scale organisation & we've been extremely inventive and clever (for various reasons we still seem to produce a disproportionate amount of talent). The Germans made two major mistakes (i) they assumed that we should give in when France was conquered (they expected France to hold a good deal longer): they had made no preparations to invade & had never given the matter a thought: it now becomes apparent that our danger in 1940 was nothing as great as it looked, provided the population stood up to bombing. It's very much to Winston's credit that he saw all this though he would never have surrendered whatever the real position, which was also important. (ii) They greatly underestimated the Russian army, God knows why. This I just don't understand. If they had stayed still in 1941, attacking neither us nor Russia, but placidly developing Europe, I believe nothing could have defeated them.

The Japanese war looks like going on for some time after the German one ends, which is bad luck for you & means that we shan't see you for a bit longer. It may go quicker than I expect when all the

84

equipment in the world rolls towards the Pacific &, of course, if Russia came in it would end in a few months. But I don't believe for a moment that Russia will come in, & I do believe that we shall have to kill more or less the whole Japanese Army, Air Force and Navy before Joe E. Brown tours round the Inland Sea [a reference to Anne and I spending a day with Brown on his tour in Western Fiji to American troops].

The world won't be comfortable for the rest of our lives. It is bound to be a struggle between the two continental units, Russia and America, with us by guile, brains and mobilising bits of the rest of the world keeping a sort of precarious balance. The Russians will never forgive the Americans & us for letting them fight the war effectively alone. It's what they always feared, & they won't be in a better temper when they finish the war with 10,000,000 young men killed & the USA practically unscathed. Chance & history & a certain amount of deliberate policy have made it certain that something like this would happen. It's difficult to see what else we should have done, & I'm glad the decision didn't rest with us. But I don't believe that after this war the two cultures are ever going to be reconciled. I'm not sure whether there'll be a gigantic trans-oceanic war in 30 years' time. My guess would be against it, largely because Russia will be so powerful that the Americans won't dare. I think the probability is of a suspicious semi-militarised inconclusive period for the rest of our lives. And it's not easy to see how the world is going to become one even after we are dead. These big continental units have gone some way towards the world-state, but ultimately make it almost impossible for the world-state to happen (something like monopoly industries in a capital country). I think we shall find Russia after the war increasingly suspicious, nationalistic and in spirit moving to the right . . . .

He went on to give his appreciation of the war situation, and news of our friends. Although Fiji was now out of danger, an end to the Pacific war seemed infinitely far away, whereas one could measure by each day's news the rate of push from all sides into Germany. I was three days by bamboo raft up a remote river opening a school when a Fijian arrived from my headquarters with a telegram from England saying that my mother had died. She was almost seventy-three and had been in poor health for some years but indomitable in spirit. I felt cheated at being denied the chance of seeing her again. This was 1944; in normal circumstances Anne and I would have been back in England in 1942. I sent back by the Fijian a message to be cabled by Anne from Naduruloulou and felt utterly miserable. It is Fijian custom to share grief and so try to diminish it. My hosts asked if they could perform a *meke* (a stylised dance) for me and after I retired to the loneliness of the thatched house vacated by the chief for me he organised a relay of young female visitors to keep me company through the night.

Although he'd retained his fellowship at Christ's, Charles didn't want to return to Cambridge. In his work for the Ministry of Labour he had become friendly with the chairman of the English Electric Company, Sir George (later Lord) Nelson, who invited him to join the staff. He became Director of Personnel (not on the Board). In 1945 he also became Second Civil Service Commissioner, his work principally having to do with scientific appointments.

In August 1945 he wrote to me from Hyde Park Place, which was to be his address up to his marriage in 1950.

Aug. 7 1945

. . . . I sent you a cable with the bare facts; the main point of this job is that I shall only be working on theoretical half-time, in fact with leave 5 months in the year; this will give 7 months free for travel and writing, & I didn't see how I could do better unless and until the books set me free altogether. Cambridge is leisurely, but one has to be there a fair amount, & also there is a certain psychological bondage. I could have got large sums from industry (for a year 1944–5 I've had a part-time job with English Electric & drawn large sums from it) – but I wanted to be as free as I could manage for the next 10 years, for I'm sure I shall write my best books now. And that remains the only real ambition I have or am likely to have. The Commission give me £1,500 for this part-time work, which is handsome for the Civil Service. I don't think I shall want to succeed Waterfield [Sir Percival, the First Commissioner], even if the Treasury asked me, which is unlikely. I want this as a not very onerous way of keeping alive while I write, & I don't mind doing a useful job for the State in the process – I am responsible for the appointment of the Scientific Civil Service though I shall also have a hand on other sides. I fancy the Treasury will always keep the First Commissionership for a regular administrative person – it carries an automatic K, which matters to them & not to me. If they leave me alone (& they all know why I've taken the job) I shall be content. Old Hankey [Lord Hankey, Secretary to the Cabinet in the First War and his immediate superior in the Ministry of Labour under Ernest Bevin, Minister] was invaluable in getting me exactly the terms I wanted. It happens that no one else is capable of doing this job properly, & I was in a strong position.

The College has, with great civility, made me a supernumerary fellow. This means I have all the rights and privileges as before, but no pay. But it is very pleasant, and the first time they've done it. If they were electing a Master tomorrow, I think they'd choose me; but they won't when *The Masters* is published. I now propose to be almost infinitely prolific as a writer. No. 2 of the *Strangers and Brothers* series is now finished and will be called *Charles March*. I expect to send [it] to Fabers this month. No. 3, *The Masters*, is between ⅓ and ¼ written; I have been in Cornwall for a month and have done 47,000 words, writing more easily than at any time before. I think these two will put me on the map and I'm pretty confident that I shall write better books afterwards.

I am in better spirits than for a long time past. I have at last recovered from W..., I am surprisingly glad to be leaving Cambridge (I never liked it as much as you did), and I can see years of comparatively successful work in front of me. And, after a month's illness in the summer, I think I've thrown off the tiredness of the war.

How are you? You clearly need a holiday. When shall you get one? We ought to talk over your books, your cricket and all your other plans. Shall you be here in 1946? It ought to be easy for me to come out to Fiji in one of my non-official periods, but I imagine you'll be in England first. I think your books and other proposals ought to wait till then: it is hard to cope properly on paper, & I doubt if you ought to begin serious writing until you've had a rest. I miss you very much, & look forward enormously to your being here. My new flat, and any other I may have, will be able to put you & Ann up at a pinch and one of you in comfort. It is about 2 mins from Marble Arch, & overlooks Hyde Park – expensive, but I believe I shall make money soon.

I was astonished & delighted by the election. It doesn't mean a new heaven and a new earth, of course, and on reflection I'm surprised how glad I was. They're a dull set of dogs and the new government is personally slightly drabber than the old. But I don't think that matters. On various important things they're bound to take a non-disastrous line as against a disastrous; & I confess I'm amused at the possibility of comedy, minor and major. It's certainly the best thing for the world since the battle of Stalingrad.

The world position is curious: Russia, nationalist-collectivist: a series of nations in Europe, mostly in distress, led by England, all tending to a sort of social democracy: and USA, nationalist-monopoly-capitalist. And unfortunately the USA has got a long start with the atomic bomb, which may complicate power politics – I've known that for some years. We had the ideas, but played our hand very badly politically.

None of our friends have done anything dramatic since you last heard. *Bert* [Howard]. I nearly got him a job as secretary of the local

87

examination syndicate at Cambridge, but again just failed. I've now given up in despair, at least temporarily. He's getting too old for people to take him. The Newton's business still rankles with me bitterly [Bert was not made headmaster]. *Harry* [Hoff] has written a most entertaining novel. Not happy, but still fun . . . . *Philip Bowden*. Back in Cambridge, more El Greco-like than ever . . . . *Trend*. Unchanged except that his moustache is grey. Should be a power in foreign relations with new govt. They ought to make him a knight . . . . *John Lomas*. Says he will qualify for Leics. if you came back and captain them. He will be a don at Oxford and could play June, July, August. Batsman of a higher class than anyone they've had since the last war but doesn't like cricket or cricketers much. [He was to die tragically four months later.]

Write a longish letter if you have the energy. I think it is important for me to get into the regular habit of regular correspondence again – at least once a month.

Give my love to Anne
P

With the atom bombs on Hiroshima and Nagasaki the Pacific war ended with staggering suddenness. I had never dared to think seriously of leave; now it was four years overdue. Charles replied as follows to the news that I was coming home.

20, Hyde Park Place, W.2.

Feb. 19 1946

My dear Philip,

I've just got your letter saying that you're definitely sailing at the end of March. You might send me a wire announcing (a) which ship you're on (b) when and where in England you arrive. If you insist on living in Leicester I shan't see as much of you as I should like: until the end of June I shall be pretty busy with Commission work. If you play for Leics. I will come and watch you on Sats – if not you'd better come to London for weekends.

I'm looking forward to your stay more than I can say. I have been rather low with the grief and troubles I told you of . . . & I've not been particularly well all winter. But I hope to be revived when you appear. By the way, does your reaction to the Fiji climate affect your plans for the future? Are you trying to get transferred? I should like to hear what you've got in mind: it might be possible to do something at this end.

Life is a bit joyless just at present, not only for us but for almost everyone I know. But there is a certain amount of interest to be got out of it: is it better to be humorously miserable or humorlessly happy?

Love to you both
CPS

8. Two Men Rebuild
Their Hopes

Full of excitement at the prospect of seeing England again, Anne and I boarded a small ship in Fiji for New Zealand. There we embarked for England on a liner just taken out of war service and now full of prisoners of war released from the Japanese and able to cope only with rice when faced with the rich variety of food on the menu.

Not surprisingly, Charles looked older than when I had last seen him. He was now forty and the strain of war showed; I was thirty, and probably hadn't changed so much, but he noticed differences. He seemed to us in good spirits, but tired. Food rationing was not helping: we had been marginally better off in the Pacific, though the food was pretty awful. Being rather run-down myself, I was going through a rare phase of not drinking. This self-imposed prohibition cramped Charles's style a little: it lasted throughout the leave which, however, worked wonders for me. A break from work, seeing Charles and my old friends again, set me up.

We stayed with Eric and his wife in Leicester so as to see something of our respective parents. My father was in fine form, extracting every item of interest about Pacific insects and crustaceans which ranked momentarily among his Rheinberger organ sonatas as all-absorbing. We also visited Charles in London frequently. We enjoyed going to 20 Hyde Park Place, with its superb view over the park. Among Charles's new friends was William Gerhardi, an entertaining eccentric; he is Julian Underwood in *In Their Wisdom*. Among old friends, Bert Howard was still himself. Invited by the new headmaster of Newton's to present the prizes at their annual speech day, six years after Charles had done so, I was able to laud him to the skies.

Cambridge, or rather Christ's, was unchanged. Raven, as Master, sat me on his right at High Table and seemed interested in what I had been doing; he had mellowed a good deal. The serene Grose was just the same. For me, it was a nostalgic return to the many happy memories of the most extroverted period of my life.

My relationship with Charles was resumed quite naturally; he told me a good deal about his wartime activities which he couldn't put into his letters. His recruitment of scientists, although a proportion was for industry, was mainly for top secret purposes. He came under Lord Hankey who, as Chancellor of the Duchy of Lancaster, was responsible for some of the most confidential projects. Decisions were in Hankey's name but they were mainly on Charles's recommendation. The first priority was radar in which England had a perceptible lead over the rest of the world. Much of what Charles told me then was later revealed in his Godkin Lecture at Harvard in 1960 on the intriguing Tizard *v*. Lindemann issue under the title 'Science and Government'. He recruited scientists at a great rate, principally from the universities, for radar development. 1940–2 were crucial years for this activity, and Charles gained an insight into government that would under normal circumstances have been closed to civil servants of his rank. He was also responsible for selecting suitable young men for university courses.

In about 1942 the top priority became the atomic bomb. Charles recruited scientists to go to New Mexico, others on highly dangerous missions to occupied Europe to find out how far behind the Germans were. They were known to be active at the heavy water plants in Norway, and Norwegians who had escaped to England were recruited to go back as agents. Some of them never returned. This naturally distressed Charles and he had to learn not to feel personally responsible. He told me that by early 1944 it was clear that, while the Germans were far ahead of us in the development of rockets, they were never in the atomic race. In his letters to me he had conveyed some of his inner optimism, without of course being able to give his reasons. However, he never expected that the Americans would use the atomic bomb. He told me in 1946 that he was in fact surprised by the speed with which the atomic bombs became available, and by America's prompt decision to use them on Hiroshima and Nagasaki. He much enjoyed the discovery after the war that he was high on the Gestapo's Black List.

We left England two days before Christmas 1946; it was an enormous wrench. I remember standing on the deck of the ship gloomily watching the yellow sodium lights of the London docks disappearing astern. But Charles was delighted to receive a letter from me en route posted from Pitcairn's Island, every aspect of which fascinated him.

We missed the terrible winter of 1947 which was a blessing, and life in England was still austere. We arranged to send food parcels home. Each month Joong Hing Loong Ltd in Suva dispatched tinned fruit and meat, tinned butter and chocolate, though we later found that these last two didn't travel well. Meanwhile Charles was fully occupied, combining his civil service activities with his part-time job at English Electric. He always said that a novelist ought to have at least two kinds of lives; certainly his experiences in the Civil Service and industry did much to strengthen his versatility.

The Light and the Dark, dedicated to Sydney Grose and banned, on the strength of its title alone, by the South African censor, was published that year. He put a lot, though not of course all, of Charles Allberry into the character of Roy Calvert. For me it is his most affecting book, a profoundly moving tribute to a close friend; but despite its sadness it is also amusing. It's astonishing that it has never been made into a film since it seems to me eminently filmable. Probably the most underestimated of his novels, I would recommend anyone coming to Charles's work for the first time to start with it. Pamela Hansford Johnson, still addressing Charles as 'Snow', told him that he could now be sure of his place in English letters.

Now that airmail was in operation the pattern of our correspondence changed; it was easier to keep up to date. A new element was a return to the old banter, an encouraging indication of Charles's state of mind. Another great joy was that he selected books for me, which Heffers, with whom I had an account, sent on. His letters, the first dated 4 February 1947, are full of what he has been reading and the books he is sending me.

I ordered the second consignment of books a few days ago . . . (1) *The Web and the Rock* by Thomas Wolfe. I cannot make up my mind about Wolfe. Sometimes he describes a mood with such intensity that I think, for all his faults, he's a great writer – perhaps the greatest American writer since Melville & Whitman. Sometimes I think that, despite these moments of power, he is too asinine to be of much value. Anyway, I should like your views . . . (2) *The Age of*

Reason by J-P Sartre. Sartre is the leader of the existentialists and the most controversial figure on the literary scene just now . . . obviously a highly intelligent man and a writer of considerable perceptiveness: I don't think he is really a very important novelist, but you should at least have read something of him. It's desirable to read what is in the mode, even if it only makes one a little irritated with the mode . . ..

He ended with the news that he was off to America on 28 February, the first of countless trips over the years, to promote his books. In April he reported that it had gone pretty well. 'If there is no serious slump I really ought to have a biggish success'. He continues:

Have you read any of Huxley's mystical works? I always get the feeling that he has no first-hand experience of what the mystical experience is and is groping about rather heavy footedly and insensitively towards it. I fancy that anyone of deep religious feeling, such as Charles Allberry, would find these works distasteful . . . I read *Ciano's Diary* on the Queen Elizabeth. I thought it was a fascinating document; my opinion of men of action, never very high, went down a peg or two . . ..

Our first child, Stefanie Dale Vivien Snow, was born on 11 June in Suva. Charles wrote as follows:

20 Hyde Park Place, W.2.

13 July 1947

My dear Philip and Anne,
I received the cable with great relief: wasn't the birth delayed? You should have had one from me in reply. Yesterday I had a letter from Anne. It is very good news that all has gone well. Is the second name 'Merle'? Surely Vivian [sic] is a boy's name? One advantage of a girl is that you don't have to bother about her education . . . [an Olympian view which now infuriates Stefanie]. Not much news here. I have been rather subfusc, with lumbago, not very severe but more or less continuous, through the months of May and June. Tedious and dispiriting, and it has prevented me from beginning Vol. 5, in which I'm all set to go and which will write itself, of course. *The Light and the Dark* comes out on 3 Oct in England, January in New York and February in Vienna. I fancy it will appear in French also in the Spring.
I sent you last month Pamela Johnson's *An Avenue of Stone* (she is my most formidable backer, and this is a good novel) and Dorothy

Carrington's *Traveller's Eye* (which I felt was right up Philip's street).

I am thinking of buying a house, but I don't know where – (a) for financial reasons (it is a good hedge against inflation) (b) I should rather like a Centre where we could all meet, even if I went to it only 2–3 months a year. I am offered one in Capri, which would suit me: presumably it wouldn't be much use to you. With your inexplicable passion for the Midland Counties I suppose you'd prefer Kirby Muxloe. I refuse to think of Leicester or Leicestershire, but I'm open to reasonable suggestions. Let me know soon.

Love to you all
P

The Capri idea fell through. The villa in fact belonged to his friend Francis Brett Young who tried to persuade him that there was room for three writers on the island – Norman Douglas and Compton Mackenzie were already there. At the end of August Charles was complaining that I hadn't written to him.

Dear Philip,
You are as silent as the fish of the Nile, as Vogliano said to Charles Allberry. Why is this? I hope it means that you are finishing off the book [a history of cricket in Fiji]. I suppose it's faintly possible that you are occupied with administrative detail.

The last two books I sent were *The Slaves of Solitude* by Patrick Hamilton – a novelist who, if he had slightly more seriousness of intention, would be very good indeed. He is naturally much more gifted than people whom the cerebrotonic young take more respectfully. Also a biography of Alexander Woolcott, one of the more incredible American phenomena. I read this book with great interest; he had an intolerable life, and was in many ways an intolerable man. I felt his life demonstrated how tough the human spirit can be . . . .

I am busy writing Vol. 5 which I should like you to see before it goes to the printer, since the first sixth of it deals with family background . . . . Leicestershire have become dimmer and dimmer and need your firm hand . . . Don't worry too much about the economic catastrophe. If anyone survives it, I shall. And you are living on an island with a favourable trade balance which means that you are sitting pretty.

Love to your wife and daughter, and to yourself
Percy

He wrote yet again before I could reply, on 22 September.

Dear Philip,
I hasten to send a cheque which covers some of my parcels: the rest can serve as a Christening present for Stephanie [she later changed the spelling to Stefanie].

I am ordering you John Gunther's *Inside USA*, a brilliant journalistic survey of each state of the Union . . ..

. . . I have had to spend a good deal of August and September in Cambridge talking to Hardy who is seriously ill. He will never be really better, but I think I left him in slightly improved spirits.

I wrote a little while ago asking why you had been so silent. I now assume this is because of your move to Taveuni. Is this a good idea? Will it prevent the tour to New Zealand?

Love to you all
Percy

I was in fact exceptionally busy, having been put in charge of the large district of Taveuni. I was also completing arrangements for the first tour since 1895 of a Fiji cricket team to New Zealand. It gave me little time to keep up with the flood of books that kept arriving. Among them was Michener's *Tales of the South Pacific* on which Charles had asked me to report for the publishers, Macmillan. I said that it captured some of the atmosphere vividly, if a little exaggeratedly; nobody at that time could have guessed that such a subject, still pretty esoteric, would be turned into one of the most successful musicals (and later a film) in the history of the stage.

Charles's next letter was dated 24 November 1947.

My dear Philip,
I'm actually writing this from Christ's: Hardy is now dying (how long it will take no one knows, but he hopes it will be soon) and I have to spend most of my spare time at his bedside. Report on *The Light and the Dark*: it has done a good deal of what you and I hoped for, but not quite all. *Sales*. Good: novel sales have been going down, but it sold out in the first edition (5,000) in very quick time. Fabers were delighted and are printing another 3,000, which should be ready by the end of the year. They are also printing another edition (3,000) of *Strangers and Brothers* [*George Passant*]. It looks as though the series will build up to very good comfortable sales: and that is important, since no front rank novelists (except Proust & Henry James) failed to get a reasonable sale in their own lifetime. *Critical reception*. To date 28 good reviews to 2 bad (a) Masterpiece: *J o'London* (Richard Church), *Sunday Chronicle* (Pamela H-J), *Scotsman, Manchester Guardian* (b) Very high praise . . . And the *private* critical reception has been very warm. But the 2 bad reviews,

though contemptible, are indicative: one was an oddly personal attack (anonymous) in the *Times Lit. Supp.* & the other some stupid abuse in the *Spectator*. These are both 'coterie' journals and I expect similar treatment from the *New Statesman* and the *Listener*. It can't affect sales, but I had hoped to conquer this kind of hostility as I must before I get a really solid reputation. I am writing in the teeth of a strong, though ridiculous, literary movement; at present I'm too 'human' for them. I'd hoped they would be outfaced by this book, but that has not yet happened. It may take several books and some years. But with good fortune I shall win through. (MacCarthy has not roused himself to review this book, which is a disappointment: he is, of course, getting old) . . . I regard ⅓ of the books sent to you as usefully spent if they keep you in touch with what is talked of in cultivated circles here – even though I don't agree with the judgement.

Hardy in fact died a few days later.

The economic muddle, mentioned in Charles's letter of 27 August, reached Fiji at the end of 1947; it had the odd effect of our being able to export by way of foodstuffs only locally tinned pineapple, home-grown brown sugar and guava jelly. We ourselves could no longer obtain what we had been sending in the parcels.

20 Hyde Park Place, W.2.

1 Jan 1948

My dear Philip,
Yes, by all means send pineapple, sugar and guava jelly. If I don't like the first and the third, I'll tell you promptly. It's a bit hard that we are in this economic mess. It may make it harder for me to get out to you in the autumn.

. . . The second edition of *The L. & the D.* is now ready but has not, I think, appeared in the shops. U.S. publishing date is 7 Feb. I am desperately busy with all these occupations hemming me in – I must finish the new book by March & it will be hard work. I am also frantically organising the final *normal* competitions for the Scientific Civil Service & there is a good deal to be done for Sir G. [Nelson]. I hope I have a literary success in America soon so that I may simplify my life. In America the expectation is either of a big success or comparative dimness: it is unlikely that I shall repeat the scale of moderate success I've had here.

Give my love to Anne and her daughter. I refuse to be associated with you in claims for extreme passivity of temperament [I had said that Stefanie took after me in placidity rather than Anne, that she is Snovian in this respect]. It isn't the least true of me, except that I

Above left: 1908. Mother, with Harold, aged ten, and Charles, aged three.
Above right: The family home, 40 Richmond Road, Leicester (left semi-detached)
Below: 1921. Charles with other prefects and the headmaster at Alderman
Newton's School.

1929. Eric, Charles (wearing the Leicester University College cricket blazer), Philip, Father and Mother and the family's only dog, Gyp. The eldest son, Harold, had died three years earlier.

Above left: Charles as a young Fellow of Christ's College, Cambridge.
Above right: Professor G.H. Hardy.
Below: 1937. Part of Christ's College governing body for sport. Left to right:
Charles, Philip, A.T. Goodrich and C.R.C. Allberry.

Above: 1950. Reception after Charles's marriage to Pamela Hansford Johnson. The bride and bridegroom with Bert Howard.

Below: 1953. At Clare, Suffolk. Left to right: Philip, Stefanie, Anne, Lindsay, Charles, Pam, Amy (Pam's mother), Andrew.

1957. Charles in the drawing room at Hillmorton Road, Rugby.

Left: 1965. Charles Snow at sixty.
Below: 1968. Charles on the House of
Lords Terrace with his niece Stefanie.

Above: 1963. Charles as an honorary Cossack with M.A. Sholokhov and Pam on the Don.
Below: 1967. Charles, Harold Macmillan and Lady Spencer-Churchill at a Foyle's literary luncheon.

1974. Charles with his cat, Gabbo.

have a certain superficial good temper – & I shouldn't have thought it very true of you. Eric's cricket history has many most interesting facts & is a triumph of scholarship . . ..

Love
P

The reference is to our middle brother Eric's history of Leicestershire cricket. When it was published in 1949 it was indeed regarded as the classic of its kind, a model for all cricket histories.

I was selected to captain the Fiji cricket team for a three-month tour of New Zealand, including matches against the first-class provinces, starting in January 1948. I enjoyed it thoroughly. Crowds were large: the bigger they were, the better we played. A great fuss was made of us by the New Zealanders whose links with Fiji in the war had been strong. I could not keep pace with the stream of letters that followed me. Anne, left with Stefanie on Taveuni, kept Charles in touch, although as it turned out he too had had his diversions.

20 Hyde Park Place, W.2.
12 Aug 1948

My dear Philip,

I ought to have written long ago, but I've been very distracted, largely owing to a violent love affair which began in May and from which I have just extricated myself. I wasn't in love, but the circumstances were melodramatic – a wild upper-class girl of 24 suddenly conceived an infatuation for me, mainly because she felt I could bring some stability into her life. Not that stability wasn't necessary, since she was (a) drunken (b) liable to sleep with any man at sight (c) fantastically extravagant (she cost me hundreds of pounds in three months). In fairness, I ought to add that she's also intelligent, has formidable character and is voluptuously attractive to a degree. Unfortunately she decided that she wanted to marry me, and being much touched by her (I can't imagine how her life will end, and don't like to think) I had to remove myself without damaging her too much. Which I believe I've done. Incidentally, she has one husband already plus an Italian lover of 46 who has been keeping her for some time (he is the most important figure in her past and I have had bizarre scenes with him) plus a very large number – really large, about fifty – of other lovers. All of which is a singular mélange for a middle-aged gentleman of quiet tastes. Poor girl. I felt desperately sorry for her. If she had been a bit more bearable I should have taken her on: which, although I should have been

97

envied when I followed her into restaurants, would have made a mess of my life.

Someone ought to produce a nice girl for me to marry: otherwise I'm still liable to get into these predicaments.

Literary news. England: *The Light and the Dark* is shortly coming out in its 3rd edition, *Strangers and Brothers* has just been reissued and appears to be selling well. USA: *The L. and the D.* had good reviews but didn't sell. Nothing is selling there at present, except book club choices. *Translations. The L. and the D.* is being translated into Danish (the whole series is being translated), Spanish, German & possibly French. What do you think of *A Traveller in the World* as a title for the whole series? And *Time of Hope* for Lewis's young manhood? . . . Write soon.

Love to you all

P

Charles had sent a draft of *Time of Hope* to Pamela Hansford Johnson. Their literary friendship went back to 1941, but they didn't meet till 1944; she still called him Snow.

I was about to join the brotherhood as the third to have a book published. Following the outstanding success of the 1948 Fiji cricket tour and its large public interest in New Zealand, a publisher in that country wanted to bring out my *Cricket in the Fiji Islands*. When the book came out in 1949 with an Introduction by Sir Pelham Warner and a Foreword by Ratu Sir Lala Sukuna, it received gratifying reviews from Sir Neville Cardus, John Arlott and other leading cricket journalists. As only 500 copies were printed its rarity value now is considerable. The royalties went to the Fiji Cricket Association. I had asked Charles for advice about its title.

20 Hyde Park Place, W.2.

3 Oct 1948

My dear Philip,

I should vote for *Cricket in the Fiji Islands* (or, just possibly, *Cricket in the South Seas*). I'm very glad that you are getting it published. I hope you won't be long about finishing *Bronze and Clay* [my proposed book on the South Seas, primarily on Fiji]. It really is an unusual book and ought to win you a kind of eccentric success. I'm sure it will be well thought of.

I've nearly finished *Time of Hope*, and this should be out in the early autumn of '49. *The Masters, Charles March* and others will compete for the next appearance, in 1950. It wouldn't have been wise to produce another Cambridge book just after *The L. and the*

D., though *The Masters* is the most certain of these books to have a very high sale. The general view, shared by Fabers and Macmillans, is that *Strangers and Brothers* is the ideal title for the series. I have gradually accumulated a little money, and must make a new will. And the copyright of the books will now in all likelihood be worth a considerable sum. If anything should happen before this will is complete, see that Anne Seagrim receives either the copyright of *Charles March* or *The Masters* or a sum of £2,000 (whichever she prefers – the copyright is the better bet). [For Anne Seagrim, see below page 182.]

I am half thinking of buying a house: if I had a competent person to run it for me I would actually buy a farm. In the world as it's going to be for the next generation, a farm is a good investment in England. The only danger is to be extinguished as Kulak Snow. If ever you get tired of the tropics and wish to transform yourself into a farmer, let me know. It's rather silly to be earning so much money and paying so much to the Exchequer. For various technical reasons, the more different business ventures one runs, the more taxation one escapes. Life is not unpicturesque in some of the circles in which I move. The general uncertainty is affecting some of the 20–30 group. I can't say that I blame them . . ..

Ever
CPS

On 27 October he wrote:

. . . No particular news. I'm very busy and have nearly finished *Time of Hope*. If I make my world tour I ought to be able to finish a fairly short work (90,000 words) on the various sea journeys. I'm still contemplating very seriously buying a largish farm. I believe it will be the best investment for the rest of our life-times . . .. At the moment I have a large income (£5,000–£6,000) but little capital (about £8,000 apart from the capital represented by unpublished MSS). A large farm with a substantial country house would cost £25,000. I think I could raise this on a mortgage from my bank. And the Income Tax law is such that (with perfect propriety) it just wouldn't matter losing money on the farm for years. It's all a tangled but interesting game.

Love to you
CPS

My savings after a decade in the Colonial Service were £200. My salary was only £750 and the cost of every imported article in Fiji was twice what it was in England. All rather inadequate; I concluded that the Colonial Administrative Service was a most unrewarding life financially. When I wrote to Charles saying that

I'd be looking round for another job when my next leave came up in 1951, he replied promptly.

20 Hyde Park Place, W.2.
22 Dec 1948

My dear Philip,
I was interested in your last letter. If any suitable job comes up I will let you know: but would you really be content to spend a good slice of your life in cricket administration? You are an odd fish, and you find a good deal of interest wherever you go. But I should have thought it would have palled after a time . . . .

As for the farm: this will probably become a serious proposition quite soon. It is the best that I can see: I shall want to run a largish (200 acres at least) & successful farm: I am too much of a born professional to play at these things. If in a year or two I can raise 20,000–30,000 pounds, I shall take expert advice and buy one, probably in Suffolk or Huntingdon or round about. Such a farm ought to pay 10%, after allowing for a reasonable salary to a resident manager such as yourself. I don't know how serious your conscientious objection to animal-murder is (are you a vegetarian now?) but the chief functionary on a large farm doesn't poleaxe animals himself, if that is your objection. Most East Anglian farming is wheat, etc., but I think all the pundits agree that mixed farming is the safest and most interesting kind for anything of the size I am imagining.

My life has been desperately overworked (I must simplify it soon). Have finished *Time of Hope*. The German *The L & the D* is having something of a success – published in Vienna in a most sumptuous edition 3 weeks ago. I'm doing novels for *The Sunday Times* for a month. Have an idea for a play. I wish you would finish *Bronze and Clay*. If we survive 10 years, we shall have some literary power.

Love to you both
CPS

A friend of long standing, Gorley Putt, was advising Charles to ease up so that he should live to be a GOM with at least twenty years' 'benign existence' after his main work was completed.

1949, when I returned to Suva on promotion as Assistant Colonial Secretary, was Charles's last year at Hyde Park Place. On 19 August he wrote:

My dear Philip,
I got your cable . . . I'm doubtful whether, even if the chance came, I could get away . . . I am fighting the hardest battles of my writing

life, with occasional reverses but with a progress that is quite substantial when one looks back 2–3 years. The chief anchor to keep me here is that I am now reviewing novels fortnightly for *The Sunday Times*. This is, of course, a most valuable strategic position, & I don't want to give it up until I have secured the major objectives. *Time of Hope* comes out on 23 Sep., the third and best of the sequence. There will be another next year. I had a play televised in July, & have now finished the final stage version. It is called *The Ends of the Earth*. I am busy with my complicated manoeuvres (more suitable to you) to get it on the West End stage. At the worst, I shall secure a very competent production at one of the small peripheral London theatres, with a chance of transfer. I believe that I can be as good a playwright as novelist, & if I have any success on the stage I shall write a play a year, as well as a novel.

I wish you were here to take a hand. By the way, I shall like to ease your next leave – so will you take a house at my expense and charge the upkeep to me ? It would be nice if you and Anne could do some entertaining for me. I don't mind where the house is, either in London or the country. I think it will be very pleasant to have somewhere for a time. I am so constantly preoccupied that I just haven't the reserve to do anything like it for myself.

Love to you all
C

He signed this letter 'C', a significance I missed at the time. Pamela Hansford Johnson was now addressing him as 'Charles dear'; it was she who caused him to change his name.

Plans for moving the play from The Lyric, Hammersmith, to the West End, were intricate indeed. *The Ends of the Earth* had gone over well on television with Cathleen Nesbitt (to whom Rupert Brooke had written adoringly from Fiji in 1913) in the principal role of Lady Hayes. Charles discovered that Lord Vivian, an impresario, wanted to read it and had hopes that The Haymarket or The Apollo would put it on. At the same time he sent it (retitled *View over the Park*) to various leading actors. His expectations of becoming a playwright were never realised, though several of his novels were successfully adapted for stage and television.

At the end of 1949 *Time of Hope* won the British Annual of Literature's first medal. It was published in the same month as Eric's *History of Leicestershire Cricket* and my *Cricket in the Fiji Islands* – three books by three brothers within a month.

Charles expressed extreme dissatisfaction to Sir Geoffrey Faber about the firm's promotion of *Time of Hope*. Faber admitted their mistake in underbinding the first edition of 3,500 but Charles pointed out that the sales record for all three books published by them had been unsatisfactory: they printed 3,000 of *Strangers and Brothers*, plus a 2000 reprint in 1948, and *Time of Hope* and *The Light and the Dark* could, he felt, all have been pushed harder. He therefore asked Faber to release him. This was coincidental with his meeting Lovat Dickson of Macmillan who wanted very much to publish for him. Reluctant at first, Faber finally realised that one cannot hang on to an unwilling author; his next book, *The Masters*, went to Macmillan, who remained his British publishers for the rest of his life.

The end of the decade saw Charles about a third of the way towards completing the great scheme which he first conceived in 1935, and firmly established as a literary figure.

At this point it seems appropriate to quote a note which he wrote on 12 March 1945.

This is a series of at least 11 novels for which I have not yet found a general title: I may call it *Strangers and Brothers* and rename Vol. 1. Each of the novels, except perhaps Vol. XI, will be intelligible if read separately, but the series is planned as one integral work of art and I should like it so considered and judged. The work has two explicit intentions – first to carry out an investigation into human nature . . . through a wide variety of characters, major and minor, second, to depict a number of social backgrounds in England in the period 1920–50 from the dispossessed to Cabinet Ministers. For each major character, the narrator is occupied with the questions: How much of his fate is due to the accident of his class and time? and how much to the essence of his nature which is unaffected by class and time? . . . All the social backgrounds are authentic. I have lived in most of them myself; and the one or two I have not lived in I know at very close second-hand.

I hope to finish the whole work by 1950.

He was wildly optimistic. *Last Things* was in fact published in 1970.

9. A New Empire

Charles and Pamela Hansford Johnson were married in Christ's College Chapel on 15 July 1950 by Ian Ramsay, later Bishop of Durham. Bert Howard was best man, resplendent in morning dress.

Pam had been publishing novels since the age of eighteen and was an able critic; she had first written to Charles nine years previously to express her admiration for his work, and they had been corresponding ever since. *Important to Me*, a splendidly evocative book and the nearest she came to an autobiography, shows that her background was not dissimilar to Charles's.

In the spring of 1951 Anne, Stefanie and I flew from Fiji to Australia to catch the liner *Orcades* for England. In the Suez Canal we were greeted by hails of stones hurled by angry Egyptians. Charles and Pam met us at Tilbury, Pam looking even better than her pictures and truly soignée; her blue eyes, the colour of a Siamese cat's, were easily amused. We were totally charmed and saw them as often as we could.

They had leased 1 Hyde Park Crescent for £5000. Charles had taken on a considerable household, with his two young step-children, Andrew and Lindsay, and Pam's mother Amy, who had worked for Henry Irving and Ellen Terry (experiences which were helping Pam with one of her most engaging books, *Catherine Carter*). She told us of Pam's affair with Dylan Thomas. They'd once got as far as the registry office steps, she said, but changed their minds – much to Amy's relief. Charles and Pam gave us a welcoming home party at which we met among other people L. P. Hartley, benign and distinguished, and Kay Dick, monocled with a 1920s foot-long cigarette holder, both matching my outmoded idea of what fashionable novelists should look like.

I returned to Leicester in the hope of being selected for the county, but it was soon clear that the chances of breaking into first class cricket were even less than in 1946. Thus an ambition of Charles's, scarcely less strong than my own, did not materialise.

Before my six months' leave was too advanced I started looking round for a job in England. I'd done reasonably well in the Colonial Service but the problem of Stefanie's education was looming up. Charles threw himself into the business of job hunting for me; since time was short it was advisable for me to meet as many people as possible. Cricket being the pleasantest way I knew of making contacts, I played a good deal.

Nigel Balchin, the writer, asked me to play for his team at Tenterden in Kent. Charles umpired. He had not seen me play for thirteen years and, officiating at my end, was convulsed when my googly repeatedly broke sharply across to smack a baffled batsman's rump. After the match we all retired to Balchin's converted oasthouse. Its low roof, in combination with Charles's somatic awkwardness, made it a safe bet that he would bang his head on a beam. Duly plastered, he spent the rest of the evening in abstruse conversation with Mark Bonham Carter that soon had me out of my depth. A little note followed:

. . . Mark Bonham Carter's match is at Oxford on Aug. 12. I should play if you can. You have won v. good opinions.

My worries much relieved. Brian [Downs] and Grose have invited us up to Cambridge next week: can Pam and you & I all go? . . .

The last reference was to a feeling of his that he was not welcome at Christ's following the appearance of *The Masters* in the middle of the year. He was indeed *persona non grata* among certain fellows, but everybody else loved it; to the ordinary Oxbridge graduate in particular it was a revelation. Paul Jago, the principal character (based generally on Canon C. E. Raven) is, after a monumental struggle, defeated for the Mastership by R. T. A. Crawford, drawn mainly from Sir Robert Watson-Watt. The latter, who claimed more than an equitable share in radar's beginnings, was later to be an adversary of Charles in a national controversy.

As a result of Macmillan publishing *The Masters*, Faber reported that sales of the other books had gone up considerably. Harold Macmillan believed that the sequence would have a long and flourishing life.

Soon after publication we were sitting in front of the pavilion at Lord's and chanced to hear two members discussing *The Masters*.

The spontaneity of their review – for they were unaware of the author's proximity – gave Charles much pleasure.

We were now planning a holiday together. Because there was no certainty that I would not have to return to Fiji in January I wanted to see something of Europe. Charles and Pam had been to Venice on their honeymoon the year before and wished to return there. It occurred to them that since I had a car I might join them there and bring them back. I did not want to drive to Venice alone. So I advertised in a Leicester paper for a travelling companion, selecting a Leicester man of about my own age. He had been a Commando and turned his training to practical if shaky moral advantage by supplementing our apple supply with raids on orchards, executed with a wicked-looking Commando knife.

Reaching Venice I caught a cold; it was October and the lagoon and canals were ruffled by a strong wind. Charles loftily commandeered my pre-war camel-hair overcoat, which he thought suited him and his black homburg better than me. Charles and Pam were intrigued by my companion and the potentialities of his Commando knife but he decided, when we started on our return journey, to make his way back by train from Milan where Charles and Pam made a call on their publishers.

The journey back along the Italian Riviera from Genoa via Monaco and the French Riviera was an eye-opener to me. I had not imagined such beauty, and fell in love with Monaco and Nice. Then we travelled inland to Aix-en-Provence, through Avignon, to Burgundy and Paris. The highlight for Pam and Charles was a route taken by their special request through villages redolent of Proust near Chartres; since neither of them drove it was a rare opportunity and their excitement on recognition of the places mentioned in Proust was intense. It added a little to Pam's great store of knowledge. The leisurely journey enabled me to get to know Pam whom I had only seen previously for a day or two at a time, and also to see Charles and Pam together. We nearly missed the ferry from Calais to Dover. I had been waiting, after a breakfast taken alone, for nearly an hour when Charles appeared with a suitcase and a sheepish, if contented, look. 'You know what women are like,' he confided. 'Punctuality doesn't matter a lot when they want something.'

On our return I received a note from him saying how immensely he had enjoyed the trip and how he hoped 'more than I can say that you will get a good job in England'.

1952 had started off badly for Pam with attacks by critics on *Catherine Carter*, in my view her best novel. But for me it had opened well. To Charles's undisguised pleasure, I was selected to be Bursar of Rugby School. The announcement came just a fortnight before we were due to return to the South Seas. I had ambivalent feelings about changing horses in mid-stream. The sacrifice of a top post, at best a governorship with an automatic knighthood, was the most obvious snag. But it would have meant waiting for years – and would the Empire last? I also lost fourteen years pensionable service, but with my mass of field notes I could write about the Pacific just as well, if not better, in England with all its research facilities and, of course, I would see more of Charles. I had many regrets at the time; it would have been strange, after fourteen years, if I had not, but I kept in close contact with my multi-racial friends in Fiji and was able to be of use to them, particularly after Independence, in return for the many kindnesses they showed me.

I found many diversions in my new life.

1 Hyde Park Crescent, W.2.
May 2 1952

My dear Philip,

I don't expect you are mobile in term time, but I thought it just worthwhile to say that Collins are giving a party in honour of Cardus's first book for 15 years, and that you are invited. If you could come, stay the night of course with us . . . .

Ever
CPS

On the slender base of my Fiji cricket book I began appearing in the Authors *v.* Publishers cricket match at the Westminster School ground in Vincent Square. Charles used to watch some of these annual matches, including the one where the Authors' scorecard read:

1. Sir Leonard Hutton (England) 2. J. H. W. Fingleton (Australia) 3. A. R. Morris (Australia) 4. Philip Snow (Fiji) 5. D. R. Jardine (England, capt.) 6. P. G. H. Fender (England) 7. I. A. R. Peebles (England) 8. Alec Waugh 9. Edmund Blunden 10. Paul Gallico 11. Laurence Meynell.

Alec Waugh was Charles's and my cherished friend but Charles, feeling himself to be a superior cricketer, expatiated on the justice of himself being No. 8 and certainly being an improvement on Nos 9 to 11. The Publishers, led exuberantly by Billy Collins, were invariably no match for the Authors. Why C. P. Snow was not selected I never could understand. Nor could he.

Savile Club
69 Brook Street, W.I.

June 21 1952

My dear Philip,
. . . I keep getting congratulated on my score v. Publishers. It appears to have been reported (in Daily Graphic & elsewhere) & people assume that Philip Snow is me.

Ever
CPS

Meanwhile Pam and Charles, with a child on the way to join Andrew and Lindsay, decided that Hyde Park Crescent was much too small and that they must have a garden for the children. They bought Nethergate, a lovely Jacobean house in the East Anglian village of Clare. It had a semi-wild garden running down to a stream with swans and moorhens gyrating round the landing-jetty. There were two gracious staircases; the drawing room was half-timbered with beams and the dining room white-panelled. Charles had a $2\frac{1}{2}$ hour train journey from London but found it otherwise convenient, spending most of the week in the metropolis. For Pam and Amy, as pure Londoners, the novelty of country life was considerable.

Soon after they had settled, I was informed of a memorable event:

Nethergate House
Clare, Suffolk

Aug. 27 1952

My dear Philip,
The baby arrived a month early, last night: we had to rush Pam into the Cambridge Maternity Home in the small hours of Sunday morning. She is very well indeed. The baby, a boy, is of course very small, under 5 lbs., but looks very nice so far as a new-born child can . . . . we are giving it 3 names Philip Charles Hansford. The Philip is after you & it will be called that . . . .

Then followed a progress report:

Civil Service Commission
Scientific Branch
Trinidad House, 7th floor
Old Burlington House, W.1.
Sep. 30 1952

My dear Philip,

Philip lailai [Fijian for small] is doing very well and put on 8 ozs last week since we got home. People think he looks like me. I think he looks like *you*. I'm taking most of October off to get somewhere near finishing the scientific novel. (I wish I had a title for it.)

Love to you all
CPS

At this time he was, rather oddly, offered the job of Head of the Appointments Board at Cambridge, one of the least flattering invitations extended to him in his career. More complimentary was Leonard Russell's invitation to write twelve reviews at twenty pounds a time for *The Sunday Times*.

Charles sent the manuscript of *The Devoted* to Macmillan and told them that the next book would be called *The New Men*, the story of Lewis Eliot's brother. He drew up a fresh plan for the whole series which was to be entitled *Strangers and Brothers*. Lovat Dickson of Macmillan thought that the order should be Vol. V the scientific book and Vol. VII *The Devoted*. In the event he was not far wrong, as Vol. V was *The New Men*, Vol. VI *Homecomings*, Vol. VII 'the Jew book' (later *The Conscience of the Rich*), *The Devoted* being absorbed into *Homecomings* and other works.

In 1954 Macmillan asked Charles to act as an adviser with a retainer of £250 a year, involving a three-hour meeting every fortnight over lunch. Scribners took over the American side of publication and have remained in close contact ever since. They reported the quaint fact that the US Army had ordered 800 copies of *The New Men*, which had just come out and was to win in 1955 the James Tait Black Memorial Prize for the best novel published the previous year. Awarded by Edinburgh University, it was worth £175.

I remember on one occasion, when driving Charles through Barford, a village between Rugby and Stratford-on-Avon, his asserting, 'This is where I shall set the locale of *The New Men*'.

In *The New Men* Martin Eliot (a leading character in that book and a subsidiary one in *Time of Hope*, *Corridors of Power*, *The Affair*, *The Sleep of Reason* and *Last Things*) proposes writing letters of outrage to *The Times* about the dropping of bombs on Hiroshima and Nagasaki while himself engaged in the bomb's development. He is stopped by Lewis Eliot from doing so at a cost to their relationship which takes some time to put right. Martin gives up science and all ambition in the wicked world and retires to academic life in Cambridge.

Though I could not see much of myself in Martin Eliot, other people have detected a good many similarities. Certainly the dialogue between Martin and Lewis Eliot rings true – Charles caught exactly the nuances of our conversation – but Martin Eliot's problems were so much more dramatic than my own, and the tension between the two brothers is charged with an electricity that we never experienced in reality. I suspect, though, that had our lives indeed followed the pattern of the fictional brothers, we might have behaved much as they did.

The last sentence is as follows: 'Of the human relations I had so far known, I had found, despite our mistakes, none more steady and comforting than that with my brother; I hoped that in time he would feel the same.' I like to think that this is a considered statement of our relationship throughout his life.

There was more good news.

Nethergate House
Clare, Suffolk.

Aug. 15 1954

My dear Philip,
I'd like to come to Lord's on Wed. about 3.30. If it is fine I will come to the back of the pavilion at 3.30 (± 5 minutes). [He was invariably that punctual.] Are you doing anything for dinner that night?

Penguins have bought *The Masters* and *The New Men* & hint that they may do the entire series, which would be nice.

Ever,
CPS

Penguin did just that and have published virtually all his works since. Although this was inevitable, I like to think that my introducing Charles to a Penguin contact may have contributed.

In October Charles and Pam went on a sea voyage:

Oct. 12 1954

My dear Anne and Philip,

We feel we shall never make fun of Philip's maritime horrors again. The moment we left the Firth of Clyde it became rough; & went on being repulsively rough until the Tuesday night, when we hit a hurricane. It really was alarming! We awoke about 2 a.m. to an awful roaring & crashing & the next thing that happened was the careering of the stateroom furniture all over the room. No more sleep was possible, so Charles tried hard to concentrate on the Lakeland Poets & I folded my hands & looked steadfastly at the opposite wall. Next day when I was on the Promenade Deck, I was even more horrified to see nothing visible but sea one side of the ship, & nothing visible but sky on the other. It was a dreadful day, but thank God we gained the Straits of Belle Isle (The Earthly Paradise) about 9.30 pm . . . . Love to you all, & we shall never laugh at anyone's hurricanes again – serve us right!

Pam

Then from Charles, whose trip was a mixture of English Electric and literary business:

John Inglis Co. Limited
Consumer Products Division
14 Strachan Avenue
Toronto 3, Canada

Oct. 24 1954

My dear Philip,

I was very sad to hear of father's death. But I believe he would have been pleased to do so so easily: I don't think life had any more meaning for him: & I find it a curious kind of comfort to see how one can slip out of life.

Do anything that is required of me. I don't see any use in flying home, which in any case would be desperately difficult. If you want any help in settling business about the house, let me know. We are having a busy & not unenjoyable time, until darkened by this news. Toronto has done us proud: I happen to be relatively well-known, especially in the intellectual anglophile circles, & it has been a round of broadcasting, TV appearances & parties. We'll tell you all when I get back. I think of appointing myself Governor-General after Massey, with you as Chief Adjutant. It is a place calling for supreme

110

& absolutely continuous tact. It is also going to be the third richest (& perhaps the first) nation in the world.

Love to you both
C

Eric had rung me in the middle of the night to say that the lodger had found that father had died in his sleep. He was in his eighty-sixth year and had never been ill in his life until he'd fallen on an icy pavement fracturing his collarbone. This had shaken him severely and he'd had to retire from St Mary de Castro. His last interest in life gone, he'd never recovered. I found it hard to bear. He is faithfully described in *The Sleep of Reason* as 'the most self-sufficient' of men as well as the 'most affable and gentle of human beings'. Though he never read any of Charles's books he would have been proud to know of his later honours.

Anne and I had moved to a large early Victorian house in Hillmorton Road, Rugby, large enough to house the odd pieces of furniture from Richmond Road. Charles had given Eric and me the Leicester house left to him by mother. We sold it for £400 and, to our regret if not surprise, it was demolished in 1959.

Homecomings came out in 1956, dedicated to William Cooper (Harry Hoff). Charles regarded the first part as his best piece of writing – though less satisfactory overall than *The Masters* – but it is not to everybody's taste, being the most sombre of his novels. There was endless discussion about the title. Scribners eventually plumped for *Homecoming*; Macmillan dithered between *Land of Day*, *The Buried Day* and *The Moment in which We Stood*, before settling for *Homecomings*.

Quite a few changes occurred that year. Charles stopped reviewing for *The Sunday Times* and his job as literary adviser to Macmillan came to an end. At this time he was earning £1750 as a part-time director of English Electric and £2000 as part-time Civil Service Commissioner, in addition to his mounting earnings from writing. He was quite happy to spend the week in London and the weekends in the solitude of Clare, but as Pam wanted to get back to London Nethergate House was sold. On 13 October Charles wrote:

Back from Scandinavia on Thursday p.m. & your letter arrived this morning. We had a tiring, interesting & valuable time: I'll tell you when we meet . . . . The book [*Homecomings*] has been a real success here: even my enemies have to concede, very grudgingly, that I'm becoming a sort of GOM. Selling v. well. Just out in US: first reviews as good or better than the English, sales promising. The total Press is the best and solidest I've had . . . . I never get into books quite as much humour as I have (or think I have). Perhaps it will come when I've got a bit further.

We leave here on Oct 22 & for a month go to Dudley Hotel, Hove, Sussex. After that in London, renting a flat until January, when we move into Cromwell Road . . . .

While they were still homeless, the Suez crisis broke upon the world:

Dudley Hotel
Hove, Sussex
Nov. 6 1956

My dear Philip,

I don't think a total war is likely, but one can't be sure that it's impossible & perhaps we ought to make emergency plans. Particularly as, if it happens at all, it will happen during the next two weeks, when we are house-less. It seems to me that our best course is to descend on you if the thing was really going to start – if necessary splitting the family between you and Eric. I don't pretend that, in a total war, any of us would stand much chance, but with children one has to take such steps as don't seem ridiculous.

It might be a useful precaution if you laid in a few days' supply of tins of food. It's no use over-insuring – the only kind of calamity we can possibly emerge from is one which is all over in a comparatively short time . . . .

Love to you all
CPS

Charles and Pam had been working on my *Bronze and Clay* which a publisher was now allowed to have a preliminary look at. Charles wrote on 11 November:

. . . . Collins completely missed the outstanding virtue of the book, its remarkably sensuous (particularly visual) actuality . . . . *Homecomings* has done v. well in England★. & Macmillans are I believe reprinting. *The Last Resort* [by Pam] has come out at the worst possible time. *Homecomings* has had a fine press in US but I've heard nothing about sales which is rather ominous.

Ever
CPS

★It will do better than any of them except *The Masters*.

Although we had discussed the possibility of a knighthood for his Civil Service Commission work, it was far from all our minds when, on 1 December 1956, the Prime Minister wrote to say that he wished to recommend Charles for the New Year's Honours List. Charles confided to me:

Civil Service Commission
Scientific Branch
Trinidad House, 7th floor
Old Burlington Street, W.1.

Dec. 6 1956

My dear Philip,

With some uncertainty I have just accepted a K. It will (if we all survive) be in the New Year's Honours; I didn't want you to see it first in the paper.

It is being given for my official career, which pleases me. These things are of course nothing but a nuisance to a writer; it will do me a slight but perceptible amount of harm. However there are inducements on the other side. People who compare me with Trollope ought to realise that I've gone much further in the public Service than he ever did. This is naturally a secret. It is death if these things get out.

Love to you both,
CPS

There was no concealing from me his and Pam's delight when I saw them a week later. But Charles reminded me of the doubts he had expressed whenever the question of a writer accepting a title had come up. It had been a strict convention from at least the beginning of the century for writers to be wary of honours; the OM was always acceptable, but knighthoods had been regarded as the kiss of death by some. Precedents for taking them are few; they include Rider Haggard, Hugh Walpole, Arthur Conan Doyle, Max Beerbohm, James Barrie and Walter Scott. Omissions have been significant: Galsworthy and Kipling (who did however have the OM), Wells (who wanted the OM more than anything else), Shaw, Arnold Bennett, Dickens, Trollope. Charles settled the dilemma by recognising that the knighthood was for his Civil Service Commission work and had nothing whatever to do with his writing; he resolved to continue to be known as C. P. Snow for all literary purposes. He did not realise how difficult it would be to enforce this, but there is no denying the uplift it gave him. He received about four hundred congratulatory letters; I saw them all. The Home Office informed him that the accolade would be conferred at Buckingham Palace on 12 February. He wrote me:

I have 2 tickets for the Investiture. Pam wants one of course & you are welcome to the other. It will mean staying with us on the night of Feb 11, since we are due at the Palace at 10.15 a.m. on the 12th ...

Pam and I had good seats from which to watch the crocodile slowly amble across the ballroom floor to the surprisingly flippant music from the Household Band in the gallery above us – excerpts from *Oklahoma*, *South Pacific* and *Carousel*. As Charles bent his knee before the Queen, I waited expectantly for the band to launch into 'When I marry Mr Snow' from *Carousel*: disappointingly, it coincided with the OBEs. Charles looked unusually tidy in his morning dress.

Generally he was renowned for a rather individual stamp of dishevelment. He had an idiosyncratic dress sense; apart from a short period in the 1960s when he was a Minister (and looked one), he could hardly have been accused of being clothes-conscious. He was known to have made an after-dinner speech in a suit over a faded blue cardigan with darned elbows, the sleeves hanging down to envelop half his hands. There were phases of wearing what passed for a square black homburg but otherwise he went bareheaded. His shoe-laces were invariably undone; he acquired a peculiar mannerism of twisting himself into a laborious position to retie them—quite ineffectively. His coats would be buttoned up in all the wrong holes; frequently he would dangle a large, white crumpled handkerchief on his knee. His sartorial waywardness was too much part of him to attract much comment.

He could be no less idiosyncratic about food. His idea of a reasonable lunch was that it should be cold, except for soup, of which he was inordinately fond. Corned beef, pork pies, ham—but on no account tomatoes—were relished above all else. Once at the Stag and Pheasant Hotel in Leicester he asked the waitress if the fruit-salad was fresh or tinned. 'Fresh, of course,' she replied indignantly. 'In that case,' said Charles, 'I won't have it.' He had a partiality for pheasant and blancmange, a passion for chocolate that lasted all his life. At Eaton Terrace he would keep some in a sideboard drawer and help himself surreptitiously after lunch, not offering it round.

114

Chocolate liqueurs were even better, and boiled sweets also found favour. His favourite hot meal was white bait, crêpes de volailles, followed by a savoury; he particularly liked chicken livers rolled in bacon. He used to protest mildly that these three never coincided; indeed he was rarely offered any one of them. He abominated Christmas and all the food that went with it, to say nothing of the lack of newspapers. 'Depression and an alcoholic haze' were the main features of his festive season.

He was once asked to contribute to a publication called *The Artists and Writers Cookbook*. He declined, saying that he quite enjoyed food in a hit-or-miss kind of way but had never cooked a dish in his life. He just ate the food when it appeared. He told me of a lunch he had with Harold Macmillan in 1964, when Macmillan had resigned as Prime Minister and was once more Charles's publisher. They went to the Ritz, Macmillan's favourite place: 'Charles, what will you have? You can have anything you like, on or off the menu.' Charles cheered up. 'I'll have a poached egg on toast.' Macmillan looked bemused. 'No,' said Charles, 'I'll change my mind, if I may.' Macmillan looked encouraged. 'I'll have two poached eggs on toast, please.' And that was that; Macmillan had caviare, roast beef, a pudding and cheese.

At the end of 1956 the family moved into the ground-floor flat at 199, Cromwell Road. There was a capacious study in which Pam and Charles could work together, though Charles preferred an office away from the house. Ideas for books, problems of title (in which Pam was disposed to have the initial inspiration) and theme, and arrangements outside writing would be discussed mainly over lunch and dinner, newspaper and journal reading taking its sanctified place in between times.

Charles and Pam frequently appeared on television, the former on Brains Trust Programmes – he'd also done them on radio during the war – and people on buses which stopped outside the flat would occasionally recognise Charles through the study window. They are probably the only married couple to appear together on the Brains Trust. Pam, looking very cool, was distinctly articulate; Charles was more hesitant, before intervening or answering with an originality that breathed depth of feeling and breadth of outlook.

I saw a great deal more of them than at any previous time. I had frequent opportunities to share Charles's confidences as he and I stayed up until two or three in the morning; it was a time of special closeness. On 26 June he wrote:

115

I meant to tell you about this but I've been so busy that more important things have got shelved. Pam & I are flying to Malta on Saturday & flying back 10 days later. [Charles had agreed to serve on the Royal University of Malta Commission for four years.] It seems to me reasonable to make a will, which I ought to do anyway. We are bound to be flying about a good deal in the next few months . . . The arrangements are . . . .

If Pam & I die together. Income of my estate to be used, in the first instance, for educating and maintaining Andy, Lindsay and Philip. I should like you, if you felt inclined, to take them into your hands; but that is for you to decide. There is considerably more money than is required for their upkeep and education, even on a lavish scale . . . . . This arrangement about the income of my estate is to continue for *8 years* – when Andrew is nearly 25 and Lindsay 21 . . . . Capital bequests of £3,000 to . . . and Anne Seagrim . . . . [See below page 182.]

If I predecease Pam. Bequests as before. Rest of the estate goes to her in trust i.e. income available to her for her lifetime . . . .

This is moderately complicated & wants administering with charity & good sense . . . . You ought to have an idea of the estate. Investments (at present market prices) about £27,000. English Electric insurance £12,000 (I think they would cough up individually more if you spoke to them thoughtfully). Insurance for the Malta trip (& presumably something similar for all such trips) £12,000. *The Conscience of the Rich*, now complete, is worth at least (probably more) £3,000. *The Devoted* (in my safe) £2,000. Income from the books ought to stay at least £500 p.a. for some years & might jump considerably . . . . Pam knows I have made a will providing for the education of her children.

Ever
CPS

On the literary front, Alan Maclean of Macmillan had commissioned Sidney Nolan to design a standard wrapper for all the Lewis Eliot novels. Charles and Pam had been among the very first to recognise his talent, filling the walls of their flat with Nolan canvasses. Nolan had in turn an admiration for Charles's work and was pleased to be associated with him.

The Conscience of the Rich was now at last published, since the person on whom a main character is compositely based had died (in his nineties) and the understanding not to publish in his life-time had been honoured. It had taken about a decade and a half for Charles's 'Jew Book', as he had long called it through the multitudinous change of titles, to be seen publicly. Dedicated to Pam, it received good reviews.

At this stage Charles was becoming the subject of constant biographical attention. In 1959 William Cooper (Harry Hoff) published a booklet with the title, *C. P. Snow*, in the *Writers and their Work* series; Robert Greacen published *The World of C. P. Snow* in 1962 and Jerome Thale's booklet *C. P. Snow* came out in 1964.

It is interesting to see the sales up to 1959 of books published or re-issued by Macmillan: *The Masters* 20,675 over the period 1951–8, *The New Men* 12,391 (1953–8), *Homecomings* 11,500 (1955–8). *The Conscience of the Rich* 11,629 (published in 1958), *The Search* 5,156 (republished in 1958), whilst those taken from Faber and Faber since 1951 were *Strangers and Brothers* 5,383, *The Light and the Dark* 5,152, and *Time of Hope* 4,692. The best seller of all was some six years away.

The 1950s were to go out with a bang. In a literary sense Charles had long been international but it was in a rather different context that he made his greatest impact to date when he gave the Rede Lecture, appropriately at Cambridge, on *The Two Cultures and the Scientific Revolution*. The fee for the lecture was 9 guineas – the same rate as in 1525 when it was established. What he had to say had long been obvious to thinking people but nothing was being done about it; now, nearly a quarter of a century later, one wonders what has been done since. Charles felt the need simply to express the fissure between intellectuals at one pole, the Arts, and at the other, Science, in the clearest possible way; but his honest account of the lack of communication between scientists and non-scientists on everyday and more critically important levels aroused the deepest feelings of anxiety. Many found the truth unpalatable, and books and articles – from the highly commendatory to unwarrantably vituperative – came pouring out.

Senator J. F. Kennedy told F. P. Miller at the University of Virginia, Charlottesville: 'I thoroughly agree with you that this is one of the most provocative discussions that I have ever read of this intellectual dilemma which at the same time is of profound consequence to our public policy. It is an essay of which I shall undoubtedly make use in future speeches.'

Charles told me that he always hoped subsequently to meet Kennedy but in fact he met few politicians in either America or Russia;

they were not, with the exception of Kennedy, interested in writers. Charles regretted this because he would have welcomed the chance of writing about them as public figures, as he did so penetratingly about other non-literary figures in *Variety of Men* years later.

Bertrand Russell expressed great interest in the Rede Lecture: 'The separation between science and culture is very much greater than it used to be.' And he was singularly experienced in both worlds. The Russian Ambassador was another who told Charles that he had read the lecture with great interest.

From now on Charles became a controversial figure. It was only the beginning of an era 'of notoriety', as he put it to me. But he enjoyed it and the prospect of more. Lord Astor invited him and Pam for the first of a number of visits. They liked Bill and Bronwen Astor and, when there was a fairly general calumny of Cliveden after the Profumo affair, Charles was ready to give any support that he could to restore some sanity and sense of proportion in the public mind.

'Of all things!' he exclaimed, when invited to open the new building for Alderman Newton's Girls' School, which had been previously housed in the Boys' School where he had first started. Anne, who had been a pupil there, and I were invited for the occasion. Charles gave one of his characteristically 'casual' speeches – entirely without notes of course. He blinked benevolently at audiences who were not slow to pick up his own brand of drollness; he had a mock-wry expression to ensure that these moments were not lost. In most public speeches he could rarely resist comparing this country with Russia and America – and Russia and America with each other. They were often staggeringly broad assertions but intuitively one felt them to be the result of his study of a good many instances first-hand or of judgements of people he trusted. On this occasion he said that Russia produced masses of competent and sometimes distinguished women engineers, and, given the historical proof of this country's ability in emergency, he could not understand why England's women were so little drawn to the profession. He knew his English engineers and had seen first-hand quite a few of Russia's. This was one of his more incontrovertible generalisations.

It was while he was enjoying in the Grand Hotel, Leicester, a very rare nostalgic evening with a handful of contemporaries from his boys' school that he was called to the telephone to hear from Pam that *The Affair*, due to come out in 1960, had been selected as the Book of the Month Club choice in America. Elated by the certainty of at least 20,000 sales, he did not recollect much of the rest of the evening.

118

It was about this time that he declared to me: 'If I had the last thirty-three years over again I might change my personal attitudes but not my works.'

Towards the end of 1959 he was invited by Lord Hill, Chancellor of the Duchy of Lancaster, to serve on a committee to help select titles of British publications for export. He took this on with enthusiasm. It was a subject on which he felt strongly.

With Pam and many others he signed a Declaration on Racial Discrimination by Christian Action; he was to take similar steps in 1963 for the Anti-Apartheid Movement when forty-eight playwrights refused to allow their work to be performed in any South African theatre where non-Europeans were discriminated against.

The 1950s had seen Charles's literary career taking giant strides. His great sequence was now about two-thirds complete. With *The Masters* he had produced what many aficionados regard as far and away his best novel, though he himself regarded *Homecomings* as the most sensitive of his creations. This apart, the Two Cultures proposition alone was likely to make the next few years lively.

10. An Edge of Darkness

At the end of 1959 Charles gave up his job with the Civil Service Commission to concentrate on his writing and lecturing. He and Pam entertained a good deal at Cromwell Road, and I remember several dinners for visiting Russians and Americans. Charles was now extremely busy, employing a secretary to cope with his vast correspondence as well as his literary output. It gave him particular pleasure to have been elected an Honorary Foreign Member of the American Academy of Arts and Letters, a rare distinction. He felt that this was much the grandest thing that had ever come his way – so grand, indeed, that most people had never heard of it. Henry Moore and Graham Greene, who were also members, told him that he'd get buttons and a sash. The buttons materialised but no sash. He was also awarded honorary degrees at Leicester and Liverpool Universities, the first of many, though he couldn't help feeling that Leicester was a bit slow off the mark. He maintained that since gaining university status Leicester had tended to obliterate the pre-war years. He couldn't be expected to like this since, as he pointed out, 'I'm part of the past. I am thus tending to give what little help I can to other Universities (such as St Andrews and one or two in the United States) where I haven't got this feeling of being unwanted'. He was uncharacteristically bitter and returned the Vice-Chancellor's welcome with some coldness. This contrasted strongly with the affability he showed towards old colleagues.

Of all his books, *The Affair*, published in 1960, made perhaps the best start. It had a wonderful reception in the United States that took Scribners by surprise, going immediately to the top of the bestseller list in New York. Charles used to say that he and Lawrence Durrell were the only English writers generally regarded as 'serious' to have broken through in America since the war. The title for the book had been taken, he explained, from the Dreyfus affair, the 'anti-hero' being as charmless as Dreyfus himself. The background had been supplied by Philip Bowden when Charles was contemplating writing it as far back as the 1930s. One or two friends were rather critical of the fraud devised in the novel, but it was based on Bowden's recollection of a sad deceit by an ambitious Swiss peasant's son who, after being exposed in a scientific journal, became clinically insane and committed suicide.

Ronald Millar telephoned Charles to say that he would like to make it into a play. It was the first of the *Strangers and Brothers* series to be considered for this treatment; Millar was enthusiastic about its dramatic possibilities and seemed to Charles very much in tune with it. From the beginning there was complete trust between them in a working relationship that lasted for the rest of Charles's life. In his preface to the edition of the three plays based on his novels, Charles wrote: 'One evening when *The Masters* was doing well at the Savoy, the pair of us walked down the Embankment and thought of Gilbert and Sullivan: they might write more admirable comedies than us but we certainly get on with each other better.'

During Charles's absence in California for six months Millar dramatised *The Affair*. Rather surprisingly, the Queen went to see it when it was put on at the Strand Theatre – 'good for business', Charles remarked. During the run Millar adapted *The New Men* for the stage. It never really caught on, unlike its successor, *The Masters*; but Charles wasn't too dismayed: 'It wasn't R.M.'s fault: it was mine. A play of the kind R.M. was writing needs above all a narrative.' Millar, after successes with his *Abélard and Héloïse*, *Robert and Elizabeth* and the Snow dramatisations, became the main writer of Heath's speeches as Prime Minister and adroitly took over the same role for Mrs Thatcher. Charles's friendship with Millar showed that politics never stood between him and those he liked. Millar recently described Charles to me as 'a lovely – and loving – man'.

'Uncle' Sydney Grose at Cambridge (the Arthur Brown, Senior Tutor, of the *Strangers and Brothers* series, who lived to his mid-nineties) showed particular appreciation for *The Affair*.

I think I would put it as your very best, considered from all angles . . . . I often think of that August day when you first appeared in my room and of some of the battles we had later to secure recognition not only for you but also for Charles [Allberry] and for Tom Burrow [later Professor of Sanskrit at Oxford] and later for Jack [Plumb]: looking back I don't think I had much but obstinacy to take into battles . . . .

When Richard Church wrote about the book, Charles reminded him: 'I owe a great deal to you as you know and I shall not forget it. Yours was the first voice raised on my behalf.' This refers to a review of *Strangers and Brothers* in 1940.

Euphoric with the reception of *The Affair*, and before its West End stage appearance, Charles went to Russia in the middle of 1960. His visit must have had considerable impact since *The Affair* sold at least 100,000 copies there. Charles always came back full of vigour from Russia: he had worked hard to absorb enough of the language to attempt to read newspapers and exchange a few words with people. Certainly the Russians took him to their hearts.

He had a favourite story illustrating the Russian sense of humour: 'A Soviet boss whom I met was induced to give his opinion of my books. "Ah!", the boss said, "I have read *Masters*." He gave a wide, Slavonic grin: "I think your politics are much like Kremlin politics. But our penalties for losing are a little more severe."'

Charles was a 'natural' for the Russians. Essentially stoical, humorous, amiable, complimentary to the point of flattery, unegotistical, he came from acceptable origins and was the unconventional Englishman. When required he could be a hard drinker. Remarkably, he was also a 'natural' for Americans. His admiration for their way of life communicated itself and his interests were wide-ranging in a way they respected; for them, too, he was the unconventional Englishman. In a speech at Pace University he was mildly self-mocking and anti-chauvinist about England; such an attitude was fresh to many Americans. He would candidly assert that, unlike the English, the American and Russian systems of education both made serious attempts to link the duality of the literary and scientific worlds.

Charles would have made a splendid ambassador to either country. Many have misunderstood his pro-Russian stance in an antipathetic climate. There are, I believe, two paramount reasons. Firstly, his admiration for them in the war was unbounded. He considered that they had saved the world from fascism by unparalleled heroism, and thought that the Allies should have attempted the invasion of Europe a year earlier even at the risk of being driven back into the sea. He was also concerned to try to understand Russia, when few seemed able or willing to, with the object of bridging the widening gap between Russia and America. He was only too well aware of each nation's imperfections, but saw himself as an interpreter of one axis to the other, searching for the good things in each.

After his visit to Russia, he visited America. Dartmouth College, New Hampshire, had offered him (and Aldous Huxley) the first of his galaxy of American honorary degrees (a Doctorate of Literature). Charles accepted with alacrity. Accompanied by Pam, he received his degree and then crossed to the University of California at Berkeley where he was Regent's Professor of English for three months.

Not much was happening in England, though *Crossbow*, the quarterly of the Bow Group, cutting across party lines, had prophetically advised life peerages for Blackett and Charles. It was a lull before a storm.

At the end of the year he delivered the Godkin Lectures on *Science and Government* at Harvard. Published in 1961, they were on the wartime clashes between Sir Henry Tizard, the leading British scientist in whom armed forces had faith, and Professor F. A. Lindemann (Lord Cherwell), Churchill's friend and scientific adviser. It was a slice of history on an important theme to which Charles, knowing both men and the background, felt impelled to give an airing.

Controversy erupted among scientists, administrators and specialists in telecommunications. It revolved round the question of how close the all-important radar development had come to being sabotaged by Lindemann poisoning the prime minister's ear. What most disturbed Charles was the possibility of an individual exercising influence of a sinister nature on governmental policy without any real administrative restraint. The controversy challenged Churchill's own sagacity and judgement. Eminent wartime figures took sides. Pro-Tizard exponents included Professor A. V. Hill, Professor P. M. S. (later Lord) Blackett, President of the Royal Society and a close friend of Charles, A. P. Rowe, secretary of Tizard's committee, Marshal of the RAF Sir Edward Ellington, Air Chief Marshal Sir Philip Joubert de la Ferté and Earl Swinton (formerly Secretary of State for Air). The Lindemannites, led by Lord Birkenhead, were less identifiable.

The controversy persisted throughout 1961. Charles would regale me with developments. He wrote to *The Times* once more providing irrefutable evidence of Tizard's battle to get the highest priority for radar, as Sir Robert Watson-Watt, who'd helped to develop it, had taken an impassioned line denying that Lindemann wanted to give it a lower priority. Air Chief Marshal Sir Philip Joubert de la Ferté supported Charles, and Sir Edward Appleton, whose contribution to radar had been enormous, told him not to worry about Watson-Watt 'who only wanted to get into the papers'. Appleton paid tribute to Tizard as 'a catalytic agent, triggering off big things for which other people got the credit'.

Charles believed that Lindemann had very poor judgement. Rowe agreed that this was true, the crime being compounded by Churchill's ignorance of all things scientific. To a professor in Puerto Rico who asked him about the significant history of radar Charles gave this interesting summary. Despite Tizard's insistence on urgency, by 1938 a chain of radar stations was only just being set up. This was one of the very few technical justifications for Chamberlain playing for time at Munich, but Charles didn't find it convincing. Radar was working well enough for advanced warning as early as 1940. From the end of 1939 until 1942 the English fighter defence was by a long way the best system in the world, infinitely better than that of the Germans. Thanks to Tizard and no thanks to Lindemann, the Battle of Britain was won before it began. Charles enjoyed this controversy quite as much as the one over the 'Two Cultures'.

The visit to America at the end of 1960, culminating in the Godkin Lectures, was an important one. Pam wrote:

3, Vine Lane, Berkeley, 8,
California.

7.11.60

My dear Philip,
We are monsters not to have written, but life has been busy beyond belief. Charles is as famous as Napoleon in the U.S. and is always lecturing his head off here, there and everywhere. We are trying to get to every campus (we have already been down to Santa Barbara, which is so lush it makes one giddy), we gave a seminar to students, we have open-house for students twice a week, and one way or another we just about manage to survive. Charles has had another streak of superlative luck – believe it or not, his Godkin Lectures ('Science and Government', which he gives in Harvard later this month) have been chosen as a dual choice of the

124

Book of the Month Club! It seems small beer to tell you that he has sold his whole series in Latin America (Spanish trans. I mean) . . . .

Much love to you all
Pam

Charles thought that the Godkin Lectures must have made more money than any other public university lectures. In 1962 he published a postscript to *Science and Government*.

His international reputation was now assured. He was known to reject an American proposal to write a number of articles with the remark that he didn't like writing about things much 'unless (a) they happened to be fantastically highly paid or (b) if they chance to catch my fancy'. If one wanted money, he said, it was much easier to reside at an American university. It was at this time that he sold his manuscripts to the University of Texas. He was sad to do so, but the proceeds were tax-free in England and he knew they would be well looked after. All later papers of whatever kind passed through me to Texas (except for a manuscript to Eton), generously enabling me to see the whole of his correspondence, some dating back to 1945 (before which year every inward letter had been destroyed in a Cambridge cellar without his knowledge).

In the course of a winter visit to America in 1960 Charles had a television discussion on The Two Cultures with Mrs Franklin D. Roosevelt. She wrote:

55 East 74th Street,
New York City 2, New York

Dear Sir Charles,

I am most grateful to you for staying on in Boston to participate in our television programme. I have felt for some time that your method and pointing to the significant breach in our society between the scientist and non-scientist holds an important lesson for all of us who are apprehensive about the destroying of mankind. I for one learnt a great deal from the program . . . .

With best wishes, Yours sincerely, Eleanor Roosevelt

He also had discussions on the same topic with Aldous Huxley, for whom he had always had a great respect, and gave the 'keynote' address on 27 December to the American Association for the Advancement of Science entitled 'The Moral Un-neutrality of Science'. By early 1962 he began to doubt the efficacy of continued debate. He did not think he had exaggerated the dangers and, feeling as he did, there was no alternative but to draw attention to them. At the same time he did not think that he had achieved very much, and recognised that the controversy might have damaged his own reputation. He believed that there was less need now for his voice to be heard, with the Washington administration showing some intellectual control and with the Khruschev administration doing much the same. He considered it possible that we were moving towards détente. If this proved true, he declared, he would give up punditry for ever.

On their return to England Charles received a letter from an unlikely petitioner, Billy Graham, the evangelist, asking for any personal gift – a painting, jewels, furniture, antiques or historical documents – to be auctioned in aid of research on multiple sclerosis. Charles replied: 'A very dear friend of mine was afflicted with the disease, and I have never been able to forget it. Unfortunately I have never acquired any possessions worth mentioning – certainly none that any sane person would want to buy.' The 'very dear friend' was the original of Margaret Davidson in *Homecomings*, *The Affair*, *Corridors of Power*, *The Sleep of Reason* and *Last Things*. Charles's remark about possessions was the literal truth: apart from the Nolan paintings, a bronze sculpture and a painting by Michael Ayrton, books in plenty, there was virtually nothing. Neither he nor Pam were interested in objects.

Indeed, Charles was as unaware of aids to physical comfort as anyone I have ever known. He would perch on the very edge of a chair and could never grasp the art of repose. Even an ordinary deck chair was made to look precarious. His method of sitting was never quite like anyone else's. Only when reclining full length on a settee did he approach a posture of relaxation.

He found travelling fatiguing. He disliked flying, describing it as either excruciatingly dull or excruciatingly dramatic. Liners gave him the only headaches he ever had. Cars he could tolerate most easily; but surprisingly he did not recognise, when time was at less of a premium, that trains could make travelling enjoyable. I used to make this point but he would simply give me an oldfashioned look. As disinterested in comfort as in material possessions, he was close to being the pure stoic.

The Library Association elected him President for 1961. Invited to the Centenary of the first Public Library in Birmingham, he reported that he could not be present as he was off to America but sent a message which included the following: 'My grandfather, who came from these parts, was born exactly a year before the Library. I should like to think of him as a young mechanic – he left school at ten – making up his education through the Library . . .' He was also too busy to accept an invitation from the Prime Minister, Harold Macmillan, to serve on the Robbins Committee of Higher Education, although it was a matter close to his heart.

However, he managed three weeks' holiday in the South of France which meant missing the first night (pre-London West End) of *The Affair* at the Theatre Royal, Brighton; he had mixed feelings about first nights anyway.

He reported how 'fantastically well' *The Affair* was doing whenever I saw him. I had gone with him to its first night at the Strand Theatre, Aldwych, and, although no judge of first nights, it seemed to me to have good prospects. I saw Charles just after a deal of £25,000 had been done with the 'libraries' – that is, the ticket agencies – which guaranteed a run of five months, with the expectation that it would go considerably longer than that. He was jubilant: 'We are literally breaking records at the theatre.' He himself had never expected it after the first night but, as he said, he just didn't understand the theatrical world. Nevertheless, he was seldom less than shrewd, even in unfamiliar situations. He told Henry Sherek, the impresario who financed the adaptations of his novels, that he had an office in Aldwych and went along each day to look at the reviews outside the theatre; he suggested that those responsible had not picked the right ones.

Like most authors, he was acutely sensitive to what was written about him; he would be enveloped in gloom while waiting for reviews to come in. With all his experience he never learnt to disregard critics, except those he could dismiss as motivated by personal spite. Conversely, he was elated by praise, particularly if it came from an unexpected quarter. He chortled for months when Prince Philip, making a widely publicised speech in Australia, quoted him. However, the pros never quite outweighed the cons. The eupeptic part that reviews played in Charles's life is immeasurable; it reached its peak at this time when his output was enormous. When depressed and anxious he could be dismissive, almost brusque. My taking him to Lord's, where he would never go except with someone who knew the game and was able to share private jokes about it, was regarded by Pam as therapeutic; it alone seemed to take his mind off reviews.

As a reviewer himself he was magnanimous. In later years, he was in a position to select those books he wanted to review, leaving aside those for which he might have found it hard to say a good word. He was singularly kind to new writers, and was in part responsible for the success of Kingsley Amis's *Lucky Jim*, defending it against an outraged attack by Willie Maugham. He found it hurtful when some writers whom he had encouraged were less than generous to him. He told me in his more pessimistic moments how fatal it was to do anyone a good turn; you could expect them never to forgive you, or anyone connected with you.

He was particularly encouraging to students. At the end of 1961 he exchanged letters with Mrs Marÿke Lanius, a student at the English–American Institute of the Humboldt University, Berlin. She had sent him a thesis, *C. P. Snow – a modern English bourgeois writer*. It was a detailed analysis and Charles told her she understood *The Masters* and *The New Men* exceptionally well. To a specific question he gave this reply:

. . . The phrase Strangers and Brothers is supposed to represent the fact that in part of our lives each person is alone (each of us lives in isolation and in such parts of the individual life we are all strangers) and in part of our lives, including social activities, we can and should feel for each other like brothers . . .. Socially I am optimistic and I believe that men are able to grapple with their social history. That is, the brothers side of the overall theme contains a completely definite hope. But some aspects of the individual life do not carry the same feeling. Have you ever seen anyone you love die of disseminated sclerosis? This is the strangers part of the thing. I don't believe we subtract from our social optimism if we see the individual tragedies with clear eyes. On the contrary, I believe we strengthen ourselves for those tasks which are within our power . . . .

1962 was a year of crisis for Charles. F. R. Leavis, who had been at the university for years but had never been elected to a Chair, had been invited to give the Richmond Lecture at his college on 28 February. He leaked the news to the press that it was going to be a flat-out attack on C. P. Snow. (He also sold the lecture before it was read to *The Spectator*.) It was consequently given much publicity in *The Times* of 1 March and *The Sunday Times* of 4 March, everyone smelling a first-class row in the offing. *The Spectator* showed it to Charles who told them to publish and be damned; they thanked him for not withholding consent to print. In the meantime, he wrote to Leavis on 5 March asking him for a full text of the lecture. It was published on 9 March.

If it contained any theme other than personal vilification, it was an attack on Charles's exposé of the division of the cultured world; but it was so abusive that Charles began to feel that the world had gone slightly mad. There were only two courses open to him; he could sue for libel, in which case he would certainly get heavy damages, or preserve a dignified silence, leaving the counter-attack to others. He found the latter course irksome but could not be persuaded to pursue the former. It was a time, he said, when one knew who one's friends were. Those who wrote to *The Spectator* denouncing Leavis roundly included Dame Edith Sitwell, William Gerhardi and Lord Boothby. Dame Edith Sitwell said that she had read the 'non-stop and malevolent attack' right to the end simply because she 'could not make out what it was all about'. Perhaps Mr Snow had offended Mr Leavis, she suggested, because of his great fame and because he could write English. Gerhardi had been a complete recluse for a dozen years but this vicious attack roused him to action; his intervention was a fine example of sustained polemic. The fact that Charles had eleven novels to his name, Leavis nil, was not lost on detached observers.

The counter-attack was spontaneous; of those who rose up in fury on his behalf Charles said that he knew only one well, excluding Gerhardi whom he had not seen for over a decade. He was touched to have what he described as a message of 'superlative generosity' from Lawrence Durrell whom he had never met. He was annoyed by the *New Yorker* claiming, very wide of the mark, that the response in *The Spectator* had been 50–50. As Charles pointed out, Leavis's only real support was from fanatical pupils who were deaf to arguments on the other side. To close friends he admitted what was already evident to them – that the affair was much more unpleasant than he admitted in public. The whole thing was so venomously personal that he might be forced to counter-attack. He asked many of the people who gave him their support if they thought it right to keep out of it himself, though it required a major effort of self-control. Cockroft, representing Churchill College, said he did not think the attack worth replying to.

J. D. Scott, who was one of those who must have shaken Leavis by their vigorous defence of Charles, congratulated him on succeeding

Pasternak as being the most controversial writer in the world. Walter Allen in the *New York Times Book Review* tried to analyse the outburst as there was no record of any previous hostility between Leavis and Charles. He guessed that 'part of the reason must lie in the role Snow plays in British life today. He is a public figure certainly as no English equivalent since Wells and Bennett have been, and he is a public figure in a way quite different from Wells and Bennett.'

My own feeling on reading *The Two Cultures. The Significance of C. P. Snow*, was that Leavis sought publicity on a scale that none of his works had achieved, or were likely to attain; his driving force was jealousy of one who possessed the creative talent he lacked. He was a critic only, and critics can turn savage.

A year or two later, Aldous Huxley, in his *Science and Literature*, was to say that the argument did not begin with Leavis and Snow. His own grandfather had strong views on the need for scientific education primarily but mixed necessarily with English literature and foreign languages.

Charles told me that this publicity would put paid to any chance of the Nobel Prize for a good while to come. It was in truth Charles's main underlying worry because the sequence of *Strangers and Brothers* seemed to be shaping up to the dimensions of the *Forsyte Saga* and Galsworthy had been one of the few Englishmen to gain the Literature prize. We had discussed his chances and Charles secretly hoped that it would come about.

Then disaster struck again – in a different form. A month after the Leavis attack Charles found that the retina of his left eye had become detached and had to lie on his back in a darkened room with both eyes covered. When staying with us a couple of years earlier Charles had got up during the night to go to the bathroom. Half-asleep and thinking that he was in the Cromwell Road flat, he had taken a wrong turn and crashed down two flights of low, wide stairs, cutting his head on a newel-post. We heard nothing, but next morning we noticed a gash above his left eyebrow, and he explained what had happened. He made light of what must have been a considerable shake-up and we wondered subsequently if this had anything to do with his eye trouble.

Towards the end of 1961 he had been elected Rector of St Andrews University and his installation was to be at the end of the week that this trouble began. By the strangest coincidence the address which he had long ago prepared and sent to St Andrews as his proposed subject was 'On Magnanimity'. In the context of Leavis's distortions it was a most fortunate choice. The inspiration for this theme had come from a previous Rector, Sir James Barrie, whose address had been 'On Courage'. His predecessors included, among others, John Stuart Mill, Balfour, Earl Haig, Kipling, Nansen, Smuts and Marconi; nothing could dissuade him from keeping the appointment.

Wearing a black eye-patch and a large dark handkerchief to keep it in position, he made his way from London via Rugby to Scotland. To avoid the risk of his eye being jolted, the traditional carriage ride over cobbled streets in St Andrews and Dundee was abandoned, and he was driven in a closed car. His reception in these circumstances was particularly cordial; everyone knew that he had to go into hospital immediately on his return. Harold Macmillan wrote on 9 April from Admiralty House commiserating about the eye: 'It is very plucky of you to give a Rectorial address under such conditions.'

Charles replied:

> 199 Cromwell Road,
> London SW5
>
> 12 April, 1962
>
> Dear Prime Minister,
> How very kind of you to write. I think there is a reasonable chance of saving the eye and if necessary I can get on well with the other one, which has always been the better of the two. I hope you will approve of the address. I think you will. It is rather in your line.
>
> Yours sincerely
> Charles Snow

Charles thoroughly enjoyed the very demanding occasion. It was a special pleasure to him to confer an honorary doctorate on Mikhail Sholokhov, an old friend whose *And Quiet Flows the Don* he regarded as the best Russian novel since the Revolution. He gave £430 from the proceeds of *On Magnanimity* to the Students' Representative Council of St Andrews, whereupon *The Sunday Times* increased the fee for the serial rights from £100 to 150 guineas.

The operation on the retina was not an entire success. Sir Compton Mackenzie sent his regrets, 'but I have been one-eyed for ten years. The main handicap is that I can't read as fast.'

Indomitable as ever, Charles was on his way to America five weeks later. He sailed on the *Mauretania* – his surgeon had forbidden

131

him to fly since the deceleration on landing could have done serious damage; that apart, the voyage ensured a period of convalescence.

The University of Washington, St Louis, Brooklyn Polytechnic and Bard College had awarded him honorary degrees; so earlier had Kenyon College. These involved further ceremonial occasions; he endured them stoically, determined not to let people down. He and Pam returned on the *Queen Mary* in time for a dinner at Admiralty House with the Prime Minister, Harold Macmillan.

Charles wanted to get back to his unfinished novel, now at a crucial stage, which had been grievously interrupted by the Leavis explosion. He was wondering whether he could call it *Corridors of Power* as it had become somewhat of a cliché. 'The fact that I invented the phrase and that it is my cliché doesn't alter the case,' he told me.

A diversion from the preoccupations with the Leavis affair and retina was when a friend suggested that he would like to get Harold Wilson and Frank Cousins together with Charles and possibly a distinguished scientist. Charles said that he would like to meet Wilson and Cousins: a dinner was duly arranged at Brown's Hotel. It was the beginning of the shape of things to come.

On the 200th performance of *The Affair*, making it the biggest hit of the current season and also its movement to Broadway a certainty, Charles had arranged for the cast to be given specially bound copies of the book. Peter Howell, who had played Martin Eliot, was very appreciative: 'Your words have edge and bite and irony and it is an honour to speak them on the stage.' *The Affair*'s success on Broadway was unpredictable. Charles's agent had suggested that an early personal appearance might be crucial. Charles asked: 'What am I supposed to do? Sing outside the theatre? If they will definitely run the play to October 6th I will fly across this Thursday, September 27th.'

The play opened in Boston on 6 September and they missed its first night when Adlai Stevenson was among those present. Early in October Charles made an appearance at the Henry Miller Theater. He told me that he sat on the stage after a performance answering questions from a lively, and very friendly, audience: 'This bizarre experience formed one of the happiest evenings of my life.'

The Affair ran for sixteen weeks, not long compared with its year's run in England; a six-month run had been anticipated but it had struck a bad time. A week before the confrontation with Russia over Cuba *The Affair* had been making a reasonable profit; it was then struck a killing blow by New York's prolonged newspaper strike.

Charles would have liked to act. It was seriously suggested to him that he should go on a four-month nation-wide tour of *The Affair* in America as Arthur Brown. The idea appealed to him greatly; but he was saved from the temptation when the tour was cancelled. Earlier in the year it had been expected that *The Affair*, after the Broadway opening in September, would open in Paris in November. But Charles never really believed this.

Meanwhile, *The New Men* had, after two weeks at the Theatre Royal, Brighton, moved to the Strand Theatre, London. It was to run for two months and 79 performances (300 less than *The Affair*) when to Charles's and Millar's chagrin it was taken off without explanation by Sherek. *The New Men* following *The Affair* at the same London theatre was unusual in itself; it can have happened only rarely for a play based on a book to be succeeded by another from the same author and adaptor.

The Leavis business was revived on the publication by Chatto and Windus of the lecture. Charles could have stopped it, but, following his earlier policy, took no action. More publicity followed; but there was worse to come.

It is best summarised in the reply to an invitation to a small cocktail party given by the Queen and Prince Philip at Buckingham Palace on 5 November:

> 199 Cromwell Road,
> London, SW5.
>
> 29th October, 1962
>
> The Master of the Household, Buckingham Palace
> Dear Sir,
> With the deepest regret I am afraid that I have to ask you, on behalf of my wife and myself, to present our duty to Her Majesty and H.R.H. The Duke of Edinburgh and ask them to excuse us from attending the party. I regret this because I have to have an operation on the left eye; there was one operation earlier this year but the trouble has revived without warning and the only chance of saving any sight is to have the operation this week.
>
> Yours faithfully,
> Charles Snow

He has written of the outcome in *Last Things*. Immediately after the operation Pam telephoned me in great distress saying that at the end of it, when the retina was being stitched, his heart stopped for two or three minutes. The eye surgeon, Lorimer Fison, had the awesome choice between external massage or making an incision in the chest to get the heart going again. Pam said that the latter had been done successfully and that she had been told by heart surgeons, brought in after the emergency, that as a result there would be no ill effects. When Charles came out of the anaesthetic the surgeon told him what had happened. Charles's first words to Pam, a devout Christian, were: 'Well, now I know what the after-life is. There isn't one.' He had never for a moment believed in any form of theological salvation, though he liked to think that his behaviour conformed to Christian ideals, making conscious efforts to love his friends and forgive his enemies. If that sounded sanctimonious he would say that he would have been a better man if he had followed the ideals more strictly.

The Times's bulletin laconically published the eye-surgeon's statement: 'During the operation there was cardiac arrest and this was treated successfully in a routine fashion. Sir Charles leaves hospital tomorrow after a successful recovery and the sight of his eye is now assured.' Few people reading this understood the implications, and almost everyone – at least those who have not read *Last Things* – have forgotten it if they ever knew it. I saw him in his darkened room at Moorfields a day or two afterwards. He was cheerful; glad to have survived would be a modest statement of his feelings. We chatted as usual about cricket and general news. He was not specially concerned whether the eye operation, so speedily concluded, was successful. Life itself was more important, though to one who lived for reading as he did sight was of vital concern.

His psychological recovery was brisker than any of us had hoped for. As he said, he could dine out on the experience as long as he lived. 'It was a narrow squeak', he would say, 'but I'm perfectly all right.' His only discomfort, he said, had been a swollen ankle where an intravenous injection had been pumped in and, in the general excitement, had been overlooked for a while.

Corridors of Power had been going very smoothly up to the Leavis interruption and the first of the eye operations. Then it stuttered along to the second operation. Within a few days after final surgery Charles started another chapter of the remaining ten. *Corridors of Power* had the most chequered career of any book in the series except for *The Conscience of the Rich*, which, though written quickly, was held up for fifteen years.

The year ended on an ironical note. Belatedly Charles allowed himself to be proposed for membership of MCC. He had always gone to Lord's as my guest. But by the time he was elected his eyesight had weakened so much that he could only take in what was happening on television.

A more significant touch of irony was that he was invited by the Downing College undergraduates (in whose power the offer lay) to give the annual Richmond Lecture in 1963, the year after the Leavis outburst. He accepted with alacrity.

At the end of 1962 Charles was affirming that he felt battered. 'A rough year,' he would say in his succinct manner, and so it was.

The pinkness returned to his face; he had long since abandoned sitting in the sun for as long as he could which used to confer an impressive bronze veneer on his baldness. It has been said that he bore a physical resemblance to Buddha; when seated, his figure bore a superficial likeness, but the eyes, behind large thick lenses, were as round and unelongated as the lenses themselves. There was also nothing Oriental about his head; it might be Russian, perhaps – the dome, rounded and broad at the front, flat and squarish from behind. I concede, however, that he had something of Buddha's impermeability, for he lived on borrowed time for a further seventeen and three-quarter years after the 'narrow squeak' of 1962.

11. Stateliness of a Man Presiding

This seems an appropriate moment to pause in the narrative to consider Charles's character. He hated holidays and never completely relaxed. Even in 'idle' moments there were newspapers and books to be devoured; he was in the best sense an eternal student. This came out in his conversation – sometimes in ironic observation, more often in a carefully marshalled line of arguments, empirical and seldom philosophical. He was never dogmatic; the reasoning, when unfolded, one knew instinctively to be right and obvious. His mind was without pomposity and packed with common sense. Of course his judgements of people switched about a bit, and of course some of them were fallible, but he was proved right by events more often than not.

He tried, whenever possible, to answer all sensible letters and questions – he replied to a fourteen-year-old American boy's question: 'When you write a novel or short story, do you get your idea from happenings or do you think them up?' with: 'The answer to your question is not entirely easy. Most characters and situations in a novel have some origin in real life: then they get transmuted, and it is often genuinely difficult to know how far they have altered from their point of origin. But imagination by itself does not take one very far.'

Patience was a feature of his correspondence, but he was uncharacteristically close to tetchiness in replying to a Hungarian who had drawn attention to others' criticism of his writing style: 'It is absurd to call my style slipshod. People do call it dry or dull or flat, if they like, providing they have no ears to hear invisible irony. But to call it slipshod is ridiculous. One might as well use the same term of Stendhal.'

He calculated that when *The New Men* was translated into Japanese

there were few languages in which his books had not been translated; offhand he could only think of Portuguese, Finnish,
Rumanian and Chinese. So far as I know, all these have been covered
since.

He was puzzled as to why, when he was celebrated in most parts
of the world, he was not known at all in France. He never understood their lack of interest in him (nor the extraordinary supremacy
that Charles Morgan enjoyed there), although he realised that there
were special problems of translation. His style, he said, looked a
good deal simpler than it was; when translated faithfully into
French he believed, as did others, that it resembled a Civil Service
minute. This was due to his habit of using a set of words with
almost, but not quite, the same sense; in French translation this
produced a repetitious effect 'both ludicrous and mechanical'. It was
clear from reading his correspondence later that he tended to use the
same expressions. Having found the right words, he would rarely
alter them while that subject was topical, and when it had ceased to
be fresh he would not recapitulate; once he'd settled an issue to his
satisfaction he would move on to something else. This is not to say
that he forgot it; little escaped his memory, even when it was inconvenient for him to remember. As I've said before, his recollection of
dates, events, sequences was almost faultless. Names used in the
Strangers and Brothers series (and novels outside it) were habitually
those of cricketers, of neighbours or those whom he had heard
people mention. I can trace the derivation of almost all of them.

As to his method of writing, he used a fountain pen until biros
came in, recording his words in notebooks with a seismographic
style of writing which almost no one else could read. The script was
nearly vertical with few loops; 'i's were mostly dotted but when
they weren't it called for close hieroglyphic study. Where he wrote
was immaterial; a dark room or a light one, a basement or attic, it
was all the same. He once said: 'If you can only write in a purple
dressing-gown, in a room facing north-east, temperature 67, then
the prognosis for your art isn't very hopeful.' He preferred to be on
his own and it was always more convenient for him to have an
office.

He and Pam would see each other's books in draft and would
discuss outlines and plots before starting, reporting progress as they
came to be written. There was much exchange of ideas on titles for
books and chapters. Charles would deal with correspondence
promptly before turning to the regular writing. In the course of a

novel he liked to have as few breaks as possible. He scarcely paused, saying how fatal it could be to do so, trapping one for hours at a time over the construction of a sentence; he never hesitated over punctuation on the first draft. Four hours a day was, as he grew older, the discipline he fixed for himself – from about ten in the morning to about two. He kept to this rigidly. He admitted that it was not always easy to stick to it; he would never say that writing was easy.

On this most important aspect of his life he had several *obiter dicta*. He came out with them almost casually; I used to make a note of them soon afterwards to retain their flavour. They were as epigrammatic, being so close to his heart, as anything he said, and contained a combination of feeling, experience and intuition. Here is a selection.

'A writer has precisely one possession of any value, which is his name. He has to be uncommonly cautious if he uses it or lets it be used for commercial purposes.'

'It's very hard for a writer to be certain of the origin of his works. My background, interests and leanings had a good deal to do with mine.'

'Nearly all writers feel dissatisfied when a book is finished. It's never as good as the book one had in one's mind.'

'I'm often accused of being entirely interested in success. Anyone who reads my books will realise that what I'm most closely in sympathy with is tragic failure.'

'The main influences on me have been Tolstoi, Dostoevksi, Balzac, Stendhal, Proust, Turgenev. Perhaps R. M. du Gard. Trollope far less so. H. G. Wells only before the *Strangers and Brothers* series started.'

'If I have any originality it is that I'm not prepared to make assumptions about the psychological or moral nature of individuals. I don't take people for granted: I want to study them in certain situations and I happen to have the good luck to know at first hand several varied social situations.'

'If a writer acquires any kind of reputation he has a social duty over and above that of an ordinary citizen: his voice can be useful.'

'Some reviewers not only depress me but astonish me. I have the feeling that a completely different review copy has somehow been sent out from the book I thought I had written.'

'My favourite poets in English are Hardy, Yeats and Browning in the last hundred years or so. Eliot and Auden, no.'

'By the age of fifteen I knew I was going to be a writer but I gradually realised that I was the sort of writer who develops late. All the same, because I knew as much about the official world as I could possibly use, I ought to have left the Civil Service life earlier than I did.'

'As a general rule, novelists like a living original to get them going, although they often depart from it or intermingle it with other originals before completing the work. Rarely are they portraits and sometimes they are only rough sketches.'

'What makes a writer write? A rough answer is that he can't help it. Sometimes, more pompously, one can say that it is because one thinks one has something to say which might make people understand their world a little better.'

'Favourite books among my own tend to be *Time of Hope*, *Homecomings*, *Last Things*, those closest to me. *Homecomings* is Lewis Eliot's personal story. But the most proficient was *The Masters*.'

'As regards evocative writers, I like those most who ride over all obstacles to reach what they think to be the truth. Tolstoi hammers away to tell the truth about a human being: that I admire. I enjoy Proust's evocative passages.'

'I should call myself a "realist" writer. I draw a sharp distinction between realism and naturalism.'

'One of my strongest dislikes is writers who make the commonplace incomprehensible.'

'Writing is a chancy business. Sometimes one does better when one is not trying too hard.'

'If I were taken back twenty years I would still have said something to the effect of what I did say. I would do it more tactfully: yet there are times when tact is self-destructive.'

'Joyce led novels up a blind alley.'

'In the top dozen of the twentieth century, Sholokhov's one great novel, early Solzhenitsyn, Bulgakov, Dreiser.'

'I've found a kind of alienation from society which is certainly foreign to my temperament. I think Pinter has obviously a real talent and Becket possibly, but I'm not engaged by them.'

'I don't really enjoy actual writing. It's a morning's work now but in earlier life I had to do it in holidays and at weekends. I start off anything with 300–400 words and then aim for 800–900 words a day. (Pam writes faster, sometimes up to 3,000 a day.) There is much revision, insertion, crossing-outs and balloons.'

'I don't envy Anthony Powell's work or that of any writer alive – just some of their gifts. This isn't because I think I'm all that good but because, as the Russians say, each man has his own word and all one has to do is to say it.'

'The gift I envy most is Tolstoi's sensuous awareness.'

'My handwriting has been described as intolerably illegible and cerebrotonic (to use a Sheldonianism).'

'I am very much against telling children that literature is something with a capital L to be approached reverently and taken in small doses. There is no substitute for books. The proper time to read them with the maximum appetite is when young.'

'When free of Lewis Eliot for the first time I felt relief because it had been an obsessive task once I'd started on the series .... [And yet] the people were very real to me–some of them [had been with me] for thirty years. A slice of my life has been parted with.'

'I took the name Eliot from Port Eliot in Cornwall, the family home of Earl St Germans which I used to visit as a friend of his daughter Liz Eliot. I came to regret the choice through the accident of its association with T. S. Eliot with whom I had little in common.'

'I have made notes for books, not for anything else like reviews or speeches–well, very occasionally for the last. The notes were to remind me of facial expressions, essential elements of characters, special or characteristic phrases.'

'I was fond of most of my major characters and I most enjoyed writing *Homecomings*. I'm best at probing into human beings.'

'It always takes a long time to write at the best of times. Nearly all my novels go through several different versions before I've finished with them. As a film producer once said to me, as though giving invaluable advice, "You've got to *sit down* to write a novel."'

'To write professionally one must not hide one's whole life in the country but must be in contact with regular sources for information, visitors, meeting new people. Cambridge, after *The Masters* had been written, was too small and the wrong place to stay in. *The Masters* had exhausted the most interesting aspect–college intrigue. Writers simply must not live in isolated places. They must never be out of touch. Many of them are: it's no good for them. They must be in the mainstream. It's sometimes a help to be doing a job which allows combining it with writing.'

These statements, some of them characteristic understatements, are revealing about what was after all the most important part of him.

He was as nearly devoid of self-consciousness as anyone could be. Rarely, if ever, overawed, the pretentious were wasting their time with him; he deflated exhibitionism by ignoring it. Only when conversing with cricketers who had been the heroes of his youth did I detect a note of exceptional deference. He addressed George Geary and Herbert Sutcliffe as 'Mr'.

His confidence gave the impression of candour. All the same, Nancy Poland, to whom he wrote one of the last letters of his life – on the day he died – suggested, in one of the best interviews recorded (for the *Harvard Magazine*), that 'he has a sensitivity that he is too open to shield and this vulnerability is very appealing'. She found his basement office in the Benjamin Franklin building in Craven Street near Charing Cross Station like his writing, 'spare, unadorned, functional'. She went on: 'He answers questions quickly, analytically, with enthusiastic detachment.' She also noticed that he laughed a lot and 'speaks more like the prose he writes than most writers do . . . talking with him is a paradox: he is so jolly in his pessimism. . . .'

Nevertheless he could appear awesome to some people, a rather ponderous figure particularly when standing; it wasn't until he sat down, or smiled, that they felt at home with him. Even so, one journalist recorded: 'There is a moody magnificence about C. P. Snow which makes him an awesome figure behind his desk.'

Charles would usually be genial and encouraging to interviewers; when it was tête-à-tête, often jocular in his special vein. But he could be lofty if piqued by the wrong sort of inference, confronted with praise for someone for whom he had no time, or if he thought the questions were silly. In his armoury, which so fundamentally kindly a man had to possess, was an old-fashioned look; it was re-served mostly for audiences of more than one and took the form of looking down his nose. In the main he expected this to be inter-preted as dignity pretending light-heartedly to be offended.

In 1975 Peter, my son-in-law, as Chairman of the Birmingham Bow Group, introduced Charles at a dinner, which he attended in a suit with a large ink mark on the breast pocket and a hole in the sleeve, with: 'He will go down in history not as scientist or novelist or anything like that, but as Peter Waine's uncle-in-law.' Charles greeted this with huge guffaws; he loved bravado.

I have already mentioned his ineptitude with things mechanical. Charles was a theoretical believer in car seat-belts but it was quite beyond him to work out how to fasten or unfasten one. He would sit there looking vague, blinking mildly and expecting someone to do the manipulation for him. Once fitted in, he would never com-ment on the marvel of the manoeuvre or the difficulty encountered.

His disinterestedness was almost sublime, as if a valet should have been on hand for something so menial. He assumed the same grandeur in the matter of handling baggage.

Setting up deck-chairs or 'sun-loungers' was as little within his capability as making use of the comfort they were designed to provide. It is not that he found fallacies of construction; he never got that far, abandoning hope of ever being able to make the right movements. He could not change a plug or repair a fuse – surprising with his scientific background. He would wait for someone else to carry out the operation. The only time, in later life, when he tried to use a dictating machine he soon relinquished it crossly – he could not master its undemanding mechanism. This lack of relationship with instruments put him to no disadvantage that he ever acknowledged. The nearest to a mechanical act that I saw him perform was to stoke perfunctorily the boiler at Clare on the handyman's day off. He was not meant for living in the country where a certain amount of self-help is essential.

His fingers and wrists never seemed strong; his hands were almost feminine. 'Percy has a surgeon's hands', mother would say proudly but not altogether accurately; nevertheless he could in his youth twist a ball with ferocious flexibility.

He was disdainful of certain forms of transport. When he lived in London he almost never used a bus, except at Cromwell Road where there were bus stops immediately outside the flat. Tubes were his principal form of transport. He did use taxis but was aghast at the cost. 'Tubes are good enough for me,' he would declare flatly.

His fascination with power struggles in any institution, however small and unimportant, in salaries of friends and acquaintances, in social origins and identifying people with them, would often take over a conversation. His interest was enthusiastic and yet detached.

Cogency and rationality were qualities important to him; but he hoped for more from people, above all for sensitivity. He had a distrust of people with 'bullet heads', alternatively described as 'metallic' or 'ivory' ones; he judged them impenetrable and liable to be militant.

Over the last forty years of his life he had a strong bias towards people of working class origins or the petty bourgeois to which he belonged. To have been poor and to have succeeded in an intellectual more than a commercial sense went a long way towards earning his approval. For him it argued fundamental spirit and energy which were close to the top of the solid human qualities that

142

he looked for. He detested people he described as 'vivacious bores' – those who were vigorously opinionated, given to monologues. He found them 'agonising', 'maddening', 'preposterous' (the last a favourite word from his early youth onwards). He did his best to avoid the company of second-rate, dull, pretentious intellectuals. He is on record as saying that he preferred decent soldiers to indifferent intellectuals. For him an intelligent person rather than an intellectual every time.

People meeting him for the first time would be slightly rocked off balance by his getting as quickly as possible to the salaries they were earning. If asked himself, he would probably have supplied only a fairly guarded, neatly generalised indication of how he stood. To his way of thinking no spurious modesty should be attached to financial status; he felt deprived if there was effective concealment. As regards manoeuvres for power, information in any sphere, however small the organisation, would seize his attention.

From the professions he expected total professionalism. But he would be pleasantly surprised by the promising or brilliant amateur – writer, player, performer.

A third party's account of some absurdity would be met with gusts of laughter which, like tidal waves, would go in threes. These explosions, so marked a feature of him in his halcyon Cambridge days and right through to the 1950s, were seldom evident in the 1960s; I think the change can be dated round about 1962, the year of trauma.

As far back as I can remember, he was always punctual and insisted on punctuality in others. It was an obsession, a rare characteristic he shared with father. Both would compulsively study their respective wrist and waistcoat watches.

Charles had none of the conventional social graces. He rarely opened doors for women and would absentmindedly stand up only if others did when they appeared. Pam's arthritic mother, carrying coal from the cellar in the Clare house to the drawing room, would often find the door punctiliously held open for her by Charles but it would never have occurred to him to relieve her of the coal bucket itself; Amy thought this particularly amusing.

Drinks at his home would never be poured out by him; this was Pam's province, *faute de mieux*. He seldom carried cigarettes; if he did, he would not offer them round but simply take one and look round, blinking, for a match. If he had no cigarettes he would ask for one, saying vaguely 'someone give me a cigarette'. Sometimes, instead of asking he would merely gesture to Pam to bring him one. Once lit, he would puff at it till only half-finished. He never smoked a cigar. When one visited him at the Lords only he could buy drinks; he would bring them across the Bishop's Bar in a rather gauche manner as though they were the first he had ever carried. It was advisable to help him.

At dinner the wine would tend to remain at his right hand after a single circuit of the table. One learned to fill up one's glass as near to the brim as possible as it was unlikely to be circulated again, although in his last years he became less absentminded about this.

In our late-night talks – Pam and Anne had gone to bed – Charles would drink a fair amount; much more than I because I don't like whisky and have never found a satisfactory drink for that hour. The conversation would invariably turn, after earlier talk on cricket or tennis, to the family; to our grandfather, the Melton Mowbray uncle and his children, the Richmond Road Library and early books. It would seldom turn to Newton's and never to Leicester University College; there would be very little on Cambridge. I came to recognise that he wanted to take himself back to Leicester purely in a family context; the rest – his early struggles; at Cambridge the Leavis association, the tragedy of Allberry, the fading of Hardy – held painful memories. We used to compose the best English, West Indian and Australian teams. His memory for these would be formidable, even after the fifth whisky. Writers would never be far away – Dostoevski, Proust, Trollope and that comparative newcomer, Galdós. We would often go over what was left of the Empire and revise our guess as to which would be the very last outpost to survive, invariably coming to the ironic conclusion that it would be the mutineers' bequest, Pitcairn's Island. By the end of the session the generalisations about countries and people would scarcely have stood up to analysis. Of course not every visit would have these substantial late night indulgences; it depended entirely on whether or not he had an early engagement the next morning. If he was in the mood for late-night talking, which was most of the time, I could not opt out, whatever I had to do the next morning. The opportunity for me was anyway much too attractive to let it pass by; and his disappointment would have been too great. Afterwards I always took the precaution of climbing the extremely steep stairs at Eaton Terrace behind Charles, ready to prop him up if he stumbled – which I always expected though it never in fact happened. Nevertheless, his drinking was almost exclusively social.

144

Returning by taxi from the Ritz after a party given by Harold Macmillan to mark the end of the *Strangers and Brothers* sequence, Pam, Stefanie, Anne and I got into the taxi first. Then Charles, who sank slowly to the floor, failing to negotiate the seat. He lay there, supremely unaware of his unconventional posture, talking with ardour, if less than coherence, about the people at the party, all the way back to Eaton Terrace. On another occasion, in a taxi after a Fishmongers' Hall dinner for an Australian team, he rather took me aback by interrupting me to say: 'Oh yes, brother Philip would be very interested to hear that.' I hadn't the heart to tell him that I *was* brother Philip and not brother Eric, who had left the dinner earlier to catch a train back to Leicester.

Unlike me, he never suffered from hangovers. It was remarkable how brisk he was in the morning. At breakfast he would devour the newspapers, bellowing out his comments. He would earlier have opened his mail, but seldom referred to it.

His breakfast tastes were versatile. For a long time it was a full breakfast, then a phase of kippers, and ultimately only toast with fish-paste or jam. When he stayed with us, particularly on Sunday mornings, we would set the papers beside him on the table, if he had not gone downstairs first to get them. He would go through them with some speed, discarding them down the sides of the chair – sometimes they would find their way underneath him or gather in heaps on the floor, pages out of order and besmirched by butter-and-marmalade. His reading would be interspersed with little grunts and hums, like Winnie the Pooh. Having the knack of simultaneously reading and taking in conversation, he would come in with some relevant comment on what was being said at the other end of the table. The dining room floor would be dominated by tents of newspapers; none would be offered to anyone else. He expected complete and utter control of them and then left them abandoned. It was agony for me; I can only tolerate papers that have the impression of having been ironed and untouched since coming off the press. On his pile of papers he reminded my daughter Stefanie of an orang-utang happily enthroned on a mound of straw. His jowls and the thick fold of flesh enveloping the back of his neck were of course beloved of cartoonists. I eventually grew wise to the need for putting books and magazines out of sight.

Charles and Pam deferred having television for a long time; then tentatively a black and white set was admitted into the Clare house and limited at first to news programmes, though in the end it got a hold. A pet aversion was to be subjected to the endlessly repetitive interviews with Trade Union leaders or shop stewards gabbling blatherskite or merely being thickly opaque. To the end, watching tennis on it was a delight for Charles. He regarded Laver and Borg and, among women, Goolagong and Evert, as the exponents of the perfect combination of temperament and technique that he looked for from all at the top.

He and Pam had an unexpected weakness for some serials which they would watch religiously – any police series like *Z Cars*, *Softly, Softly*, *Kojak*, *Perry Mason* and *Ironside*. Charles would sit on the edge of a pouffe very close to the set for a couple of hours at a time, often with his handkerchief in his hand or on his knee, sometimes with Gabbo, the stray cat faithfully attached to the household. He would talk to Gabbo after the news: 'Yes, Gabbo, you think Peter Carrington a very sound man, don't you? We are all right in his hands, you feel? Yes, a very sound man, Gabbo dear'.

Anything competitive attracted him. This extended to the Olympics, the Eurovision Song Contest (for which he made out his own list although immune to melody – perhaps this helped), Miss World; he was susceptible to the international competition whatever the theme. He enjoyed Benny Hill. Peter, my son-in-law, visiting Charles at Eaton Terrace, once had to wait until the end of the Muppet Show before being able to speak to him.

In 1957 Charles and Pam had been on the Brains Trust together. If there had been earlier quiz games Charles would have been a natural for them. I didn't appreciate his interest in these competitions until after a broadcast of *What Do You Know* (Brain of Britain) for which I had been selected for the Midlands panel. I had not told him I would be in it because I thought he would be scornful. On the contrary, he was peeved at having missed it.

His general knowledge was immense; he might have been weak in Greek mythology of which these games are so fond, but he would quickly have mastered that. He was fascinated when a Canadian woman on *Mastermind* took the novels of C. P. Snow as her subject, and said that he would have found difficulty in doing better. (She scored 10 out of a possible 17.)

Charles would have excelled in programmes like *Question Time* or *Any Questions* that require statements rather than one-word answers, not through lack of celerity in the latter – he was cue-sharp – but because the former would have been the ideal form for his easy articulateness. He took most of the opportunities that offered to appear on television but I wish he had done more.

At the end of 1963 the Royal Institution formed a fine television setting for Charles's talk on '*The Two Cultures and The Sorcerer's Apprentice*'. Charles's explanation for the title was that he felt a little like the Sorcerer's Apprentice: he had done something innocent yet the flood came in and in and in. In white tie, he gave a dignified performance in front of the cameras and his equally elegant audience. The setting might have been high Victorian but the lecture and style of delivery were utterly contemporary. Although the lecture was delivered in November 1963, it was not transmitted until February 1964, and then only in abridged form. Charles found his 'modest' lecture being talked about wherever he went. Abuse was mixed with praise. He gave a simple account of The Two Cultures; our education and methods of encouraging professional people had been so arranged that the more intensively instructed among us were ceasing to be able to communicate at all on the level which made up our working lives. This was distorting creative, intellectual and moral life as much as the view of what should be done about the world. For the practical purpose of demonstrating his axioms he had chosen two polar groups of educated men who had ceased to be able to talk to each other at all. It was a splendidly clear, definitive exposition, his *tour de force* in that medium, if one excludes the biographical study directed by Alan Wallis fourteen years later.

Except for his repeated bursts of laughter, I would describe Charles as a quiet person. Even his indignation was never loud; it would be mostly over inefficiency or third-ratedness or plain stupidity. He scarcely ever raised his voice; rather, he spoke at times close to a mumble, and a gruff one at that. Few things merited a row. His attitude to the world was reflected in his charitability. His restraint in replying *to agents-provocateurs* like Leavis and, to a lesser degree, Watson-Watt, was a by-word. He would say with justification: 'I am the least quarrelsome of men'.

As in his novels, Charles could be melancholy but with a radiance breaking through. He told Priestley, after saying: 'You and I have got on well all our lives, though we differ somewhat on the plane of reason', that this streak of melancholy was pretty strong, that he had to struggle with it, which was part of the incentive for leading an active life. His moderately high spirits were tempered by stoical gloom. He was intolerant of intolerance. He was not fussy; for instance, he would without demur, however busy, respond to mailed requests for autographs and would sign any number of books for anyone anywhere. He was also reasonably ready, given the time, to write Introductions and Prefaces for people. His contributions were always first class but he was at his most expansive for Ronald Millar's three plays based on his novels and for Hardy's *A Mathematician's Apology*.

Unexpectedly for so rational a mind he was superstitious – fearful of expressing too much optimism lest this very indulgence should cause his luck to break. It was a long time before I realised that he held quite common superstitions; he concealed them as he knew that I would laugh at him; I would never have admitted to my own.

Numbered among his dislikes were lethargy, most food, and misused words, for example, 'industrial action' meaning, of course, industrial inaction, and 'expertise', superseding the perfectly good 'expertness'.

Among his likes he would put classical detective stories, conversation and claret. Although his principal drink was whisky it was not until he visited America regularly that he became perceptibly diverted from wine. He also caught the American habit of smoking between courses.

'Any news?' was his prelude to almost every conversation I had with him. He almost invariably had some when the question was reversed.

As a writer he had to have his ear to the ground for trends, however recherché, but he was only mildly curious about them and never succumbed to a major use of new fashioned propensities except perhaps in *The Malcontents*.

His crisp sense of irony is neatly typified by a story he told me. With the twinkle in his eye that was always a prelude to something choice, he said that he'd read that Dreyfus, playing bridge one day when he was an old man, was told that someone was suspected of giving away secret information. 'Ah well!' said Dreyfus. 'There's no smoke without fire.'

His stories were brief and ironic. At the dinner table he would appear physically to offer his listeners some choice tit-bit by holding his hands forward and curved inwards. His repertoire would be based around understatements or overstatements, self-delusions or pretentiousness. The social background of the person talked about was important to the story: '. . . Remember that X was one of the grandest of land-owners' or '. . . Remember that Y was of the very humblest origin.' His anecdotes mostly came from others; he would say that X had told him . . ., or more notably, 'Hardy used to tell this story. . . .' Comedy for him unfailingly lay in statements made by people unconsciously or in absurd attitudes. He would have a selection of stories about eminent people which he seldom repeated. He rarely made use of an accent in telling a story – though he sometimes stretched to a heavy Russian or East European one. He would deliver the story dead-pan and with unfailing certainty on the punch-line. Then, with his hands doing little flips, he would end with: 'Don't you think that *very* funny?' Or 'bizarre' or 'comic' or 'picturesque' – those favoured words. The explosion of laughter or convulsive chuckles would follow immediately. He would think the anecdote quite as funny as the hearer, often more so, and sometimes it would be embarrassingly difficult to sustain the laughter. But he would only keep the story in his head for a short time. He once said that he was absolutely stupified when asked to produce jokes in cold blood; he couldn't remember a single one.

Charles ruefully told me that he thought that Jews, for some reason, tended to be mystified by his kind of jokes. He found this baffling. His instinct for detecting Jewishness when it was not obvious was acute. He would often start a biographical sketch conversationally on these lines: 'He is a Jew of Central or Eastern European origin, from somewhere like Hungary or the Baltic States, a very clever man. . . .' He admired Hebraic shrewdness, among many other gifts, although he might react against excessive sharpness.

He was himself admired for his good sense, together with a combination of shrewdness and humour. Indeed, he had a shrewd business mind and would have been a successful investor. He reckoned that imagination was the best aid to investment. I often heard these qualities extolled, sometimes in front of him by someone bold enough to tell him. He tended to shrug it off and change the subject. He expected men to be of good will – Adlai Stevenson was one of the public examples he liked to mention – and was quick to detect its lack and to take avoiding action.

It was a kind of writing joke amid the directness, the clarity and what his enemies like Leavis would stigmatise as his poverty of language, to throw into his novels every now and again an obscure word. 'Lanthanine', in *The Light and the Dark*, is a prime example, untraceable in most dictionaries. It means obscure or secret, and was used to indicate that Roy Calvert was not well known. This word was one that he and Charles Allberry shared as a private joke. There is a similarly obscure word in all the *Strangers and Brothers* novels planted there for fun.

He hated the telephone, neither making nor receiving calls if he could possibly help it. My advice to people wanting to telephone him was: 'Don't'. He could, even with those closest to him, be disconcertingly brusque when confronted with the instrument, omitting to say 'goodbye'. Chat was conducted between people, not with an instrument listening in. On the rare occasions I did have to telephone I did so with something approaching trepidation. He complained that he was forced to go ex-directory because so many people would ring him up asking about the end of the world or with 'similarly unhelpful questions'.

Physically Charles did not fit into any of the three well-known divisions of W. H. Sheldon, the American medic-psychologist in whom he had some belief. Charles's speech could be described as deliberate, effortless and unhurried, his arms often showing the limp relaxation of a seal's flippers. His hands were soft and flaccid. His gait was a dignified amble, with no vigorous assertiveness. The voice was lacking in stridency; it was even but not constrained. All this complied with Sheldon's viscerotonic category but nothing else did. For example, no love of physical comfort and eating, no love of public ceremony, no greed for affection and approval, no complacency, no ability for deep sleep. He might have described himself as cerebrotonic but on analysis he was only so in one or two respects – restrained posture, lack of ability to sleep well. Although most of his life a bad sleeper it didn't seem to affect his energy.

Watching him, one would focus initially on his alert, lens-defended but frequently smiling blue eyes and large head. In later years a characteristic was to adjust his glasses repeatedly in the course of conversation, pressing his finger against the bridge. After the retina operation he would lift one side of his glasses to peer at reading matter, his face almost touching the page. In the days when he had hair he would constantly curl a strand round a finger, a mannerism he'd inherited from our father. He would gesticulate – more often than not with a handkerchief – not in the Gallic manner but with very restricted, sudden flapping movements. In public speaking he used his hands more frequently, but with the same gestures as for private conversation. Sometimes he would place his small, very delicate fingers and thumbs together to press a point home. A remarkable feature of his fingers, most marked when smoking or writing, was that the tips curved outwards from the end joints. He had the soft, shiny hands of our father. Antipodeans, believing in excruciating squeezes to denote mateyness, were very disappointed in Charles's handshake. His wrists were highly flexible, useful for bowling and deck-tennis. He would sometimes hold his hands rather like a kangaroo's front paws, bent over and hanging downwards as though perpetually resting. Unadroit and inadequate as they were with things mechanical, they were eye-fixing hands. Little else of him would move when talking, bar perhaps a shoulder. Like all the male Snows (except his own son Philip) he had almost no neck. The high forehead under the huge dome that had riveted Lloyd George in Antibes (described in *Variety of Men*) was well creased. His ears were not unlike our father's, flat and long-lobed. There was a marked tendency to deafness in his last three or four years: he acquired a hearing aid in his last year but never used it.

For a large man who had in his youth been a great walker, he took extremely short steps – as short as father's, himself a walker of necessity, who was a much smaller man. His elongated trunk and huge head made the quick movement of his feet seem the more incongruous.

Charles was asked often enough if he would have chosen any other time to live in. Priestley had suggested that they were both a century too early or too late; but Charles insisted that while the nineteenth century had its attractions this was the one for him. In particular he believed that the National Health Service (which he used far less than most in his lifetime) was at least one outstanding advantage over the previous century. What he sensed about the twenty-first century he was to express in 1969 in *The State of Siege*.

Adjectives he liked to apply to himself and to others whom he found interesting were 'sardonic', 'sarcastic', 'suspicious' (in the meaning opposite to 'naïve'), 'pessimistic'. He intensely disliked moral vanity and had no casuistical postures of his own outside his strong personal ethics. He would say: 'If I worried overmuch about my *amour propre* I'd have been dead a long time ago.'

He had no use for people saying that they accepted honours because their wives wanted them to. There was nothing of the poseur about him, he could not pretend to be what he was not. He was surprised that when he had a title people tended to look at him as though he was not quite human.

His sense of irony was acute, in his own life and that of others. It amused him that he should follow *Corridors of Power* by going into politics. Not in the least inflated himself, he had the ability to buoy

151

other people up. At first meetings people would be surprised by the encouragement and flattery they received. He would say: 'Your strong points are . . .' 'You have clearly a gift for . . .' This was the result of the thousands of interviews he had given in his Civil Service posts, integrated with his novelist's sixth sense. He would be very diplomatic about aspects of character that his friends and acquaintances might improve on. They would often tell me that they had gone away with a spring in their step as a result of his discerning analysis. I frequently had the same experience; few men in my life have had this effect.

He had no small talk; I often saw conversations dry up after a few perfunctory enquiries as to what people did and what salaries they earned. He looked for astringency; that would set him going. Those who could not succeed in getting through, due perhaps to no fault of their own, might judge him to be cold, which was far from the truth. He had less egotism than most; it gave him the endearing (and flattering) power to absorb himself in listening to others and analysing them, often to their advantage. He would almost never hold forth on himself unless pressed determinedly.

He used to declare, 'There are times when I actively dislike my surname.' The puns on it irritated him; he had also come to the conclusion that the two letters 'sn' precede an extraordinary number of unattractive words – snivel, sneer, snoop, snarl, sneak, snore, snub, sneeze, snob, snide.

With animals his contact was dignified amiability. When his last attack of 'migratory arthritis' subsided at the beginning of 1980 he had hoped to visit us again in Sussex; he wanted to feed one of a series of robins I had regularly tamed. The last time he had done it was a couple of years earlier and it had left an indelible impression on him. He would murmur softly to the robin as it took cream crackers from the palm of his hand. This sentimentality extended to cats and dogs whom he liked to have about.

But most of the time he took care to disguise any suggestion of softness; he reserved it for phases of his youth, aspects of America and, less explicably, Russia. I believe that he had a large share of sentiment which he seldom thought wise to reveal. He was obsessionally secretive about himself; only a handful of people were allowed to know what he felt deeply about. His business was to analyse the present and look into the future, even if, or because, his writing was mostly about the past.

He was not especially generous in small things, but very generous in bigger ones; Anne's fare from England to Australia during the war, the twenty-first birthday party for our daughter Stefanie in the House of Lords, payment of bills I couldn't meet at Cambridge, help for Bert and Cecil Howard and their sister Marjorie, and others. He gave up his very limited spare time to help writers with their work when he felt they were worth it. He was always concerned for his protégés.

He was more responsive to kindness than he cared to show. 'How very kind . . .' he would say and then appeared to forget the act. But it had lodged in his prodigious memory and he would seldom fail to reciprocate, if not always directly. This was a small but telling indication of his complexity.

12. Corridors of Power

1963 was a gentler year. The second operation on the eye was at least partially successful, but Charles did admit that he'd been working too hard over the past two years and – this was most unlike him – that 'the prospect of making even one more speech becomes something of a drag'.

Nevertheless he kept his promise to deliver the Richmond Lecture – on 'Education and Sacrifice'. He didn't make a single reference to Leavis; indeed it was not until 1970 that he broke his public silence in a long article in *The Times Literary Supplement* entitled 'The Case of Leavis and the Serious Case'.

Charles had taken heart in 1963 from his personal resilience and also from the state of the world. Walter Lippman, Patrick Blackett and he, over a dinner at the end of 1962, had all come to the conclusion that, barring accidents, we were in for twenty years of relative peace. They had not felt so optimistic since the end of the war. The real problem was thought to be China; here Charles was influenced by his Russian acquaintances who had nightmares about what they thought was the inevitable Chinese invasion.

Charles's thoughts were being drawn to domestic politics, the possibility of Labour winning the next election. He told Lippman that if Harold Wilson became prime minister Blackett would be 'the chief grey eminence' in military and connected matters as he had the coolest judgement of anyone he knew. Through Blackett Charles was closely in touch with Wilson and was, he estimated, something of a 'grey eminence behind a grey eminence'. R. H. S. Crossman had told him that Wilson had Blackett in mind for Minister of Science and Higher Education, and Charles had told Crossman that he estimated Wilson to be quite abnormally impressive – 'more so than any Western politician I have met'.

Charles recognised that he would have to impose limitations on himself, particularly over conferences and lectures: 'I am so over-worked and generally busy that I am having to refuse all commit-ments. Otherwise I shall go mad.' This implied that he was finding life exciting in the way he liked it – plenty of activity of his own choosing. He had come to the conclusion that lecturing was intolerably hard work; not so much the lecture itself but the associated activity, meeting hundreds of people he would never see again. 'I tend to make public utterances from the front of my head, whereas my writings come from the back of it,' he told me.

There were aggravations which he could have done without and he felt obliged to bring three libel actions all of which were settled out of court and in his favour. The British Migraine Association and the Freedom from Hunger Fund gained the modest sums for which he asked.

The Masters, adapted by Ronald Millar, had opened on 14 May at Golders Green; rather like opening in the Bronx, Charles felt. He was given a cheer as he went to his seat for the first night – 'The most pleasurable one I've spent in the theatre,' he told me. When I saw it on its first night at the Savoy Theatre on 29 May, I agreed with him that this was the best of the three plays by Ronald Millar; with John Clements as Paul Jago it came over remarkably well. After the Savoy it transferred to the Piccadilly Theatre and had one of the longest runs of 1963.

Time of Hope had also been adapted for the stage – by Arthur and Violet Ketels in Philadelphia. It had excellent notices. Violet later visited us in Rugby; she wanted to see Leicester first-hand, so ab-sorbed was she in the *Strangers and Brothers* sequence. When we showed her round she found it very close to the idea that she had formed of it.

In the early autumn of 1963 Charles made a memorable visit to Mikhail Aleksandrovich Sholokhov, one of Khruschev's oldest friends. He had received this cable: 'Hon. Degree, Doctor of Philo-logical Science, Rostov-on Don. . . . Being old enthusiasts for beat-ing records we hope that the high and warm hospitality offered at St Andrews will be beaten by Rostov-on-Don. Heartily yours, M. A. Sholokhov.' Charles replied by cable, thanking him for the honour and saying: '. . . . We shall see you on your own Don this year and hope to survive Cossack hospitality.' So far as I know, he is the only person to have received honorary doctorates from both Russian and American universities. On his return, Charles wrote to Sholokhov:

199 Cromwell Road, London, SW5
23rd October, 1963

Dear Mikhail,

. . . It was a magical experience to be with you, by the side of your own Don, in that golden October weather. Love and thanks both to you and . . . I embrace you with affection and admiration.

Charles

Ceremonies for honorary degrees in Russia are not like those in this country and America; gowns and caps are not worn. As a joke Charles was given at the end of the ceremony at Rostov-on-Don a *burka*, a cloak of black sheepskin about which there was nothing remotely academic. Apparently its enormous width was so that Cossacks on horseback could sweep up a woman at full gallop and conceal her beneath it. Charles was persuaded without difficulty to wear it on the BBC programme 'Tonight' and for press photographs, walking along Cromwell Road with as much indifference as he'd shown in Leicester under his top hat nearly fifty years before.

The Russian visit was a huge success; Charles had hardly ever enjoyed anything quite so much, although he admitted that it was 'intolerably exhausting'. Sholokhov lived in feudal style in a mansion full of retainers. One night, host, family and friends sat down to dinner at 7 p.m.; they staggered up from the table at 2 a.m. Charles claimed that he had outdrunk the Russians – but Sholokhov began his tippling very early that day.

Charles told Bertrand Russell that there was an extraordinary occasion at an altogether remarkable breakfast, with about forty present, when Sholokhov chose to make a passionate speech denouncing anti-semitism. Quite why was not clear unless, as I suggested, Sholokhov thought that Charles was Jewish. Charles doubted that; the outburst was all the more remarkable for being in Cossack country where anti-semitism was traditional.

The hospitality there was overwhelming and Charles was not allowed to spend a rouble. He had accumulated a considerable number of them from the sales of his books; after Jack London and A. J. Cronin he was the biggest selling foreign writer in the Soviet Union. All royalties were paid in blocked roubles and his account at the Moscow bank mounted. (The assertion made in the *Daily Telegraph* obituary of Pam that she and Charles were given a small house by the Black Sea is untrue.)

In 1964 Charles and Pam jointly urged the Swedish Academy that

Sholokhov be considered for the Nobel Prize for Literature. This was particularly generous because, although friends, Charles and Sholokhov were competitors for this coveted award. It was a successful plea, Sholokhov receiving it the following year.

Soon after his return Kennedy was assassinated. Charles wrote to an American friend: 'I don't think I have ever known a death, except perhaps Roosevelt's, to spread such gloom over this country. Several of my Russian diplomatic friends were in tears. In curious contrast to their theory, Russians personalise politics, much more than the English do.'

At this time Bert Howard died in Hilversum, Holland. He'd had a mild stroke, followed by a severe one. Before he became seriously ill he had been extravagant, luxuriating in what Amsterdam had to offer a man of his ambivalent tastes. Charles sent £200 towards the expense of doctors, nursing, his burial and debts. He also wrote his obituary in *The Times*.

Charles wished that he had been of more than tenuous use to Bert. Somehow, he said, Bert's life ought to have taken a different course. In recent years they'd seen little of each other, Bert having become more and more self-absorbed and Charles increasingly busy. Yet he, along with Hardy and Allberry, formed the male triumvirate who exercised the greatest influence on Charles.

Charles had been gathering material for *Corridors of Power*, a field as yet outside his experience. In March he told an MP, Maurice Edelman, that he wanted 'to prowl around the House with you if you can spend a few hours. . . . I hate to be a nuisance but. . . . I very much want to get everything right.' He also wanted the answer to some procedural questions. When it was finished Edelman declared the book the greatest political work of this century: 'And if Mr Macmillan, publisher, cares to quote this, he is at liberty to do so.'

Charles certainly did his homework in the Commons with extreme care: he was always sure that the book would make a considerable impact. Because it was so different from any of his other novels he discussed it incessantly in case he could pick up anything. I knew nothing of that world and could not make the slightest contribution but this did not deter him from talking to me about it during its preparation – I think, more than anything else he wrote.

Charles, who had collected honorary degrees the year before from Michigan (Ann Arbor), Syracuse and Temple Universities, went off to America in March 1964 for an honorary Doctorate of

Letters from the University of Pittsburgh. Asked in advance if he had any special requirements, he replied: 'No, except an occasional Scotch.' Anything he could do by way of meeting students and members of the faculty, he added, he would be glad to fall in with, provided that he had a couple of hours to himself each day.

He returned from the trip very overtired and determined to take life more quietly. Luckily he could afford to. *Corridors of Power*, another Book of the Month Club choice, outsold all his other novels. He assigned the copyright to Philip junior in trust; I was one of the trustees. 'It can't earn less than £20,000 . . . . We shall all be borrowing off Philip when he's twenty-one, if we live so long,' Charles told me.

He was pleased to become a Vice President of the H. G. Wells Society. He could never express his liking for H.G. often enough. Wells had certainly influenced Charles's first novel, *The Search*, but not, Charles believed, later ones directly, though he felt that he had always been a general influence. Later he was inordinately pleased to be invited to unveil the GLC plaque on Wells's last London home at 13 Hanover Terrace.

A libel action had to be taken against *The New Daily* and Anthony Lejeune who had written: '. . . That conspicuous non anti-Communist, C. P. Snow himself, who once said he could happily have lived in the Soviet Union, but not in France, Spain, Portugal, Rhodesia or South Africa.' Charles made frequent visits to France, and he had promised to make a prolonged visit to Johannesburg in the spring of 1965 and to deliver a public university lecture there. His books were translated into Spanish, and he was well known in the Peninsula. An apology was printed in the paper, affirming that Charles had never made such a statement, and a payment of £100 made to the Students' Union at St Andrews. It was yet another example of the extent to which Charles was in the public eye.

Charles and I discussed the probability of Labour winning the General Election in October after so long a Conservative run. As he had eschewed active politics we neither of us envisaged his ever being offered a political appointment. Following Labour's win, I was reading in the Sunday paper conjectures as to possible appointments by the Prime Minister, including Sir Charles Snow as Permanent Representative of Great Britain at the United Nations, when the telephone rang. It was Charles, saying that he had just returned from No. 10 Downing Street where Wilson had summoned him to offer him the post of Parliamentary Secretary to the Minister of Technology. Since the Minister, Frank Cousins, would be in the Commons, Charles had been asked to accept a Life Peerage and to be the Government's spokesman for Technology in the Lords. He had accepted and asked me not to tell anyone except Anne and Stefanie until it was announced the following day. So as to keep the press guessing, he had been asked to visit No. 10 by the garden door and to return by that route. It struck me, I recall, as odd that the press had not grown wise to that ruse.

Charles wrote to the new Prime Minister:

Dear Harold,
In general I take a fairly Tolstoian view of human affairs and I don't believe that human individual people have a decisive effect. But this was one of the occasions when those rules do not apply and I think only you could have done it.

Yours ever
Charles

To which he received the reply:

10 Downing Street, Whitehall
28 October, 1964

Dear Charles,
Thank you very much for your letter of 16 October. I'm so sorry not to have written before to thank you for all that you have said. I am delighted that you are able to accept the invitation to join the Government.

Yours ever
Harold

Charles had sent commiserations to Maurice Macmillan on his loss of office and the defeat of his party: 'There is not much to be said for the literary life, but I think that on balance I would sooner be a writer than a politician, which is not saying much.'

He also wrote to John Freeman, Editor of *The New Statesman*:

199 Cromwell Road, London, SW5
22 October, 1964

159

I suppose that I ought to resign from the Board of the Statesman Publishing Company. I shall do so very reluctantly but if Gerald Gardiner has gone [to be Lord Chancellor] I think I must too. We must be rather overcareful about these things, don't you think.

Yours ever
Charles

Political opponents were charitable. Harold Macmillan wrote in his own hand:

Birch Grove House, Chelwood Gate,
Haywards Heath, Sussex

20.x.64

Dear Charles,
You will have received so many letters about where Corridors of Power lead that I shall content myself with sending my warmest congratulations and good wishes.

Yours
Harold Macmillan

And Sydney Grose wrote from Christ's:

Distressed though I am – for I will be quite open with you – at having to live again under a Labour Government, I must write to offer my most heartfelt good wishes for success in your new adventure. And I am sure that, if anybody, you are the man to make good. How remote in time; yet seeming so recent the day when you first appeared in my study to ask for admission! I still remember it as though it were yesterday, the lateness of your application, talk about physics, Menzies, cricket – it seems much closer than some of the fights we had to secure your recognition here as Fellow and Tutor. Unhappily some of us have not been able to secure a fuller recognition in more recent years.

The last sentence was a reference to the college having failed to make Charles an Honorary Fellow, a recognition that was, like the honorary doctorate at Leicester University, deferred beyond all reason. Charles replied:

I think you will find that this Government will cope pretty manfully with the economic situation. It was because I believe them and further believe that this country must earn a living that I took the job. It means a good deal of hardship and a very large financial loss, as you can guess. I owe a great deal to you, my dear friend. I think I have proved that in print, haven't I? You will be amused by the coat of arms. It contains two remarkable puns.

A consolation for his loss in income was the allowance for attending daily at the House of Lords, which was tax-free, and also the low, presumably subsidised, cost of its meals.

Garter Principal King of Arms, Sir Anthony Wagner, who happened to be a friend, wrote on 21 October:

Dear Charles,

I have been advised by the Prime Minister's Office that Her Majesty the Queen has been pleased to approve that the dignity of a Barony for Life of the United Kingdom be conferred upon you. May I offer you my best congratulations on this well deserved honour. It will be necessary for you to sign certain papers stating what title and design you wish to take for your Barony and I should therefore be happy to hear if you could arrange to call here by appointment so that we might discuss and settle the matter.

Yours sincerely
Anthony Wagner

Pam wrote to Anne:

Thank you so much for the congratulations. It is all great fun at present, but rather breathless. The induction will probably be on Nov. 4 and C. will look into the business of tickets. It would be fine if you could be with us.

We had a great afternoon's mummery at the College of Heralds, which would have made Philip laugh like a drain. We were choosing our Coat of Arms (for which, by the bye, one pays through the nose) Shield; symbols of 2 Cultures, telescope crossed with pen. Supporters: 2 Siamese cats, because we love them, and because they pun on Colleges of Advanced Technology. Crest: a snow crystal. Motto: Aut Inveniam Viam Aut Faciam, 'I will either find a way or make one', a motto I chose for myself when I was eighteen and have hung on to with adolescent romanticism. It is fun to see it come true . . .

Love to all
Pam

From Charles:

199 Cromwell Road, London, SW5
28th October, 1964

Dear Philip,

Would you and Anne like to come and have lunch with me and my Sponsors in the House of Lords next Wednesday? Then you can see the Introduction in comfort. I don't know quite where the lunch will be, but if you ring up when you arrive we can all go together.

Yours ever
Charles

On 4 November Anne and I had a most entertaining lunch in a special room at the Lords. Besides ourselves there were Sir Anthony and Lady Wagner, Lord Bowden and Lord Boothby. The last named was in full flow of ripe reminiscence. He and Lord Bowden were the sponsors.

After lunch we took our seats in the Gallery above the Lord Chancellor. Charles wore hired scarlet and ermine robes and a tricorn hat. Garter was in multi-coloured medieval costume, tight and emblazoned. Flanked by the two robed sponsors, Charles followed Garter's much bowing to the Lord Chancellor, all doffing and donning hats on a circuitous route to the book in which his signature marked Introduction. Charles, carrying his Writ of Summons without which he could not have been introduced, performed with a solemnity not so easy to share in the Gallery.

He was now officially styled Rt. Hon. Baron Snow, of the City of Leicester, CBE.

Lord Longford soon followed the Introduction with a down-to-business letter.

As Leader I am now considering the allocation of duties in the House of Lords. As Parliamentary Secretary you will of course be spokesman for Technology in this House. Would you also be good enough to assist Vivian Bowden with Education and Science and Charles Hobson with the Post Office.

Charles replied: '. . . It is going to be pleasant to become one of your boys. I'll do my best on the jobs you mention.'

He found the tempo fast from the start. To his American agent he wrote:

. . . 'am almost insanely busy for the moment . . . . I am the No. 2 Minister in the most original part of the new Government – the new

162

Ministry of Technology. The idea of this is simply to try to rejuve-
nate a certain amount of our economy. With good luck we may be
able to do something. Anyway it was, I thought, my duty to try
. . . .

Charles was glad to have a break from writing and reviews. To his
American publisher he confessed: 'It is lucky for me I can turn to
some months of practical politics as a kind of nepenthe.'
  Anthony Powell wrote on 2 November.

My dear Snow,
Do let me add my congratulations to the flood you must be receiving. I like to think that, prophetically, the subject of Supporters
came up at some stage in the course of the evening when we last met.
Your case offers all sorts of alternative possibilities to the herald. Do
not rule out a stranger or a brother, which would tax the artist's
invention and have enigmatic charm as that part of the achievement.
Yours
Anthony Powell

Charles replied:

My dear Powell,
It was like you to write so generously. I only wish that I had your
ingenious idea about Supporters. It would have made Anthony
Wagner more than usually thoughtful. In fact I got weakened by the
atmosphere of punning facetiousness which pervades the College of
Heralds and settled for two Siamese cats; and the initials CAT stand
for Colleges of Advanced Technology – which I am supposed, quite
wrongly as usual – to be a passionate advocate of. By the way,
wouldn't Leavis be proud of the construction of that sentence?
Yours ever
Charles Snow

Amid all these pleasantries, but no doubt as a result of his having
been very much in the forefront of the news, there was some
abrasiveness. He was attacked by *Private Eye*. It was suggested, in
reference to a lunch for J. B. Priestley, that Charles had agreed to
attend only on condition that he took the chair for the purpose of
self-advertisement. In fact Charles made no such condition and
agreed to take the chair at the express request of Priestley and the
organisers of the lunch. An apology was published by *Private Eye*.

Undeterred, the same paper said that Lord Snurd (previous allusions had been to 'C. P. Snurd' or 'Sir Charles Snurd') had invited the whole Swedish Academy out to dinner to increase his chances of a Nobel Prize. Charles had not set foot in Scandinavia for ten years. He was in Government office which made counter-attack invidious. Innuendoes, however, gained exasperating momentum and it was decided that they should not be ignored. *Private Eye*, from whom an explanation was demanded, said:

There is a mention of him in the issue of *Private Eye* dated 3 February [1965] in a list of names of those from whom readers are invited to select the ugliest men – a competition intended to be funny but which we fear may be regarded by Lord Snow as adding insult to injury. As we have had no intention to harm Lord Snow in any way or to hurt his feelings we very greatly regret. . . .

They were asked to pay £1000 for the references made over a period of time and to undertake not to make further references to Charles in any way. *Private Eye* moaned that £1000 was far beyond their means and offered £200. They enclosed a 'cheque for £200 to Lord Snow which we agreed to pay on the undertaking never to mention Lord Snow again'. An apology plus costs of £147 followed. As there was a more than sour mention in *Private Eye* nearly five months later, the solicitors asked why the paper's undertaking had been broken. A letter arrived signed by Richard Ingrams:

I regret to say that the reference was included during my absence on holiday in an article by an outside contributor who was unaware of the undertaking not to mention Lord Snow. Apologies.

It was a lingering end to the sniping from a number of quarters. He had of course won, and latterly at little mental cost to himself.

Charles's office precluded his being able to accept an invitation from the BBC to join 'The Critics' programme:

I have however only taken on this job for a finite time and I hope to be free before the end of 1965. This is not to be taken as a political forecast.

Surprisingly early after having taken office he felt a little detached from the literary world. When Anthony Storr congratulated him on

Corridors of Power and suggested that he take no notice of an acid reviewer Charles, after only a month in office, wrote:

. . . No one is ever indifferent to attacks, or at least no one I've ever met. But it is clear enough that most literary intellectuals have become alienated from the rest of the world and have ceased to communicate except with each other. It will probably take a big change in society before this process is altered. Until this change happens most art is going to remain solipsistic.

He regarded taking a job in the Government, like Roger Quaife in *Corridors of Power*, as 'one of the most bizarre ironies' that had ever happened to any writer. When he'd had time to draw breath I asked him again if he had had any inkling of what was to come. He consistently maintained that it was all completely unexpected. Charles certainly never anticipated that he would be checking his imagined impressions of *Corridors of Power* with direct personal experience; he only regretted that he had not written it after his own involvement in politics. He told me that most of the high-ranking politicians who had read *Corridors of Power* believed that it was in essence about right. To a Swedish friend he remarked that he was surprised how close the book was to the reality.

Charles wanted to make his maiden speech at the earliest opportunity. He took the precaution of consulting his friend Lord Astor as to style. Bill Astor told him that the way in which the Lords reacted was different from that in the Commons. In the Lords a high level of courtesy is demanded from both sides. Also, unlike the Commons, the Lords' experience is that speeches influence votes. Very long speeches are not palatable; 'their Lordships like to get home in time for dinner'. A good collective sense of humour of a quiet type tends to prevail; abuse is unacceptable. It is courteous to remain in the House for the whole speech following one's own.

Charles complied with this advice to the letter; he was on his best behaviour. He had promised Astor that he would not display much of his particular brand of humour in his maiden speech. Delivered with deference and aplomb studiedly combined and of course without notes, it was a most impressive speech to a full House when he followed the opening speaker on Business Education on 18 November. Pam, Anne, Stefanie and I were in the Gallery and were held, no less than his peers, by the fluency of delivery and clarity of expression. The House can have heard few like it, at least in recent year when speaking from notes has become the practice; but then there were few more practised speakers than Charles. Bob Boothby, who was no mean speaker himself, described it as superb. Lord Longford, the Leader, wrote: 'You really gripped the House.' From 10 Downing Street in the Prime Minister's own hand:

Dear Charles,
Magnificent maiden speech. Congratulations. I have read it in Hansard and can see why you got such a good Press. And all without notes – something I could not have done. All best wishes,
Yours ever
Harold

Charles replied the next day:

Dear Harold,
This is just a private note. Pamela is typing it because neither you nor anyone else could read my handwriting. I just don't know how you find time to read speeches in Hansard but it is nice to be praised by a master. We listened to your Guildhall speech with rapt admiration, and made our guests do so too.

As for speaking without notes, that is an old parlour trick of mine. I don't think it saves any time, by the way. I have to go for a walk beforehand to clear up in my mind what I am going to say. I am rather enjoying myself just now.
Yours ever
Charles

He told a Long Island friend that his simple trick of speaking without notes seemed to have an hypnotic effect on the House. He had a favourite phrase of mild sarcasm beginning: 'X has a singular passion for. . . .' He would say of his colleagues in the Lords that 'They have a singular passion, when they know I am to speak, for coming in to be mesmerised by my not referring even to the back of an envelope.'

It was a shock when, later, he was personally attacked by the Conservative Lord Eccles for sending his son to Eton and not to a comprehensive school. Astounded by this breach of conventional behaviour and furious that a boy of twelve should be brought into a political discussion, Charles gave a badly phrased reply which he instantly regretted and paid for dearly.

166

He was, for a short time, deluged with more correspondence than on any other controversy involving himself. This was, he and I agreed, because the public could understand a public (in America, private) school *v.* comprehensive school argument better than the others. Many of the letters were vitriolically abusive and were ignored. To more reasoned ones he gave the reply he would have liked to have made to Eccles.

Charles had a strong view about written lectures – extremely boring to listen to, even more boring to give. As for reading a speech, he would say, 'the worst spoken speech is better than the best read one.' Off the cuff, after thinking about it in advance, was his doctrine. He composed many of his speeches in his head – not all, because so many institutions wanted to print them afterwards and neglected to have shorthand reporters on the spot. Though junior Minister for Technology, he was distrustful of the simplest technical gadgets, such as tape recorders. He asked Kansas University: 'Why aren't there a few people trained in shorthand scattered over your Continent?' This was after an extemporaneous speech on the steps of a new Research Laboratory had been let down by the recording device. In those circumstances when he had not been recorded he could always reproduce the main points, but was a little incensed to be asked to repeat a speech verbatim. He did not mind if reporters asked him what he was going to say beforehand – that was useful.

Although he had respect for great debaters (in his estimation Lloyd George and Aneurin Bevan were the finest parliamentary examples) he would warn that debating, like acting, had its frailties. Politicians, after making a good speech, would feel that they had done something, but debate was no substitute for action, only a valuable step to achieving it.

We asked Charles and Pam to take a break in their Christmas holidays. Pam replied:

Charles says he thinks there's little hope of us getting to you during the Christmas holidays, much as we'd love it, as even with Parliament in recess he daren't risk being away overnight. Perhaps he is taking all this too heavily, but, anyway, he does. . . .

I must say C. thrives on politics. He is out far earlier and back far later; but always comes in looking chuffed as hell. [These of course were early days; he became disillusioned as time went on.]

We look forward to seeing you and Stefanie on New Year's Eve
. . . . H. Wilson can't come as he will be back in Huyton, but apparently everyone else can. I am getting to the stage of praying for a few
refusals!

Love to you all
Pam

Charles had bought new suits and was now positively smart. His
was largely an office existence at the top of Millbank Tower with a
superb view over the Thames. There were a good many official functions, including being host at H.M.G. luncheons for visiting
ministers. Large luncheons being anathema to him, he nibbled at the
food. He made himself generally unpopular by telling two hundred
businessmen at one such lunch that the business lunch wastes a large
amount of time: 'I believe it does no good.' He was invited to no
more lunches, a deprivation he could bear with equanimity.

There were official missions to Hungary, Bulgaria, Italy,
Belgium. He worked long hours, but obviously relished the miscellaneous eupeptic company of the Lords when he had a moment's
leisure.

There were times when Charles had to keep vigil in late-night
sessions for voting in the Lords. He would like company for this;
Stefanie and I were soon able to recognise many faces in that strange
cross-section – law lords, bishops, heads of universities, miners,
tycoons, eccentrics (these more often among the hereditary peers
avidly putting in time for their daily allowances and inexpensive
victualling). We recognised the merit in debates where there could
be half-a-dozen world experts, which the Commons could seldom
claim. It was ironical that the Lords had powers on condition that
they did not use them. Separation between parties in the plush scarlet and brass and gilt corridors and rooms was not noticeable.
Charles's friends were from all sides; most prominent among them
were the Conservatives, Peter Carrington, George Jellicoe and Bob
Boothby and the Liberal, Owen Lloyd-George. It was the nicest
club in the country, he maintained.

There were enquiries from friends in America as to how to
address him. To the Dean of the College of William and Mary in
Williamsburg he replied:

Formally I am addressed as Lord Snow and on envelopes curiously
enough as The Lord Snow. But if you and any other friends call me
anything but Charles I shall pour Scotch over your head.

Meanwhile the serialisation of *Corridors of Power* in the *Daily Express* was judged to have helped rather than hindered sales. It was top of the best-seller list and by the New Year had sold 45,000 copies. He told his American publisher: 'If one has the bizarre good fortune I've had in the US, earnings on that side are bound to swamp anything that happens here.'

Charles had in mind a work to be called *Men Who Have Changed the World* or *Nine Originals*. Eventually changed to *Variety of Men*, the biographical essays were just the sort of thing he liked doing and did easily. He had more or less written six, dealing with people he had known personally – Lloyd George, Einstein (no one commanded Charles's unqualified admiration so much), Churchill, Rutherford, G. H. Hardy, Wells. His American publishers wanted him to add about four more whom he did not know but who had been influential in our century: suggestions were Freud, Lenin or Stalin, Roosevelt or Kennedy. They paid him an advance on the strength of his being able, when free, to complete *Variety of Men*. Charles had an almost neurotic obsession about receiving money for something he had not completed. He put this down to his old-fashioned conscience, and felt a weight of responsibility until he had written the last word of the last chapter. He finally opted for Stalin, Hammarskjöld and Robert Frost – to complete what in my view was one of the most eminently readable of all his books. The essays were published in 1967 and Charles regarded them as 'rather fun to do'. Dedicated to Philip junior, *Variety of Men* was unique in being the only one of his books, apart from *Corridors of Power*, to be serialised.

He was pressed for a second volume. Some of the names selected were Kapitza, Aldington, Bernal, Sholokhov, Dirac, Harold Macmillan (in the fullness of time), Blackett, Nehru, Heisenberg, Lionel Trilling, Ian Ramsey, Alexander Tvardovsky and the American Nobel Prize-winning scientist, Isidore Isaac Rabi. Charles warned Kapitza: 'I should very much like to write something about you. You can trust me to be both warm and entirely discreet.' He asked me to help him research a little on the first three and we began work in the 1970s. Regrettably, we stopped because the list was thought to be of only marginal interest in America, and the second collection of portraits never materialised.

Meanwhile, he had written an entertaining and illuminating study of leading novelists: Balzac, Stendhal, Proust, Dostoevski, Tolstoi, Henry James, Dickens and Galdós – the last a surprising and fascinating choice. After tentatively being called *Variety of Writers*, it was eventually entitled *The Realists: Portraits of Eight Novelists*, was published in 1978 and dedicated to me. The work was typical of his facility to encapsulate character with a minimum of research and an absolute economy of words. Charles had thought Jane Austen a possibility but flatly refused to include James Joyce. Thomas Hardy, a favourite poet of his, was one whose novels he could not come to terms with.

In 1965 there were personal trips to America, collecting doctorates from Pennsylvania Military College and the University of Bridgeport, Connecticut; and official ones, with speeches to the Committee on Science and Aeronautics in the US House of Representatives and to an invited audience in the British Embassy, where he and Pam stayed with Sir Patrick Dean, the Ambassador (and later my Chairman at Rugby), and Lady Dean.

On his sixtieth birthday, this telegram came from the Rector of Rostov-on-Don State University:

Our dear Honorary Doctor. We from the Don wish you many happy returns of the days good health and new success in your creative work. We are sure that our Honorary Doctor will always struggle for the peace and progress of mankind.

Via the Russian Ambassador, who had it translated, came a euphoric acclamation from Sholokhov after taking his Nobel Prize, which was awarded on Charles's birthday:

Dear faraway friends . . . . And now being in Stockholm we managed to find a few minutes to congratulate our dear young man Charles on his 60th birthday (young, due to his character, optimism, ability to laugh and enjoy life). Charles's laughter is a sound-tracked illustration of his ever young soul. We wish him many happy returns of the day, good health and happiness which he is to share with Pamela only without Cossack girls, English, Indian, Chinese or other girls of any nationality! Many thanks for the kind words said in connection with the Nobel Prize I received. Embracing and wishing you all the best and most sacred in your lives. As Charles is not a common person any longer but a Lord (and I congratulate him most sincerely) I have made up my mind to sign this letter respectfully.

M. Sholokhov
Esquire

His personal keeper of the seal, treasurer and keeper of the keys to all
the drawers and wine cellars

M. Sholokhova

Towards the end of the year he felt that there was too much work
and the rewards were not worth the effort; he told me that he had
not worked so hard since the early days of the war. He had joined the
Government on the clear understanding that it was for a finite
period, not beyond the end of 1965; in fact he could not resign until
early 1966. He was glad to be released. The job had meant an estimated cut in income of eighty per cent. The amenities and
friendships in the House were a compensation, but the actual work,
after the initial glamour had worn off, left much to be desired. He
had joined Frank Cousins, the great trade union figure whom he
found 'rather fun' but tending to 'play his own hand', out of duty
and 'some personal ties'. Charles could not get a 'free hand to do
much, if in fact there was anything to be done'. In the end his experience in government brought a sense of disillusion; he came to the
conclusion that too much power lay in the hands of the Prime
Minister. He felt stifled in the ministry; he had expected to be restricted but had underestimated the amount of red tape. He was too
old to be No. 2.

The correspondence between Charles and the Prime Minister on
the subject of his resignation ran into the beginning of 1966:

199 Cromwell Road, London SW5

10 February, 1966

Dear Prime Minister,
Sixteen months ago you did me the honour of asking me to join the
Government. I said that I could not come in for long, but that I
should be glad to try to help Frank Cousins get the new Ministry
going. Well, the Ministry is now going: some of the results are
manifest and within the next year there will be much more to show
for our efforts. So I think the time has come when I can ask you to
release me. As you understood at the start, I want to write some
more books. May I say how proud I have been to serve under you.

Yours ever
Charles

171

199 Cromwell Road, London, SW5

10 February 1966

Personal

Dear Harold,

I have written you a formal letter, but I should like to add a personal note. This has been a fascinating experience, and as I told a Congressional Committee in Washington a fortnight ago you have given me a most privileged ring-side seat. But it has been something of a sacrifice. I don't begrudge that in the least, but, now things are getting into order, the sacrifice will not be justified in terms of anything I am able to do for you.

As for the timing of my departure, I should have thought – from a good many points of view – the sooner the better. If anyone notices, it will baffle them more about election dates. The mobility report is effectively complete, and whether I sign it or someone else does, does not really matter.

I am plain astonished at the way you have prevailed since October 1964. It is one of the great facts of political history. I am lost in admiration. You will be at No. 10 long after I am dead. I had a talk with Robin [Wilson] in Philadelphia. He is most intelligent and highly thought of there. We were both at a dinner when the Hull result came through: tumultuous applause from the assembly.

Yours ever

Charles

The reply which concluded Charles's passage through the corridors of power was belated:

10 Downing Street,
Whitehall

April 5 1966

My dear Charles,

A month or two ago you told me that now the Ministry of Technology was well underway you would like to leave the Government in order to resume writing. At my request you were good enough to stay with us a little longer but now is obviously the moment to release you.

I am grateful for the work that you have done at the crucial phase of our policy of modernising British industry. I know how much you have enjoyed it but I fully understand that you want to take up your literary work again. I hope that you will contribute from time to time to debates in the House of Lords and that in this way the

Government and the country will continue to benefit from your wisdom and experience.

With every good wish for the future,
Yours
Harold Wilson

Charles was the least envious of men. He liked money but, disdaining material objects, he was oblivious of the trappings which money or positions of authority could provide. From his boyhood, however, he had depended on scholarships and marks of 'recognition' both as material aids to progress and as reassurance that he was moving up towards attaining the standards he had set for himself. Like most writers he was suspicious of honours but he also realised that he needed, even more than most of his contemporaries, the recognition represented by them.

On the writing side, in his estimation, the only British award worth having was the OM. At the International level he could not be blamed for hoping that the Nobel Prize for literature might be given on completion of the STRANGERS AND BROTHERS sequence – a unique cycle of eleven interconnected novels, the longest in literary history. I myself always hoped that the Royal Society would elect him a Fellow for his coordinating interpretative work for science, and it always seemed odd that he was never offered the Chancellorship of any of the new Universities.

Although any or all of these recognitions would have given him great pleasure he knew at the end of his life that his achievements were considerable and that his contribution to literature and to *both* cultures was of lasting value.

13. Last Things

Released from government office, Charles was flooded by offers from lecture agencies for American trips, but declared that from now on he would occupy himself with the written word.

In fact he went frequently to America and Canada, bringing his score of honorary degrees to thirty. At Fulton, where Churchill had given his famous address, Charles also made an important speech. Entitled *The State of Siege*, it discussed the problems of the underdeveloped countries and the future of the world. Its impact was less than he could have wished; people wanted to shut their eyes to this inconvenient problem. He ended his lecture with the questions posed by the sixth century Rabbi Hillel:

Sometimes I console myself with a piece of rabbinical wisdom. If I am not for myself, who am I? If I am for myself alone, what am I? If not now, when?

At Hebrew Union College in 1968 his address was entitled *A Gentile's Questions*. In it he referred to the higher than average genetic endowment of the Jews, gauged by the somewhat crude test of the number of Jewish Nobel Prize winners. Charles received many vilifying letters, mostly accusing him of being in the pay of Jews. He was also scathingly attacked by a fellow member of the Labour party, the Education Minister Edward Short, who declared perplexingly that Lord Snow was a racist with 'a completely spurious doctrine, reminiscent of Dr Goebbels'. Charles's reply in *The Times* was that he would have been relieved during the 1930s if Dr Goebbels had taken that line:

I persevere with my first question about why Jewish people have made such an inexplicably large contribution to the world. . . . Mr Short's reminiscences appear to be different from mine.

174

The Association of Jewish ex-Servicemen's Journal, *Ajex*, was irate with Short:

> To have likened the thought-provoking remarks of a noted academic and scientist humanist to the bloody vituperation of a race maniac was both outrageous and irresponsible, even from a Minister of Government.

Harry Hoff pulled his leg about his status as an 'honorary Jew', reminding Charles that he only lacked the 'little operation'.

Charles still travelled a great deal. He visited Sweden and Denmark, and travelled the length of Russia from Leningrad to Georgia and across to Riga and Poland. He made his first visit to Africa – to Tanzania. He found the programme too full 'for an elderly man . . . . one's receptivity gets fairly quickly saturated. . . . The most valuable feature, I have always found, rests in the personal contacts'. He told Philip junior that a procession of animals in a game reserve going at dusk to a water-hole was a 'sight I'll remember till I go to Valhalla'. He was impressed by the 'earnest, rather beautiful tone' of Tanzanian society, but was not sure how long it would last. A first (and last) visit to India, initially cancelled by riots, came off for the Sarabhai Memorial Lectures at Ahmedabad and then on to Baroda and Bombay.

Christ's at last made him an Honorary Fellow – only a moment before Churchill College made him an Extraordinary Fellow. He was also made an Honorary Fellow of Hatfield Polytechnic College and had a building named after him.

His correspondence was still as varied as ever. In June 1967 Gerhardi wrote:

> I have reverted to an early ancestral spelling of my name, the reason being that Dante has an 'e', Shakespeare has an 'e', Racine has an 'e', Goethe has an 'e' and who am I not to have an 'e' . . . .

Charles replied:

> Dear William
> I feel about your new spelling exactly as I should have done if requested by the author of The Divine Comedy to address him as Dant.
>
> Love from us all
Charles

The D.Litt. conferred on Charles at Louisville University, Kentucky, gave him especial pleasure. People who had graduated more than thirty years before (some of them in their sixties, including wealthy bankers) formed themselves into a body, The Snowflakes, and retraced in England the scenes of the Cambridge novels and *Corridors of Power*.He was invited by the Governor of Kentucky to the Governor's mansion for lunch, followed by a bestowal in the State Theater of the honorary award of Kentucky Colonel. 'I'm the only person alive', he told me, 'to be a Kentucky Colonel and an Honorary Cossack.'

He gave his approval to a C. P. Snow College in the State University of Buffalo, whose curriculum was aimed specifically at bridging the Two Cultures.

In 1969 he left the office which he had occupied for so long at English Electric House on the corner of Aldwych. Thanking Lord Nelson for having been so generous in letting him have it, Charles expressed his regret at leaving. It meant also separation from a faithful secretary, Freda Haddy, who had helped him over many years, some of them frenetically busy.

He was putting in a lot of time at the Lords. He told my son-in-law, Peter Waine: 'Life in the Lords is moderately picturesque and there is plenty of suppressed excitement. There is also plenty of very heavy drinking, particularly by illustrious members of the present Government.'

The world view looked gloomy in 1968. The Vietnam war, antagonism between Russia and America, the unsettled state of the Third World were all causes for concern. The future for the young was very much on Charles's mind. In an address to Kingston-upon-Hull School of Education, he said:

The more one has lived in the world, the more important luck, pure luck, seems to you to be . . . . I haven't met any honest man who had any kind of future in this world who didn't think luck had been desperately and often vitally important. Conrad said that 'a man who doesn't believe in luck if he had made a tiny bit of a name must be abnormally unfeeling or stupid'. I'm sure this is true.

Perhaps this was an indication of his pessimism at that time.

In 1968 when the lease of the flat at 199 Cromwell Road had only three years to run , Charles and Pam purchased the lease of 85 Eaton Terrace in Belgravia with forty years to run. A tall, thin, red brick house in a terrace of stuccoed ones, it had the right number of rooms

176

for the three children who were still at home and the housekeeper. Charles was finally to abandon an office outside the house.

The Sleep of Reason was published in 1968, and was a Book of the Month Club choice in America. It had 'cannibalised' much of *The Devoted*, parts of which had long been lying in reserve. It is partly concerned with sadistic tendencies, particularly in the young; Charles thought it curious that the more affluent society became the more violence there was. He believed that if he were going to be judged by any single work in the series this would be it. He considered that the description of the death of Lewis Eliot's father was the best single piece of writing he had ever done. Not everybody agreed with him about *The Sleep of Reason*; its reception both by the critics and the book buying public depressed him. To an American Rabbi friend he confided:

I have been feeling unusually low. *Sleep of Reason* seems to me much the best of what I have yet done. . . . I can't comprehend what some reviewers are thinking of, but they have reduced me to a state of depression which I don't think I shall easily shake off. This has been a temperamental difficulty all my life although I think I conceal it from the outside world. But now I am finding it hard to drag my feet around.

I sent him a copy of my *Bibliography of Fiji, Tonga and Rotuma*, published in 1969, which I had been working on for thirty years. He wrote back, 'I was delighted to get your major piece of Old Brandy. It slightly lacks narrative suspense but makes up for it through the richness of material.'

Charles had started the 1970s with what was to be a literary task calling for considerable stamina; it was to last till the end of his life. His weekly reviews for the *Financial Times* were eagerly looked forward to by many who did not normally take an interest in literature. He had total freedom, only reviewing books which really interested him. His choices were mainly non-fiction – he professed diminishing interest in new fiction. For the next ten years no book page of a national newspaper can have been better served.

1970 also saw the end of the *Strangers and Brothers* series. *L Things* was a Book of the Month Club choice in America. It contained descriptions of the retina operations and heart stoppage eight years back, giving an edge to the end of the sequence. Har Macmillan marked the achievement with a party at the Ritz. Or October he wrote:

Dear Charles

I think you must be pleased with the wonderful reception given by the critics from almost every quarter to your last novel *Last Things*. . . . Looking back upon the whole story you must feel, I would suppose, sometimes almost surprised and even incredulous about what you have done. Yet you have reason for pride as well as gratitude. You have done fine work as others have done before you and the public has recognised the sincerity of your writing and its deep meaning in the tortured world in which men and women live today. I feel it a great privilege that my family and I have been associated with this massive enterprise.

Yours ever
Harold Macmillan

Charles replied:

Dear Harold,

Of course I am delighted and slightly overwhelmed. As you know I had a very rough time critically all through the 60s – in fact almost from the time when I began to have a commercial success – so I was very apprehensive at what they would do to the conclusion of the work. It has gone far better than I expected. It was through you that I came to the house of Macmillan, and your support and friendship have been more important to me than you can realise. I like to think that our association will be carried on by the younger generation.

Yours ever
Charles

A revised edition of the whole sequence of *Strangers and Brothers* was now, after strenuous editing by Charles of the 1½ million words put together over thirty years, to be published by Macmillan in three volumes, in the order in which Charles considered they should be read, rather than that in which they had originally been published.

The Malcontents, published in 1972, was the first novel outside the *Strangers and Brothers* sequence since *The Search* in 1934. Concerned wholly with youth, it was, in the opinion of many, not Charles's métier. Charles thought that it required careful reading and that it might be better understood later. He launched immediately on what was first called *The Onlookers* and became *In Their Wisdom* (published in 1974) which brought in many court-room and House of Lords scenes. Lord Sedgwick is in part the left-wing Desmond Bernal; Lord Ryle is based on Charles himself and he could not resist combining maternal ancestral names in a firm of solicitors called Robinson and Wigmore.

1975 was a special year marking his 70th birthday of which there was handsome recognition in some quarters. An anonymous donor, understood to be American, set up a triennial C. P. Snow Lecture in Christ's to be delivered on his birthday. The first lecturer was Sir Peter Medawar and there was a congenial feast in Christ's Hall to mark the occasion.

At the Stationers' Hall in London, Macmillan and Penguin gave what Charles described as a gigantic party for his seventieth birthday and the publication of *Trollope*, Charles's first illustrated book and a beautiful production. Harold Macmillan made a graceful speech. The audience was a galaxy of literary and miscellaneous notoriety.

Ronald Millar adapted *In Their Wisdom* for the theatre under the title *The Case in Question*, with Sir John Clements again in the lead. It opened at the Theatre Royal, Haymarket, and got an excellent press.

Pam was gravely ill at the start of 1976. Since an initial stroke five years earlier there had been further strokes and acute bronchial attacks. Charles was deterred by the severity of her illness from thinking further about a 'doctor' novel he had intended to write. Instead he turned his attention to the therapeutic theme of *The Realists* and simultaneously to a detective novel – to be published in 1979 and entitled *A Coat of Varnish*.

An excellent television film under the direction of Alan Wallis was completed in 1977, with scenes in London and Cambridge and interviews with Pam and me and one or two friends.

Priestley received the OM, filling a vacancy that certainly ruled out Charles himself for the time being. As Priestley said, in reply to congratulations from Charles: 'It is all the more generous coming from you. I feel you are more the OM kind of man than I am.'

After their last trip to America in 1978 Charles and Pam were both in wheel chairs on their return to London Airport. She from fatigue, he from what he insisted on calling 'lumbago'; he had had several attacks over the last ten years. He had been working far too hard for a man of his age.

He now conceded that he had suffered attacks of what he variously called lumbago, gout, fibrositis and different kinds of rheumatic complaints, all of which, with his usual stoicism, he had suffered in silence. They were not 'lethal', he assured us, but made life very difficult. In mid-September 1979 the pain started again and

179

from then to December he was unable to leave the house. These were by far the worst attacks he had suffered: painful indigestion and nausea, which made one fear the worst. He was confined to his bedroom and study which were next to each other at the top of the house. There he was forced to have recourse to the telephone and scrupulously kept up his correspondence; he also finished a very long synopsis for a work on scientific biographical themes entitled *The Physicists*. This was published in 1981 with an introduction by Harry Hoff; it was dedicated to Stefanie. *A Coat of Varnish* had come out earlier in the year, and received a very friendly press. Charles was uncharacteristically morose about the sales which he found acutely disappointing.

By now there was no relief from the pain. 'Any kind of locomotion is hell.' It was a glum Christmas, but when Anne and I visited him at Eaton Terrace on the last day of 1979 he seemed to be in better shape than he had been for years. It was a relief; in October he'd been hugging a hot water bottle to the small of his back and sitting, transfixed, on the edge of his chair at a sideways angle to keep the pain at bay. He looked pale, strained and thin, and was becoming progressively deaf. But he derived some benefit from a course of physiotherapy and at the start of 1980 he was active again. I remember him saying at this time, 'On the whole I usually regret the things I haven't done rather than things I've done.'

Hull University wanted to confer on him the honorary degree of Doctorate of Letters on 11 July: it was rather surprisingly his first such appointment in this country since 1962 (St Andrews).

The highest Bulgarian cultural honour had been awarded to him – the International Dimitrov Prize – for his 'outstanding contribution to the better understanding among the peoples and the intellectuals of the different countries'. In the event Georgi Djagarov, prominent poet and playwright and Vice-President of Bulgaria, presented the prize to Philip junior at the Bulgarian Embassy in June 1981, as Pam was desperately ill in hospital.

There was much to do – to finish *The Physicists*, on which good progress had been made, and to start on a novel deriving from *A Coat of Varnish* with a hi-jacking theme which he expected to be commercially successful. He was also still reviewing for the *Financial Times*.

Ronald Millar began his adaptation of *A Coat of Varnish* for the stage. It opened at the Theatre Royal, Haymarket, in 1982 with Peter Barkworth and Anthony Quayle in the leading parts.

At last the contract was signed for the BBC to make a television series from the *Strangers and Brothers* sequence. Charles took Julian Bond, the scriptwriter, to Cambridge and to meet various heads of departments of the Civil Service in Whitehall. Charles enjoyed these excursions very much.

On 19 June he was struck down by a bout, which he described as a particularly violent one, of his 'old affliction'. It was so bad that he had to leave everything, saying how maddening it was for a disciplined writer and that he had no idea at all when he would be fit for work.

On 24 June he wrote to Jacques Barzun:

I have taken such medical advice as might be useful and they say in effect all one can do is endure. As I don't think I am likely to have long pain-free intervals I shall have to revert to a new strategy for working....

To others he said that the exceptionally aggravated attack of fibrositis or migratory arthritis ('what our ancestors would call lumbago' ... 'entirely undangerous' and 'not dramatic') was so painful that most of the time he could neither eat nor sleep.

Anne, Stefanie, Peter and I last saw Charles on 24 April at an Arts Council reception at New Zealand House, London, to announce the winners of the first National Book Award for history/biography. The book which Stefanie and I had collaborated on, *The People from the Horizon: an Illustrated History of the Europeans among the South Sea Islanders*, was short-listed; Charles had helped to reshape it. We were placed third in a short list of six and when we were talking afterwards to the judge, Dame Veronica Wedgwood, Charles and Pam (not looking well) came up to join us. It was our last sight of him. I did not know that his symptoms had returned in mid-June. On the morning of 1 July he dictated letters to Janet Nalder, his admirable secretary over the last four years, interspersed with amused comments over the current tennis at Wimbledon in which, of later years, he had taken almost as much interest as cricket. He was in good form when she left him at midday but was due to go into hospital straightaway for further checks; he had previously been implacably opposed to any suggestion of hospital treatment.

At 4.30 p.m. that afternoon Pam telephoned to say that Charles had died from a massive haemorrhage. The post-mortem revealed

181

that the cause of death was a perforated gastric ulcer. The private cremation followed three days later at Putney Vale, attended only by the immediate family and Harry Hoff.

The estate was £286,000 net, a quarter or more of this being the value of the leasehold of 85 Eaton Terrace; Pam was the chief beneficiary, after her Philip junior and, in the event of Philip not surviving Pam, the estate fell to me. Michael Rubinstein (his solicitor) and I had been appointed executors; Pam, Harry Hoff and I the literary executors.

His will included a provision for his post-war secretary, Anne Seagrim. Charles had resumed in 1957 his close relationship with Anne Seagrim, broken off in 1950 before his marriage to Pam. The existence of this relationship did not bring about any estrangement between Charles and Pam, and indeed Pam was unaware of it. Charles told me in 1960 that I was at that time his sole confidant and whenever he could not communicate with Anne in an emergency I was to telephone to her. This I had done immediately after I heard of the heart stoppage in late 1962. But this time, eighteen years later, I could not trace the ex-directory number and had to ask the police to go to an address I vaguely remembered Charles giving me years before. She was still there but had heard an hour before from Charles's secretary. I had not met her since 1946 but Charles had arranged that I should be the reliquary of her letters to him in his last years. There can be no doubt that if Pam had predeceased him (as seemed likely in 1976) Charles and Anne would have married.

Anne Seagrim, a daughter of an Inspector-General of Police, Indore and Central Provinces, India, became secretary to the Duke of Windsor from 1950 to 1954, and then to Field-Marshal Earl Alexander of Tunis. She is partly characterised as Betty Cooke, née Vane, in *Homecomings* and *The Sleep of Reason*. Anne, with his mother and Pam, were the predominant female influences in Charles's life.

A year after Charles's death his ashes were incorporated in the base of a memorial urn in the Fellows' Garden at Christ's in company with John Milton and three other distinguished members of the college, none later than the eighteenth century. Under the inscription 'Charles Percy, Baron Snow, 1905–1980' are the concluding words of his lecture at Fulton, Missouri, in 1968 (see p. 174). Invited by the Master, Jack Plumb, Philip junior unveiled it on 12 July 1981, the thirty-first anniversary of Charles's marriage to Pam, also at Christ's. Pam had selected that day for the ceremony. Among those present were her daughter Lindsay, Eric and Jess, Anne and myself, Stefanie and her baby daughter Philippa, representing the future generation; Charles would certainly have approved.

Pam had fallen the day after the cremation and fractured her shoulder. She had a further stroke before the Memorial Service for Charles in St Martin-in-the-Fields at which Harry Hoff gave the address. She died nearly a year later on 18 June 1981 at the age of sixty-nine. She had an almost identical private cremation.

As I write, it is nearly two years since Charles's death and I am bereft.

SOME CHARACTERS IDENTIFIED IN C. P. SNOW'S NOVELS

Characters	*Persons on whom characters based mainly, partly or vaguely* (Some are combinations or elements only)

Strangers and Brothers

Bevill, Thomas P.C., MP (later Grampound, Lord)	The Right Honourable M. P. A. Hankey, 1st Lord Hankey of the Chart, Secretary of the Imperial War Cabinet 1917–18. Secretary of the Cabinet 1919–38. Clerk of the Privy Council 1922–38. Chancellor of the Duchy of Lancaster 1940–1. Paymaster General 1941–2. Charles's chief, 1940–1. Appears in *The New Men* and *Homecomings*.
Brown, Arthur, MA	Sydney William Grose, MA. Senior Tutor and friend of Charles at Christ's College, Cambridge. Appears in *The Masters*, *The Light and the Dark*, *The Affair* and *Last Things*.
Calvert, Roy, MA	Charles Robert Cecil Allberry, MA Fellow of Christ's. Cambridge Orientalist and close friend of Charles. Killed in the RAF. Principal character in *The Light and the Dark*. Appears in *The Masters*, *George Passant* and *Time of Hope*.
Chrystal, Charles P., MA	Travors Carey Wyatt, OBE, MA, Fellow and Bursar of Christ's College,

184

Cambridge. Appears in
The Masters and *The
Light and the Dark*.

Constantine, Leo — Professor John Desmond Bernal, FRS.
Marxist. Professor of Physics and
Crystallography at London University
1963–8, and assistant to Lord Mountbatten
in World War II. Appears in *The Search*.

Cooke (née Vane), — Anne Seagrim. Close friend of Charles.
Elizabeth (Betty) — Appears in *Homecomings* and *The Sleep of
Reason*.

Cornford, Adam — Dr Anthony Storr, MD. Psychiatrist.
Charles was his tutor at Cambridge.
Appears in *The Sleep of Reason*.

Crawford, R. Thomas — Sir Robert Alexander Watson-Watt, CB,
A., — FRS. Associated with the development of
CBE, MA, FRS — radar. Scientific Adviser to the Air
Ministry 1940. Appears in *The Masters* and
The Affair.

Davidson, Austin — Professor Godfrey Harold Hardy, FRS.
Professor of Geometry, Oxford 1919–31
and Hon. Fellow of New College, Oxford.
Professor of Pure Mathematics,
Cambridge 1932–42. Fellow of Trinity
College, Cambridge, and close friend of
Charles. Appears in *Homecomings*, *The
Sleep of Reason* and *Last Things*.

Eliot, Charles — Hon. Philip Charles Hansford Snow, BA.
Son of Charles. Chinese scholar. Principal
character in *The Sleep of Reason*. Appears in
Last Things.

Eliot, Hubert Edward — William Edward Snow, FRCO. Father of
(Bertie) — Charles. Organist, teacher of music and
clerk in boot and shoe factory. Appears in
Time of Hope and *Last Things*.

Eliot, Lena — Ada Sophia Snow. Mother of Charles.
Appears in *Time of Hope*.

185

Eliot, Sir Lewis, KBE, MA	Rt. Hon. Charles Percy Snow, Lord Snow of Leicester. Appears in all books. Also Dr Arthur R. Miles in *The Search*.
Eliot, Martin F., PhD	Philip Albert Snow, MBE, JP, MA. Brother of Charles. Administrator, author and bibliographer. Principal character in *The New Men*. Appears in *The Affair*, *Time of Hope*, *Corridors of Power*, *The Sleep of Reason* and *Last Things*.
Gay, M. H. L., MA, FBA	Professor John Holland Rose. Professor of Naval History, Cambridge, 1919–33, and Fellow of Christ's College. Appears in *The Masters*, *The Light and the Dark* and *The Affair*.
Getliffe, Francis (later Lord Getliffe), CBE, ScD, FRS	Professor Frank Philip Bowden, CBE, FRS, DSc, PhD. Professor of Surface Physics, Cambridge, 1966–8 and Fellow of Caius College, Cambridge. Director of English Electric Company 1953–68. Appears in *The Conscience of the Rich*, *The Light and the Dark*, *The Masters*, *The New Men*, *The Affair*, *Corridors of Power*, *The Sleep of Reason* and *Last Things*. Also Professor Desmond in *The Search*.
Jago, Paul, MA, Litt.D	Professor Canon Charles Earle Raven. Professor of Divinity, Cambridge, 1932–50. Fellow and Master of Christ's College, Cambridge. Chaplain to Kings George V and George VI and the Queen. Principal character in *The Masters*. Appears in *The Light and the Dark* and *The Affair*.
Knight, Laurence	Francis Brett Young, MB. Author. Appears in *Time of Hope* and *Homecomings*.
Knight, Mrs	Jessica Brett Young. Wife of Francis Brett Young. Appears in *Time of Hope* and *Homecomings*.
Nightingale, R. E. Alec, MA, PhD	Arthur Leslie Peck, MA, PhD. Fellow and Librarian, Christ's College, Cambridge.

	Principal character in *The Affair* and *The Masters*. Appears in *The Light and the Dark* and *Last Things*.
Passant, George	Herbert Edmund Howard, MA. Schoolmaster in Leicester and close friend of Charles. Principal character in *George Passant*. Appears in *Time of Hope*, *Homecomings* and *The Sleep of Reason*.
Pilbrow, Eustace, MA, Litt.D	Professor John Brande Trend, MA. Professor of Spanish, Cambridge, and Fellow of Christ's College, Cambridge. Appears in *The Masters*.
Riddington, Mrs (Aunt Milly)	Kate Emily Armstrong, sister of W. E. Snow. Aunt of Charles. Appears in *Time of Hope*.
Timberlake, Sir Horace (later Bridgewater, Viscount)	Rt. Hon. George Horatio Nelson, 1st Lord Nelson of Stafford. Chairman of English Electric Company 1933–62 and of other companies. Appears in *The Masters* and *Corridors of Power*.

In Their Wisdom

Hillmorton, Lord	Rt. Hon. Harold Maurice Macmillan. (Vaguely, Charles said.) Prime Minister 1957–63. Charles's publisher.
Swaffield, Reginald	1. Professor J. H. Plumb. Professor of Modern English History, Cambridge 1966–76. Fellow and Master of Christ's College, Cambridge. 2. Rt. Hon. William Maxwell Aitken, First Lord Beaverbrook.
Underwood, Julian	William Gerhardi. Author.

The Malcontents

The Bishop	Rt Rev Ian Thomas Ramsey, MA. Fellow and Chaplain of Christ's College, Cambridge, and Bishop of Durham. Hon Fellow, Oriel College, Oxford.

SELECT BIBLIOGRAPHY

For a full bibliography, Paul Boytinck's excellent *C. P. Snow. A Reference Guide* (Boston, Mass., G. K. Hall, 1980) should be consulted.

The following select bibliography gives the principal works of C. P. Snow in chronological order under their various categories; books about him or to which he contributed are in alphabetical order of author. Original material is at the Humanities Research Center, Austin, University of Texas, except letters from Charles to me.

The Works of C. P. Snow

1. Novels outside the *Strangers and Brothers* series:

Death Under Sail (London, Heinemann, 1932).
(Anonymously) *New Lives for Old* (London, Gollancz, 1933).
The Search (London, Gollancz, 1934).
The Malcontents (London, Macmillan, 1972).
In Their Wisdom (London, Macmillan, 1974).
In Their Wisdom (London, Macmillan, 1974).
A Coat of Varnish (London, Macmillan, 1978).

2. *Strangers and Brothers* series:

Strangers and Brothers (later retitled *George Passant*) (London, Faber and Faber, 1940).
The Light and the Dark (London, Faber and Faber, 1947).
Time of Hope (London, Faber and Faber, 1949).
The Masters (London, Macmillan, 1951).
The New Men (London, Macmillan, 1954).

Homecomings (London, Macmillan, 1956).
The Conscience of the Rich (London, Macmillan, 1958).
The Affair (London, Macmillan, 1960).
Corridors of Power (London, Macmillan, 1964).
The Sleep of Reason (London, Macmillan, 1968).
Last Things (London, Macmillan, 1970).
Strangers and Brothers (Omnibus edition. 3 volumes.) (London, Macmillan, 1972).

3. Non-fiction:

Richard Aldington: An Appreciation (London, Heinemann, 1938).
The Two Cultures and the Scientific Revolution (Cambridge, Cambridge University Press, 1959).
Science and Government (Cambridge, Mass., Harvard University Press, 1961).
A Postscript to Science and Government (Cambridge, Mass., Harvard University Press, 1962).
On Magnanimity (London, University of St Andrews, 1962).
The Two Cultures: and a Second Look (Cambridge, Cambridge University Press, 1964).
Variety of Men. Rutherford, G. H. Hardy, H. G. Wells, Einstein, Lloyd George, Winston Churchill, Robert Frost, Dag Hammarskjöld, Stalin (London, Macmillan, 1967).
The State of Siege (New York, Scribner, 1969).
Public Affairs (London, Macmillan, 1971).
Trollope; His Life and Art (London, Macmillan, 1975).
The Realists. Portraits of Eight Novelists. Stendhal, Balzac, Dickens, Dostoevsky, Tolstoy, Galdós, Henry James, Proust (London, Macmillan, 1978).
The Physicists: A Generation that Changed the World (London, Macmillan, 1981).

4. Articles, lectures, etc.:

In issues of *The Newtonian* (Leicester, 1923–5).
In issues of *The Luciad* (Leicester, 1926–8).
'H. G. Wells and Ourselves'. In *Cambridge Review*, 1934.
In issues of *Discovery* (Cambridge, 1938–40).
'The Mathematician on Cricket'. *The Saturday Book*, No. 8, 1948.
'The Wisdom of Niels Bohr'. *The Saturday Book*, No. 9, 1949.

(Anonymously) 'New Minds for the New World'. *New Statesman and*
Nation, 52, No. 1330, 8 September 1956.
'An Object of Love'. *Meanjin*, 19, No. 3, 9 September 1960.
'The Moral Un-Neutrality of Science'. *Science*, 133, No. 3448, 27
January 1961.
'Writer's Luck'. *American Academy of Arts and Letters and the National
Institute of Arts and Letters Proceedings*, Series 2, No. 12,
April–November 1961.
'Presidential Address'. *Library Association Record*, 63, November
1961.
'Quarter Century: Its Great Delusions'. *Look*, 25, No. 26, 19
December 1961.
'Government, Science and Public Policy'. *Science,* 151, No. 3711, 11
February 1966.
'The Moon Landing'. *Look*, 33, 26 August 1969.
'The Case of Leavis and the Serious Case'. *Times Literary
Supplement*, 9 July 1970.
'Medical Possibilities and Human Conscience'. University of North
Carolina School of Medicine, 1974.

5. Plays:

Nights Ahead (Cyclostyled, no date c. 1930).
With Gerhardi, William. *The Fool of the Family* (Cyclostyled, 1949).
With Johnson, Pamela Hansford. *Family Party* (London, Evans,
1951).
Her Best Foot Forward (London, Evans, 1951).
Spare the Rod (London, Evans, 1951).
The Pigeon with the Silver Foot (London, Evans, 1951).
The Supper Dance (London, Evans, 1951).
To Murder Mrs Mortimer (London, Evans, 1951).
The Young and Antient (sic) Men. A Chronicle of the Pilgrim Fathers
(Broadcast, 1952).

6. Books to which C. P. Snow contributed or which he edited:

Benedikz, B. S. (editor), *On the Novel: A Present for Walter Allen on
his 60th Birthday from his Friends and Colleagues*. Trollope: The
Psychological Stream (London, Dent, 1971).
Bryant, Arthur (editor), *Imaginary Biographies*. The Original of the
Mona Lisa. (London, Allen and Unwin, 1936).

Djagarov, Georgi, *The Public Prosecutor; A Play*. Introduction by C. P. Snow. Adapted by C. P. Snow and Pamela Hansford Johnson. (London, Owen, 1969).

Doyle, Sir Arthur Conan, *The Case-Book of Sherlock Holmes*. Introduction by C. P. Snow (London, Murray and Cape, 1974).

Goldsmith, Maurice, *The Science of Society*. J. D. Bernal; a Personal Portrait. (Harmondsworth, Penguin, 1966).

Hardy, Godfrey Harold, *A Mathematician's Apology*. Foreword by C. P. Snow (London, Cambridge University Press, 1967).

Kershaw, Alister and Temple, Frédéric-Jacques, *Richard Aldington. An Intimate Portrait*. Chapter by C. P. Snow. (Carbondale, Southern Illinois University Press, 1965.)

Millar, Sir Ronald, *The Affair, The New Men and The Masters*. Three plays based on the novels. Preface by C. P. Snow (London, Macmillan, 1964).

Reznikoff, Charles, *By the Waters of Manhatten; Selected Verse*. Introduction by C. P. Snow. (New York, New Directions, 1962.)

Rogow, Arnold A., *The Jew in a Gentile World*. Introduction by C. P. Snow (New York, Macmillan, 1961).

Snow, Charles Percy and Johnson, Pamela Hansford (editors), *Winter's Tales: Stories from Modern Russia*. (London, Macmillan, 1961).

Weiner, Dora B. and Keylor, William R. (editors) *From Parnassus. Essays in Honor of Jacques Barzun*. The Classical Detective Story (New York, Harper and Row, 1976).

Young, Jessica Brett, *Francis Brett Young: a Biography*. Preface by C. P. Snow (London, Heinemann, 1962).

7. Plays based on C. P. Snow's novels:

Ketels, Arthur and Ketels, Violet. *Time of Hope* (Cyclostyled, 1962).

Millar, Ronald, *The Affair; A Play*. From the novel of C. P. Snow (New York, Scribner, 1962).

Millar, Ronald, *The Affair. A Play in Three Acts*. From the novel of C. P. Snow (London, S. French, 1962).

Millar, Ronald, *The Affair, The New Men and The Masters*. Three plays based on the novels and with a preface by C. P. Snow (London, Macmillan, 1964).

Millar, Ronald, *The Case in Question; A Play*. Based on C. P. Snow's novel *In Their Wisdom* (London, S. French, 1975).

Millar, Ronald, *A Coat of Varnish. A Play in Two Acts.* Suggested by the novel by C. P. Snow. (London, Scripts Ltd., 1982).

8. Books or pamphlets about C. P. Snow

Atkins, John, *Six Novelists Look at Society* (London, Calder, 1977).

Cooper, William (Hoff, Harry Summerfield), *C. P. Snow* (London, Longmans Green, 1958).

——, *Scenes from Later Life* (London, Macmillan, 1982).

——, *Scenes from Metropolitan Life* (to be published).

——, *Scenes from Provincial Life* (London, Cape, 1950).

——, *Young People* (London, Macmillan, 1958).

Davis, Robert Gorham, *C. P. Snow* (New York, Columbia University Press, 1965).

Greacen, Robert, *The World of C. P. Snow* (Lowestoft, Scorpion Press, 1962).

Johnson, Pamela Hansford, *Important to Me: Personalia* (London, Macmillan, 1974).

Petelin, G. and Simkin, J., *Charles Percy Snow (———CHOY), writer and man* (Moscow, 1963).

Philmore, R. (Howard, Herbert Edmund), *Journey Downstairs* (London, Gollancz, 1934).

——, *No Mourning in the Family* (London, Crime Club, 1937).

Putt, Samuel Gorley, Technique and Culture: Three Cambridge Portraits. In *Essays and Studies* (London, Murray, 1961).

Rabinowitz, Robin, *The Reaction against Experiment in the English Novel 1958–1960* (New York, Columbia University Press, 1967).

Ramanthan, Suguna, *The Novels of C. P. Snow* (London, Macmillan, 1978).

Raymond, John (editor), *The Baldwin Age* (London, Eyre and Spottiswoode, 1960).

Shusterman, David, *C. P. Snow* (Boston, Mass., Twayne, 1975).

Thale, Jerome, *C. P. Snow* (New York, Scribner, 1965).

Weintraub, Stanley (editor), *C. P. Snow, a Spectrum: Science, Criticism, Fiction* (New York, Scribner, 1963).

HONOURS, AWARDS AND DEGREES

Honorary Doctorates

1959	Leicester University, England	LLD
1960	Liverpool University, England	LLD
	Dartmouth College, New Hampshire, USA	DLitt
1961	Kenyon College, Ohio, USA	D Humane Letters
1962	Brooklyn Polytechnic Institute, USA	LLD
	Bard College, New York, USA	DLitt
	St Andrews University, Scotland	LLD
1963	Temple University, Pensylvania, USA	DLitt
	Syracuse University, New York, USA	DLitt
	Michigan University, USA	D Humane Letters
	Rostov-on-Don University, Russia	D Philological Science
	Washington University, St Louis, Missouri, USA	D Humane Letters
1964	Pittsburgh University, Pennsylvania, USA	DLitt
1966	Bridgeport University, Connecticut, USA	LLD
	Pennsylvania Military College, USA	DSc
1967	Ithaca College, New York, USA	DLitt
	York University, Toronto, Canada	LLD
1968	Hebrew Union College, Jewish Institution of Religion, Ohio, USA	D Humane Letters
	Westminster College, Fulton, Missouri, USA	DLitt
1969	Alfred University, New York, USA	D Humane Letters
	Akron University, Ohio, USA	D Humane Letters

193

1970	Loyola University, Chicago, USA	LLD
1971	Western Ontario University, Canada	DLitt
1973	Newfoundland University, Canada	LLD
1976	Louisville University, Kentucky, USA	D Humane Letters
	Cincinnati University, USA	D Litt
	New York University, USA	DLitt
1977	Pace University, New York, USA	D Humane Letters
1978	Widener University, Pennsylvania, USA	DLitt
1979	Union College, Schenectady, New York, USA	DLitt
1980	Hull University, England	D Letters

(conferment unable to be made before death)

Other Awards, Degrees, Honours, etc.

1927 BSc, London University, England
1928 MSc, London University, England
1930 PhD, Cambridge University, England
1930 Fellow, Christ's College, Cambridge University, England
1943 CBE, UK
1949 British Annual of Literature Medal, UK
1954 James Tait Black Memorial Prize, Scotland
1957 Knighthood, UK
1959 Rede Lecturer, Cambridge University, England
1960 Godkin Lecturer, Harvard University, USA
     Regent's Professor, Berkeley University of California, USA
1961 President, Library Association, UK
     Rector, University of St Andrews, Scotland
1962 Fellow, Morse Collage, Yale University, USA
     Hon. Member, American Academy Institute, USA
     Foreign Hon. Member, American Academy of Arts and Sciences, USA
     Membre, Société Européenne de Culture, Europe
1964 Barony of United Kingdom
     Diamond Jubilee Medal, Catholic University of America, USA
1965 President, British Migraine Association, UK
     Centennial Corporation Award, Albert Einstein Medical Center, USA

1966   Centennial Engineering Medal, Pennsylvania Military College, USA
Resolution of Esteem, Congressional Committee on Science and Aeronautics, USA
Hon Fellow, Christ's College, Cambridge University, England
Extraordinary Fellow, Churchill College, Cambridge University, England
1967   Hon Fellow, Hatfield Polytechnic College, England
Hon Fellow, Founder's College, York University, Toronto, Canada
1969   Award for Creative Leadership in Education, New York University School of Education, USA
1980   International Dmitrov Prize, Bulgaria

INDEX

203